Photographing the Unseen Mexico
Maya Goded's Socially Engaged Documentaries

LEGENDA

LEGENDA is the Modern Humanities Research Association's book imprint for new research in the Humanities. Founded in 1995 by Malcolm Bowie and others within the University of Oxford, Legenda has always been a collaborative publishing enterprise, directly governed by scholars. The Modern Humanities Research Association (MHRA) joined this collaboration in 1998, became half-owner in 2004, in partnership with Maney Publishing and then Routledge, and has since 2016 been sole owner. Titles range from medieval texts to contemporary cinema and form a widely comparative view of the modern humanities, including works on Arabic, Catalan, English, French, German, Greek, Italian, Portuguese, Russian, Spanish, and Yiddish literature. Editorial boards and committees of more than 60 leading academic specialists work in collaboration with bodies such as the Society for French Studies, the British Comparative Literature Association and the Association of Hispanists of Great Britain & Ireland.

The MHRA encourages and promotes advanced study and research in the field of the modern humanities, especially modern European languages and literature, including English, and also cinema. It aims to break down the barriers between scholars working in different disciplines and to maintain the unity of humanistic scholarship. The Association fulfils this purpose through the publication of journals, bibliographies, monographs, critical editions, and the MHRA Style Guide, and by making grants in support of research. Membership is open to all who work in the Humanities, whether independent or in a University post, and the participation of younger colleagues entering the field is especially welcomed.

ALSO PUBLISHED BY THE ASSOCIATION

Critical Texts
Tudor and Stuart Translations • *New Translations* • *European Translations*
MHRA Library of Medieval Welsh Literature

MHRA Bibliographies
Publications of the Modern Humanities Research Association

The Annual Bibliography of English Language & Literature
Austrian Studies
Modern Language Review
Portuguese Studies
The Slavonic and East European Review
Working Papers in the Humanities
The Yearbook of English Studies

www.mhra.org.uk
www.legendabooks.com

STUDIES IN HISPANIC AND LUSOPHONE CULTURES

Studies in Hispanic and Lusophone Cultures are selected and edited by the Association of Hispanists of Great Britain & Ireland. The series seeks to publish the best new research in all areas of the literature, thought, history, culture, film, and languages of Spain, Spanish America, and the Portuguese-speaking world.

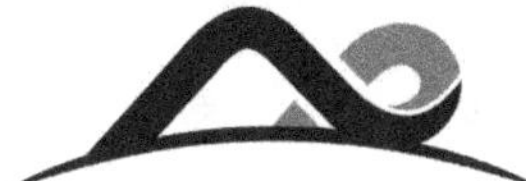

The Association of Hispanists of Great Britain & Ireland is a professional association which represents a very diverse discipline, in terms of both geographical coverage and objects of study. Its website showcases new work by members, and publicises jobs, conferences and grants in the field.

www.legendabooks.com/series/shlc

STUDIES IN HISPANIC AND LUSOPHONE CULTURES

1. *Unamuno's Theory of the Novel*, by C. A. Longhurst
2. *Pessoa's Geometry of the Abyss: Modernity and the* Book of Disquiet, by Paulo de Medeiros
3. *Artifice and Invention in the Spanish Golden Age*, edited by Stephen Boyd and Terence O'Reilly
4. *The Latin American Short Story at its Limits: Fragmentation, Hybridity and Intermediality*, by Lucy Bell
5. *Spanish New York Narratives 1898–1936: Modernisation, Otherness and Nation*, by David Miranda-Barreiro
6. *The Art of Ana Clavel: Ghosts, Urinals, Dolls, Shadows and Outlaw Desires*, by Jane Elizabeth Lavery
7. *Alejo Carpentier and the Musical Text*, by Katia Chornik
8. *Britain, Spain and the Treaty of Utrecht 1713-2013*, edited by Trevor J. Dadson and J. H. Elliott
9. *Books and Periodicals in Brazil 1768-1930: A Transatlantic Perspective*, edited by Ana Cláudia Suriani da Silva and Sandra Guardini Vasconcelos
10. *Lisbon Revisited: Urban Masculinities in Twentieth-Century Portuguese Fiction*, by Rhian Atkin
11. *Urban Space, Identity and Postmodernity in 1980s Spain: Rethinking the Movida*, by Maite Usoz de la Fuente
12. *Santería, Vodou and Resistance in Caribbean Literature: Daughters of the Spirits*, by Paul Humphrey
13. *Reprojecting the City: Urban Space and Dissident Sexualities in Recent Latin American Cinema*, by Benedict Hoff
14. *Rethinking Juan Rulfo's Creative World: Prose, Photography, Film*, edited by Dylan Brennan and Nuala Finnegan
15. *The Last Days of Humanism: A Reappraisal of Quevedo's Thought*, by Alfonso Rey
16. *Catalan Narrative 1875-2015*, edited by Jordi Larios and Montserrat Lunati
17. *Islamic Culture in Spain to 1614: Essays and Studies*, by L. P. Harvey
18. *Film Festivals: Cinema and Cultural Exchange*, by Mar Diestro-Dópido
19. *St Teresa of Avila: Her Writings and Life*, edited by Terence O'Reilly, Colin Thompson and Lesley Twomey
20. *(Un)veiling Bodies: A Trajectory of Chilean Post-Dictatorship Documentary*, by Elizabeth Ramírez Soto

Photographing the Unseen Mexico

Maya Goded's Socially Engaged Documentaries

❖

Dominika Gasiorowski

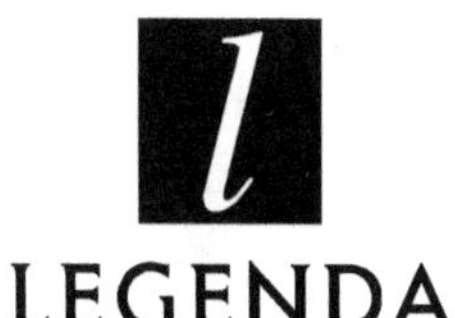

LEGENDA
Studies in Hispanic and Lusophone Cultures 21
Modern Humanities Research Association
2018

Published by Legenda
an imprint of the Modern Humanities Research Association
Salisbury House, Station Road, Cambridge CB1 2LA

ISBN 978-1-78188-795-0 (HB)
ISBN 978-1-78188-796-7 (PB)

First published 2018
Paperback edition 2021

Copy-Editor: Nigel Hope

CONTENTS

To my mother Maria Cyrankowska
and my grandmother Aniela Bukowska (1929–2018)
in deep gratitude for their private championing of women's education. Thank you.

ACKNOWLEDGEMENTS

This book began its life as my PhD thesis in 2009. In the following decade, I defended my doctorate at Queen Mary University of London, had two children and negotiated the precarity of early career academic life. I have been very lucky to receive a lot of support along the way, without which this project would have been impossible.

Prof Parvati Nair was the wisest and kindest PhD supervisor. I will always be grateful for her patience, understanding, and encouragement and for teaching me how to make the challenging process of writing positively enjoyable. I am indebted to her for the help in shaping this work and for teaching me so many valuable life lessons in the process. My life is richer and fuller for having been her student and I cherish her friendship to this day.

I was also fortunate to benefit from the expertise of several other outstanding scholars working at QMUL, including Prof Elza Adamowicz and Prof Omar García. For a very insightful and encouraging viva voce examination in 2014, I am grateful to the late Prof Andrea Noble and Dr Miriam Haddu.

Maya Goded generously agreed to numerous interviews and kindly allowed me to reproduce her photographs in this book. I am thankful for her patience and her kindness in sharing her time and her work with me. It was a pleasure to experience first-hand her ability to make connections with people and a privilege to have her guidance and company in navigating Mexico City's nightlife. Through her work and her openness, she has shown me many aspects of Mexican culture I would otherwise have remained blind to. For her expansion of my private horizon of vision, I will be eternally grateful.

The work undertaken would have been impossible without the financial backing of the QMUL Westfield Trust. I have benefitted from the Westfield Trust Research Studentship in Hispanic Studies, as well as the academic and administrative support of the School of Languages, Linguistics and Film at Queen Mary University of London.

My thanks go to the Modern Humanities Research Association for their support of this project and to Prof John London for suggesting I send my manuscript to Legenda. I am grateful to my editor Dr Graham Nelson for his advice and encouragement and to Nigel Hope for his meticulous copyediting. I am also indebted to Prof Trevor Dadson, Prof John Mraz and Legenda's editorial board for their careful reading and generous support of this book. For helping to publish colour photographs in the hardback edition of this book, I want to thank the Society for Latin American Studies and the MHRA for their financial backing.

An earlier version of a section of Chapter Four was published as an article entitled

'Bodies That Do Not Matter: Marginality in Maya Goded's Photographs of Sex-workers in Mexico City' in the Journal of Latin American Cultural Studies in 2015. A short paragraph on the figure of a fallen woman in Mexican culture from the same chapter also features in my article entitled 'Photographing Children in Mexico City's Red-Light Districts' published in the Bulletin of Latin American Research in 2018.

As an extroverted writer, I relied on my friends for their company and good humour. My thanks go to Stella Corradi, Liz Cundy, Joy Janaros, Sophie Johnson, Jules Hill, Ruth Hill, Claire Khalifa, Dr Emily McTernan, Berglind Rafnsdottir-Teasdale, Karin Thayer, Kate Tittley and the vibrant community of teachers and students of yoga in my local gym. Thank you for your love and encouragement.

I am grateful to my mother and my late grandmother for everything they taught me and for their unconditional love and belief in me. For their love, company and endless laughter I am grateful to my sisters. In providing practical support and helping me combine domestic responsibilities with research and teaching ones, I would like to thank my loving parents-in-law. To my uncle and grandfather I am grateful for their love and support.

For his unparalleled ability to provide emotional, practical, and financial support all at once, I am most grateful to my husband, Dr Ted Gasiorowski. I am thankful for his company in sharing the joys and the challenges of everyday life and for making my life happier and richer. I will always be grateful for his kind understanding, patience, support and belief in this project.

I would like to thank my children, Sebastian and Charlotte, for all the joy, love and learning they bring my way. I love you more than words can say.

Notwithstanding all of the above support for this project, any errors and omissions remain solely my own.

D.G., January 2019

LIST OF FIGURES

INTRODUCTION

If one can fall in love with images, then my initial encounter with Maya Goded's work can only be described as love at first sight. In 2009, I was a graduate student at the University of Cambridge when Erica Segre brought Goded's album entitled *Plaza de la soledad* (2006) into a seminar on Mexican women photographers. I was immediately drawn to the closely cropped black and white images, which captured women in ways I had not seen before — intimate, vulnerable, sensual and powerful, all at the same time. This was the start of my fascination with Goded's documentary work, which always prompts more questions than it answers. In trying to understand why I found Goded's work so powerfully disquieting and compelling, I sought out opportunities that would allow me to focus my doctoral research on her photography. After Professor Parvati Nair agreed to supervise my project, I began the journey of finding my voice as a researcher navigating complex visual epistemologies and mapping out new avenues of critical inquiry. Nearly a decade later, this book is the result of the potent combination of love and opportunity. It has shaped my ideas about representation and gender and taught me a new appreciation of ways in which images construct and influence our lives.

My intense visual pleasure provoked by Goded's work was all the more compelling for its accompanying ethical questions. At the time when the visual field is being saturated with images due to galloping information technology creating an illusion that everything can be seen, Goded turns her camera and her attention to people excluded from the privilege of representation, clearly pointing at gaps, omissions and exclusions in our apparently full visual horizons. Was photographing people hitherto excluded from visual, political or cultural representation a starting point for addressing that exclusion? Or was it instead a way of using their previous lack of representation to produce compelling images for elite consumption which reinforce their marginalisation? This book came from the need to account for Goded's groundbreaking intervention in what is seen and what is known about unseen lives of people absent from historical as well as visual narratives. In this accounting, I found that her photography could be a starting point for seeing people hitherto invisible and for challenging theoretical stratagems for the divergences and convergences between visibility and knowledge.

It was this encounter with Goded's imagery and the subsequent research into her practice that informed my thinking of visibility and representation as functions of power, mediated through photography. The main focus of this book is to analyse representations of subalternity in relation to socio-visual cultural hegemony that impedes such representations. In examining the correlation between hegemony and subalternity, I frame documentary photography as an intermediary, which challenges hegemonic horizons of vision. In a move away from negative aesthetics, which has dominated photography criticism for much of the twentieth century, this volume examines the work done by controversial images, where their subjects had been hitherto excluded from the arena of socio-cultural or political representation. The aim is to build a conceptual argument transferable across different cultural contexts. In doing so, I consider aspects of photographic representation, using Maya Goded's photo-documentary work as an example. I examine photography's role in expanding current horizons of visibility, particularly in terms of its influence on political and ethical climates. Problematising the representational role of photographs as a means of historical record emphasises the indispensable but elusive and unstable role of interpretation in relation to photography. In a cultural environment increasingly saturated with images, invisibility remains one of the cruellest forms of social ostracism, as it precludes any political or social forms of resistance to subjugation and marginalisation. I conceptualise documentary photography as a form of creative resistance to such invisibility.

As an introduction to this book, Chapter 1 serves as a biographical and cultural anchoring of Goded's work in outlining her personal and professional influences as well as contextualising her photography within the framework of Mexican visual culture. Critical analysis is not the primary objective of this chapter, which aims instead to set the context, both in personal and national terms, for analysing Goded's photographic output in the rest of this volume and, therefore, helping determine Goded's position as an agent, who creates art that influences the socio-visual landscape at home and abroad.

In order to engage subaltern representations, I build a framework within which they can be anchored. Chapter 2 examines the challenges inherent in representing the subaltern by problematising concepts of subalternity and representation in relation to photography. It is examined as a historicising medium, which demonstrates a capacity to change subaltern invisibility into documentary permanence. This is also where I engage with ethical debates surrounding documentary photography by examining the intellectual legacy of the Frankfurt School and its impact on critical approaches to photography during the last century. The theoretical triad of subalternity, representation and photography is the basis for analysing specific modes through which the subaltern subject can be represented, making apparent the intertwining of materiality and meaning.

In Chapter 3, liminality provides a theoretical platform for addressing Mexico's position on the global geopolitical scene through critically referring to colonial legacies from a post-colonial perspective. Therein, I examine neoliberal policies and the influence of twentieth- and twenty-first century imperialistic globalisation on Mexico and its people in relation to the concept of the global south. I frame Mexico's liminal position on the world scene in relation to its rich photographic legacy, historically chiefly produced and framed by foreign photographers. Within the discussion of the concept of liminality in Goded's work, I theorise photography as a liminal medium par excellence. Its intervention in Mexico's liminal spaces, understood both locally and globally, reveals the uprooted, liminal and vulnerable experiences of space in Mexico.

The discussion of visualising social and spatial liminality leads me to considering the bodily presence of people who inhabit those liminal spaces. In Chapter 4, I examine representations of the subaltern body in Goded's work through the prisms of race, gender and death, with an emphasis on bodily effects of subalternity and their portrayal. I frame her photographs of absence as visual evidence of the invisibility of subalterns in hegemonic scopic regimes.

After examining Maya Goded's photographic interventions in representing subaltern groups, which would otherwise remain invisible, in Chapter 5 the focus shifts onto the critical analysis of visibility and invisibility in relation to photo-documentaries and their representation of subalternity. I analyse necessary blindness inherent in every act of seeing, photographic or otherwise, and its consequences for socio-cultural visibility. Likewise, I examine the connection between language and vision — the blindness of the latter and the influence of the former — and the ways in which they interact, which shapes individual and collective perspectives. These reflections help to position Maya Goded's interest in the subaltern as an attempt to challenge not just the regimes of visibility, but also epistemic systems, which enable their cognition.

The concepts of liminality, embodiment and visibility in relation to subalternity and representation illuminate pertinent aspects of Goded's documentary practice. By putting them together, I create a framework where subaltern representation can be analysed in relation to hegemonic horizons of vision without being rendered powerless or complicit in creating them. The critical potential of the concepts of liminality, embodiment and vision lies in their necessarily dynamic nature, allowing me to frame subalternity as an unstable site of visual questioning and potential for seeing otherwise. Together, these concepts build a context around Goded's images by theoretically anchoring their subaltern representations, and mount a defence against the loss of meaning in documentary photography more generally. To paraphrase John Berger in his introduction to the 1970s BBC TV series *Ways of Seeing*, I hope you will consider what I wrote, but remain sceptical of it.

CHAPTER 1

Maya Goded and Mexican Photography

Maya Goded was born in 1967 in Mexico City and is today one of the most renowned contemporary Mexican photographers. Her contribution to the Mexican visual culture is particularly significant because of her photographic focus on communities and places that are rarely represented, and whose subaltern position within hegemonic cultural discourses consists of their socio-cultural invisibility. Visual mediation in this case involves widening the scope of what it means to be Mexican in the twenty-first century, shedding light on national and gender stereotypes that are productively engaged in Goded's photographs. Her exposure of marginalised lives explicitly probes exclusions created by normative standards, providing a visual counter-narrative that features hitherto unseen people and places, and resists their omission from mainstream culture as well as the social imaginary and consciousness.

Maya Goded has lived in Mexico City nearly all her life and her home environment had a significant impact on her interest in the visual arts. During her formative years, her father was a Mexican political activist whose leftist sympathies led to his imprisonment (Goded in Carreras 2004: 89). His political affiliations were something of a family tradition, since Goded's paternal grandparents were Spanish Civil War refugees (Light 2000: 251). The family's clandestine political activity prevented the young Goded from sharing stories of her domestic life with other children (Goded in Carreras 2004: 251). In several interviews she also hints at language problems she suffered from as a child, which made it difficult for her to communicate with others (Goded in Light 2000: 253, Goded in Carreras 2004: 89). She associated talking with trouble, since dissident political narratives were the reasons why her parental grandparents had to leave Spain and why her father was imprisoned when she was a six-month-old baby. It was particularly her father's three-year imprisonment, and the subsequent distress it created within the family, which made Goded search for a method of communicating that would circumvent the silence created by trauma (Goded 2013). Consequently, visual art appealed to her from the very beginning and she enjoyed painting in her youth.

Goded's interest in art and design became more apparent during her sociology degree, when she took a photography course that inspired her to pursue image-making as a career (Goded in Light 2000: 253–54). She contacted another renowned Mexican photographer, Graciela Iturbide, who, after seeing Goded's images, recommended that she should pursue photography to the exclusion of other activities. Goded then abandoned her sociology degree to study photography in Mexico City, and at the International Center of Photography in New York. Subsequently, she started working as Graciela Iturbide's assistant, and the latter had a profound influence on her development as a photographer (Goded in Carreras 2004: 89). To this day, Iturbide is still one of the first people to see Goded's new images and one of her closest critics (Goded 2013). Nonetheless, Goded also had a desire to develop her personal style in order to move on from being a protégée of a famous photographer to becoming an independent visual artist in her own right, which meant widening her scope of visual influences to other photographers. She is inspired by the strong aesthetic of portraits by Anders Petersen, and Rio Branco's colour usage as well as Saul Laiter's and Gillian Wearing's work (Goded 2008).

Maya Goded's projects tackle the questions of gender, social justice, national identity, and violence. Her interests lie mainly in documenting the lives of others, who have little or no visual presence within the mainstream horizons of vision in Mexico as well as abroad. Her international appeal and success is somewhat at odds with the fact that she is a very local artist, primarily interested in representing communities within her own country. Her first photographic project focused on the Tarahumara indigenous community (Goded 2013). Prompted by Iturbide, Goded then found her first job as a photographer in the Instituto Nacional Indigenista [National Indigenist Institute] and was paid to photograph Indian villages subsidised by the Instituto (Goded in Light 2000: 253). The job led her to her first personal photographic project, which was published in 1994 by Consejo Nacional para la Cultura y las Artes [National Council for Arts and Culture] entitled *Tierra Negra* [Black Earth]. It was an album picturing black communities living around the Costa Chica, which had been hitherto visually, culturally, and socio-economically ignored by the normative Mexican focus on *mestizaje*. Goded's second solo publication, an album comprising pictures of sex workers entitled *Plaza de la soledad* [Loneliness's Square] and *Good Girls* in English published in 2006 gained her worldwide recognition and was a formative achievement in her career (Goded in Carreras 2004: 93). Since then she has been involved in various visual projects, the majority of them photographic, although in the last few years she has also started to make documentary films. Her photographic projects are often very lengthy, lasting years rather than days or months, as Goded takes her time building relationships with her subjects. Her most widely disseminated and critically acclaimed projects feature the black community in the Costa Chica, prostitutes in La Merced, and disappearing women in Chihuahua. Her website, www.mayagoded.net, showcases her lesser-known projects, such as her photographic essay on sorcery in northern Mexico (*Tierra de brujas* [Land of the Witches]). She has also been working on various photographic projects for the Comisión de Derechos Humanos del Distrito Federal [Human Rights Commission] in Mexico City for the last two decades. Goded's involvement with local NGOs and her output as a photographer are evidence of her straddling humanitarian and artistic work, which prompts questions about the ethical ambiguity of her interventions in her marginalised subjects' lives.

It is important to consider the specificity of the medium of photography in terms of technical equipment Goded uses for her projects. So far, there has been a distinct lack of information about the cameras she uses in the interviews she has given and in the albums she has published. This may be because when talking about her photography, Goded more often than not focuses on the content of her visual communication instead of its technical aspects (Goded 2013). On the one hand, she admits to the camera being a tool that is central to one's photographic practice, which determines and circumscribes the work one is able to produce. On the other hand, she primarily sees it as a communication tool, where the content of that communication is more important than the tool itself (Goded 2013).

Her first camera was a Pentax, which she then replaced with a Nikon; both were stolen. After the second theft, she saved enough money for a Leica, thereby joining in the ranks of many renowned photo-documentary makers such as Eugene Smith and Henri Cartier-Bresson (Nair 2011: 12). As Parvati Nair states in her book *A Different Light* (2011), the Leica was introduced into the context of Mexican photography by Spanish Civil War exiles the Hermanos Mayo and its usage has become 'a trademark of photodocumentary across generations' (Nair 2011: 12). Goded enjoys the camera's small dimensions and its discreet appearance, which is not obvious in potentially dangerous situations and helps to avoid another theft. Another camera Goded has a special affinity to is Rolleiflex TLR 6x6, an old camera with a viewfinder situated at the top of the body, which requires it to be held at chest level. Goded reports that this type of camera helps to put her subjects at ease, since she finds it easier to talk to people and look them in the eye when she is not obscuring her face with the camera (Goded 2013). Moreover, although her subjects are conscious of the camera's presence and of the fact that Goded is taking photographs, they do not always know the exact moment when a shot is being taken, which, according to Goded, helps them feel less self-conscious. Finally, the use of the Rolleiflex avoids the necessity of a potentially aggressive and divisive act of putting a barrier up between the photographer's face and the subject of the photograph by having to raise a camera to one's eye.

At the start of her career as a photographer, Goded used to have her own darkroom and developed her photographs herself, which used to form an integral part of her practice as a photographer (Goded 2013). Nonetheless, technical developments in digital photography and economic considerations contributed to her closing down the darkroom and beginning to rely on digital postproduction editing. The loss of space to develop her photographs also brought with it different opportunities, as Goded's move to using digital SLRs meant that she found her recent leap to making documentary films relatively easy (Goded 2013). Goded's declared commitment to embracing change and resisting stagnation reveals itself through her lack of attachment to a specific camera.

Goded describes herself as a lone photographer who values her artistic freedom (Goded 2013). She completes all of her photographic projects by travelling alone and is solely in charge of most of the aspects of her photographic output, which is not without its practical risks. Owing to an escalation of conflict between the government and the drug cartels since Felipe Calderón's war on drugs was declared in 2006, violence is on the rise in Mexico. Some of the areas Goded spent years travelling through by herself, such as the region of Jalisco, which was the setting of her series *Tierra de brujas*, are now too dangerous to travel through because of the escalating violence (Goded 2013). While Goded follows local advice in order to stay safe and to be accepted in the communities she photographs, some level of risk is unavoidable in the type of work she does. As she aptly puts it, 'yo soy muy miedosa, pero siempre me meto en situaciones de miedo' [I am very fearful but I always put myself in scary situations] (Goded 2013).

Some of Goded's projects were entirely thwarted by challenges, such as kidnappings and assaults she suffered when trying to photograph communities in Chiapas; others were delayed or postponed because of stolen cameras or risks associated with continuing them. Others, again, such as her unfinished work on the murders in Ciudad Juárez, proved too difficult for Goded to cope with on an emotional level, because of the way they started to affect her own life and the way she related to her family, particularly her daughter, who was a teenager at that time. It is important to note, however, that while Goded puts herself at risk in her work as a photographer, her subjects face even greater dangers, which stem from their precarious socio-cultural position and from their limited agency over Goded's representation of them. Moreover, the photographer remains able to return to her privileged lifestyle and thus escape the risks of her job, while her subjects endure their disadvantaged position regardless of her visual intervention. That is not to diminish the risks faced by Goded, but merely to point out that her subjects face an altogether different category of danger because of their socio-cultural and economic vulnerability.

Goded's choice of subjects and her clear affinity for people and phenomena from the margins of normative experiences earned her a notorious reputation in elite cultural circles in Mexico as a risk-taking, adventurous woman who travels alone, and has a keen understanding of the socio-cultural underworld of Mexico. While this romanticised image forms part of her national and international appeal, it is also worth emphasising that Goded is also firmly part of that cultural elite not only in her own right, but also as the wife of a popular Spanish-born Mexican actor, Daniel Giménez Cacho. They share a detached villa in the middle of the exclusive Coyoacán district in Mexico City, but recent financial difficulties, as well as their two children becoming more independent, have led them to begin construction work on the house in July 2013 in order to make it smaller and easier to maintain. Although this is rarely mentioned in her interviews, her husband and his popularity constitute part of her privileged cultural capital. Moreover, Goded confesses that occasionally his contacts will make her projects possible, either by facilitating them through his associates or by introducing her to her subjects.

Goded's marriage and her home in Coyoacán is only part of her privilege. Many interviewers, particularly from Mexico and other Latin American countries, often ask her about how her appearance and the apparent racial heritage it reflects influence her job as a photographer (Goded 2008). In a country where the majority of the population identify as *mestizo*, but where social and economic divisions run alongside perceived racial ones, looks are an important marker of difference. Nonetheless, discussions of race are difficult within Mexico because of an unwillingness to admit to a problem with racism in the country, both within Mexican academia (Warren and Twine 2002: 550) and at the level of everyday experience (Moreno Figueroa 2010: 388). Still, Goded's interviewers' persistent interest in how she fares as a blonde, white woman among the subaltern groups she photographs points to a certain desire to exoticise Goded's photographic process and render both her and her subjects as outsiders in relation to the Mexican normative identity template of *mestizaje*.

Although Goded is aware of the privileges of her social position as well as her appearance, she also states that it is not always an advantage (Goded 2013). In particular, she recalls her time as a young photographer at the Instituto Nacional Indigenista. As someone who could not claim the *mestizo* identity for herself, she was often lumbered with uninteresting projects, while those who could make a bodily claim to indigenous heritage were given more challenging assignments. That perceived discrimination shows how complex race relations can be in post-colonial Mexico, where Goded's apparent European heritage, despite its being also part of her country's heritage, becomes a systemic obstacle in her building connections with indigenous communities. Again, however, it is important to stress that although Goded may have suffered some prejudice because of her appearance, the systemic everyday racism encountered by the majority of her subjects, which significantly contributes to their precarious socio-cultural position, is strikingly more debilitating. As she is the daughter of a US anthropologist and a second-generation Spanish immigrant, Goded's position in the Mexican socio-cultural hierarchy is privileged.

Goded's links with the United States, whether familial or cultural, are crucial in analysing her photography, not least because her chosen medium is commonly associated with that country (Mitchell 2005: 272). Indeed, it is impossible to analyse *mexicanidad* and its photographic representations without taking into account the neo-imperial connection between Mexico and its northern, vastly more powerful neighbour. John Mraz in *Looking for Mexico* describes it as a love-hate relationship (Mraz 2009: 161), but it is more productive to see it as a hegemonic liaison where Mexico is in a subaltern position. The contradictory sentiments of admiration and animosity towards the United States permeating the Mexican psyche are a logical consequence of being in a weaker and more vulnerable position, where resentment and veneration expressed simultaneously are not mutually exclusive, but a cogent expression of subalternity. Goded's position as a maker of images, who personally and artistically straddles the divide between the two countries, illuminates that relationship further and allows her to circumvent the muteness and invisibility consistent with a subaltern position.

Moreover, there are practical economic considerations in regarding Maya Goded's associations with the United States. Her American education in the New York International Center of Photography in New York, as well as many American awards she received, most notably the W. Eugene Smith Grant in Humanistic

Photography and the Guggenheim Fellowship, supported her in becoming the well-regarded photographer she is today. The publisher of her most widely available book, *Good Girls*, is also American. The contrast between the global obtainability of her album *Tierra Negra*, published in Mexico by Consejo Nacional para La Cultura y Las Artes [National Council for Culture and Arts] and *Good Girls*, published by Umbrage Books in the United States, is a very telling illustration of the workings of cultural hegemony in the digital era. *Tierra Negra* has been very difficult to trace for some years now, cannot be purchased online, and has been acquired by very few libraries outside Mexico. Even specialist art bookshops in Mexico City no longer stock it. In contrast, *Good Girls* can easily be ordered from Amazon. Hence Goded's links to the United States are pivotal to her visibility and global recognition as a documentary photographer. Goded's situation is symptomatic of that of many photographers who live in the global south, since it is impossible to garner an international reputation without exhibiting or publishing one's photographs in the hubs of Western power and privilege, such as London, Paris, or New York. This configuring of control over global cultural production reflects the workings of neo-colonial cultural and economic hegemony in the flows of transnational information that persist into the twenty-first century.

Goded and the Magnum Photographic Agency

An important part of Goded's global recognition is her past membership of the prestigious Magnum Photographic Agency. She joined the agency as a nominee member in 2002, but after the AGM of Magnum Photos in 2008, the agency announced it no longer represented her (Canon Professional Network 2008). Although she is no longer a member, it is still relevant to consider Magnum's power as one of the most influential photographic agencies in relation to her photography. Founded in 1947 by Robert Capa, Henri Cartier-Bresson, George Rodger, and David 'Chim' Seymour it is a prestigious photographic co-operative where member photographers retain copyright for their images (Magnum Photos 2012). Magnum's website describes in detail the impact that the Second World War had on its founding members, particularly Chim and Capa, and the humanistic concern of their photo reportage. Goded's membership of the agency is therefore not just an acknowledgement of her photographic talent, but also an implicit alignment between her own humanistic interests and those of other Magnum photographers.

Nonetheless, Magnum is also self-consciously elitist. Its founding members, although originating from different countries and backgrounds, became one of the most recognisable names in photography and rubbed shoulders with the world's cultural and political elites. Magnum represents the majority of photography greats, dead or alive, and is very influential in its creation and sustenance of photographic hierarchies, which inevitably coincide with other power structures as well as cultural, social, and economic inequalities. Based in the global power hubs of New York, London, Paris, and Tokyo, but taking on assignments the world over, the agency's photographers are mostly male, white, and privileged. Goded is one of the few women among Magnum photographers past or present. Her relatively brief presence in the Magnum's elite is notable, especially when one considers that among the agency's member photographers seventy-five are male and ten are female, two of whom are nominees without voting rights, and four of whom are deceased (Magnum Photos 2012). This in itself is evidence of women photographers' underrepresentation and makes Goded's past associate membership all the more noteworthy. The male-dominated agency was a very different environment for a photographer who spent all her life in a country where the tradition of the female visual artist is very strong and where their vision is significant in terms of its socio-cultural impact, both at home and abroad. Goded was also the only Mexican photographer ever to have been represented by Magnum, while the list of its US members reaches over thirty. Despite this remarkable absence of Mexican photographers, photographs of Mexico abound on the Magnum website, where a search term 'Mexico' results in over 5,000 photographs. This privileging of the foreign gaze is one of the most pervasive post-colonial legacies, supported not just through repeating old visual patterns but also underpinned by contemporary neo-colonial power imbalances. Therefore, in spite of Maya Goded's successes and recognition, it becomes apparent that her nationality has a significant impact on her perception as a photographer rooted in the global south.

Although Goded's artistic independence is paramount to her ability to produce compelling work, being an unaffiliated photographer within an increasingly competitive global market is not without its difficulties. Even though Goded declares that her favourite way of sharing her photographs is through albums, until now she has only published two, namely *Tierra Negra* and *Plaza de la soledad*. Moreover, the latter was then republished by Umbrage Editions without consultation with her and renamed *Good Girls* for the English-speaking markets. Despite being fluent in English, she was not consulted about this significant change of title and not informed about the editorial process, although both editions retain the same order of photographs and the same format. Goded is uncertain of her legal rights with regard to that body of work and she has not benefited financially from the publication of the English edition, apart from having been sent a copy of her own album. Although the wider dissemination of her work resulting from the publication of *Good Girls* pleases her, she finds the situation where her own photographs are renamed and repackaged without her consultation regrettable (Goded 2013). Moreover, it is partly her inability to benefit fully from the commercial success of her work which lies at the root of her financial difficulties, which forced her to close down her website at the beginning of 2013; it was then relaunched at the beginning of 2014 under a different URL address (mayagoded.net). Goded's struggle to maintain control over her own artistic output and its dissemination, particularly abroad, is evidence that photographers who originate from the global south not only find it harder to find an audience for their images, but are also at a legal and financial disadvantage when faced with legally savvy publishers, who are focused on their own profits. The ease with which photography crosses national and cultural boundaries is in stark contrast with Goded's difficulties in retaining her copyrights within global legal frameworks.

Photographic Concerns

Goded's repeated statement that photography is her way of communicating with the world prompts questions as to the content of that communication. In an interview with Claudi Carreras, in his book entitled *Conversaciones con fotógrafos mexicanos* (2004), Goded claims that photography is for her a way of understanding people, their society and environment (Carreras 2004: 90), and describes herself as a committed photographer (Carreras 2004: 92). This is also reflected in the praises she receives with awards that focus specifically on her status as a concerned photographer. To use just one example, the jury of the Dutch Prince Claus Award presented to her in 2010 specifies that her photography is chosen for 'challenging preconceptions and giving unique insight into little-known realities, and for celebrating otherness and human commonalities that transcend socially constructed barriers' (Prince Claus Fund 2010). Goded uses the higher-truth value commonly associated with photography to shed light on communities and social groups that are culturally marginalised and excluded from mainstream visual production, which is a significant factor in their subaltern position. Much of her work focuses on women, but that interest did not stem from a premeditated desire to represent femininity, but rather from her interest in invisible communities and people who are shunned, both socially and visually (Goded 2013). Women living in marginalised communities will often suffer from multiple marginalisations, some of these deriving from their belonging to an ostracised community, others connected to their status as women with fewer political, economic, cultural, and social powers than men across different sectors of society. Goded admits to initially being resistant to being labelled as a feminist photographer, but as her body of work grew, she began to identify her work as feminist, since her concern with women and femininity in Mexico remains central to her practice as a photographer (Goded 2013).

More broadly, Goded photographically exposes poverty, social injustice, and ostracism suffered by others because of the ways in which they fail to fit into conventional expectations. In that sense, her art is politically important, because it depicts the stigmatisation suffered by subaltern people and communities and visually challenges implicit prejudices. Moreover, it also questions social and cultural preconceptions, which are partly a result of the subalterns' cultural invisibility. By putting the subaltern at the centre of her photography, she includes those normally ignored in visual media and forges a cultural as well as political space for them through her photography. Her aim, as she states in conversation with Carreras, is to provoke discussion and generate interest in issues that would otherwise be ignored, phenomena that are difficult to discuss and comprehend (Goded in Carreras 2004: 91).

It is crucial to note, however, that when Goded exposes underrepresented people, she does so from a privileged position. Indeed, she admits that this is often the crux of the disapproval she faces in her own country.

> En México me critican porque yo, rubia, blanca, se me ocurre fotografiar prostitutas. Piensan que no tengo derecho de hablar de los demás que ganan menos y son de diferentes clases sociales. (Goded 2013)

> [In Mexico I am criticised because it occurs to me to photograph prostitutes although I am white and blond. People think I have no right to talk about people from different social clases or those poorer than me.]

This sentiment is also indicative of challenges that come with rebelling against representational regimes and commonly accepted notions of what is and what is not suitable for public exhibition in Mexico. Goded's photography also encounters academic criticism, particularly in relation to *Tierra Negra*, where it is not her choice of subject matter, but rather the way in which it is represented, which raises concerns. Laura Lewis (2004), Mariana Ortega (2013) and Wendy Phillips (2009) are unequivocal in deeming her images problematic in representing exoticised versions of Mexican blackness and objectifying her subjects (Ortega 2013: 171). These concerns will be addressed further throughout the book as part of examining the challenging nature of visually mediating subaltern subjects.

Goded's persistence in linking every one of her photographic projects either to her own experience or to the experiences of her immediate family is relevant for two reasons. First of all, it acknowledges the personal nature of her photography, clearly marking her as an artist whose endeavours are visceral and affectively linked to her own lived experience. Secondly, these repeated declarations of affinity help to bridge the divides between Goded and her subjects, and emphasise that cooperation is an essential part of her practice (Goded 2013). However, this stress on visceral motivations, which help the photographer empathise with her subjects, to some extent contradicts Goded's practice of thoroughly researching her projects. She declares that she is very slow as a photographer, but the slowness of her creative process is partly due to the fact that she is a thorough researcher, reading anthropological, sociological, psychological, and philosophical materials in order to gain a wider perspective and a wider understanding of the subjects she wants to photograph (Goded 2013). The knowledge she acquires in the process starts to form a part of her way of seeing, although she states that it is also necessary to leave the reading behind and be open to new experiences as a photographer. 'Hay que dejarlo todo y salir a enfrentarse a la vida, a la foto' [You have to leave everything behind and go out to confront life and photography] (Goded 2013). Nonetheless, it is important to recognise that any such conscious leaving behind of acquired knowledge is impossible to achieve, because the information that is absorbed and remembered starts actively to form parts of an individual's point of view and cannot be un-learnt at will. This incongruity between Goded's visceral motivations, which are then thoroughly researched as part of photographic pre-production, is at the heart of her photographic endeavours.

From a hegemonic perspective, it is challenging to examine what lies behind someone's consent to being part of a photographic project that clearly designates its subjects as, for example, sex workers or witches, particularly in a country where gendered expectations of women are rigidly defined and stigmatise such identifications. It is a theoretical question fraught with misrepresentations as well as potential assumptions, and better suited for an ethnographic study. However, in principle it is important to underline that to deny Goded's subjects the agency to make their own decisions about being represented because of their extreme restrictions is to dehumanise them further by categorising them as victims in such a rigid way that the possibility of their exercising personal agency is difficult to conceive. Goded is conscious of her responsibility in publicly sharing the lives of others.

> Todos los días que haces [trabajo] documental te enfrentas a la ética. Para mi, fotografía es una forma de comunicación social, y no una herramienta de aprovecharse de los demás. (Goded 2013)
>
> [When working on documentary photography, you confront ethical questions all the time. For me, photography is a form of social communication and not a way of taking advantage of others.]

She declares that her subjects want to share their lives and be looked at, because it gives them a chance to show what they want to the camera, to portray an image on their own terms, at least to some extent. Underlying that desire, particularly in the case of subaltern subjects with little socio-cultural presence, is the faith in the possibility of defining oneself against the grain of discriminatory social categories and a belief that Goded, as well as viewers of her photography, will be able to appreciate that portrayal.

Nonetheless, Goded is also acutely aware that in her practice as a documentary photographer she is transforming the reality she witnesses by representing it through her own point of view (Carreras 2004: 92–93). Therefore, the potential for ethical conflict arises between the point of view of the photographer and the point of view of the subjects. Moreover, Goded also points to the fact that, in the process of photographing people through collaborative practice, her subjects consciously portray an image of themselves that they would like others to see (Goded 2013). There occurs, therefore, a multiple layering of representations in every photographic instance, where a portrayal mediated by the subject for the benefit of the photographer is then filtered through their lens. This filtering will inevitably lead to a degree of distortion, one that is an inextricable part of photography, which is a transformative practice. Goded's awareness of her subjects' expectations in terms of their portrayal does not diminish her own transformative visual power, since one's self-image does not always align with how one is perceived by others or portrayed in photographs. Photography is a learning process for the photographer as well as for her subjects, where the spectre of how social norms influence behaviours and appearances comes to the fore through individual subjectivities that create the image through collaboration. However, it is pertinent to consider the subaltern subjects' vulnerability in any such encounter.

The main artistic aim of Goded is to widen the collective imaginary and make it more inclusive by broadening its scope to incorporate communities and identities with little or no representation, therefore challenging preconceptions and prejudices. In order to examine Goded's contribution to the Mexican visual environment, I reference the history of photography in Mexico and its relationship to such fundamental notions as those of national identity, postcolonial identity and gender. My aim here is not to provide a comprehensive history of photography in

Mexico, a task that is too large and multifaceted to be accomplished in a single project. It is rather to examine aspects of that history in a way that resonates with Goded's photographic interests and discursively roots her art in historical and contemporary Mexican contexts.

The Nation and the Image

The history of photography and the history of nation-formation in Mexico are inextricably linked. Andrea Noble in her book entitled *Photography and Memory in Mexico: Icons of Revolution* (2010) points out the fact that Mexico gained independence 'as the result of a collapse of an empire', and not due to a collective aspiration towards national independence (Lomnitz 2001, in Noble 2010: 16). As much as imagery plays a very important role in the formation of personal and collective identities in every culture (Mitchell 2005: xiv), in Mexico the process of developing post-colonial national identity coincided with technological advances in photography, which influenced its trajectory. Mraz (2009: 2) claims that the visual media of photography, cinema, and picture histories have largely carried out identity construction in Mexico. They are all the more important because of historically low literacy levels in the country, and the widespread influence of Catholicism, which Mraz describes as a theology of images, especially in comparison to iconoclastic religions. In such a context, nation formation and its relationship to photography becomes a process that constitutes socio-cultural meanings with political ends.

During the nineteenth century, two traumatic events had a significant influence on the emerging nation (Noble 2010: 17). One of them was the invasion of US troops in 1846 and the occupation that followed and lasted until 1848. John Mraz describes it as a pivotal event in developing Mexican national identity and set the stage for the neo-colonial relationship between Mexico and the United States (Mraz 2009: 13). The other significant event was the intervention of Napoleon III and his installation of the Austrian archduke Maximilian von Habsburg-Lorraine as emperor of Mexico in 1864 and his violent demise in 1867 (Noble 2010: 17). The two events provide a historical snapshot of the hostile international environment in which Mexican nationhood began to be forged in resistance to foreign claims on its land and sovereignty.

The war of 1846–48 in which the country lost half its territory to the United States was the first historical occasion when Mexicans became acutely aware of their subaltern status in the power relationship between their country and its powerful northern neighbour (Mraz 2009: 13). Decades later, philosophers such as Samuel Ramos and Leopoldo Zea wrote about the Mexican inferiority complex, which Zea characterised as being an effect of the country's 'fearful vicinity to the United States' (Zea in Mraz 2009: 159). Crucially, the Mexican War coincided with the onset of modern visual culture, since it was in 1839 that daguerreotypes began to arrive in Mexico after their invention in France and were widely known by the time of the conflict (Gabara 2008: 13).

Mexico's struggle for self-representation was hampered even at the very dawn of photographic technology, when the dice was already loaded against Mexican interest, despite the apparent neutrality of the medium. Although the Mexican War happened decades before newspapers and magazines became major cultural and political players, the public interest in seeing reliable reports from the war was significant in the United States (Mraz 2009: 13–14). Mexico's subaltern status did not just hinge on its military inability to successfully repel the northern invaders. Critically, Mexicans were unable to produce a visual counter-narrative, which could rival that constructed by the aggressors in the conflict. Therefore, Mexico's subalternity in relation to the United States emerges here as a complicated effect of the country's military vulnerability, which is compounded and reinforced by its inability to defend its national interests on a symbolic level and produce a counter-narrative to the US hegemonic perspective. Roberto Tejada in his book *National Camera: Photography and Mexico's Image Environment* (2009) stresses that the space of Mexican nationhood was delimitated by an economic and symbolic foreign exchange with the United States (Tejada 2009: Location 290).

Power balances notwithstanding, these new photographic technologies also provided an opportunity for questioning and contesting identity politics through mechanical representation. Esther Gabara in her book entitled *Errant Modernism: The Ethos of Photography in Mexico and Brazil* (2008) underlines the importance of gaining the ability to produce representations of one's own nation in the wake of independence.

> Once the camera changed hands [in Latin America] from foreigner to native [...] modernists retook photography's naturalized function as a privileged medium of modern representation and used it to alter the very image of modernity. The act of taking this tool in to one's hands became both a triumphant gesture of acquisition and created a deep trauma of representation. (Gabara 2008: 1)

It is precisely this transfer of power in both political and artistic terms which marks the beginnings of Mexico as a modern nation.

The relative political and social stability of the presidency of Porfirio Díaz (Noble 2010: 17) offered the right socio-economic environment for photography to spread as a social practice. The late nineteenth century saw the European fashion for *cartes de visite* spread across Mexico, where they became known as *tarjetas de visita* and were what can only be described as a pre-digital precursor of twenty-first-century social networks that rely heavily on personal photographs being posted online. *Tarjetas* gave Mexicans an opportunity to express their personal and national identity, and to present in a photograph what they would like others to see (Cano 2006: 35). They were a very performative photographic genre, where use of props, special backgrounds, and best outfits was *de rigueur. Tarjetas de visita* were cherished possessions, which respectable families would display in albums dedicated to evidencing their lineage and connections, often incorporating celebrities and including them in their domestic sphere (Cano 2006: 38). Photography's ability to afford the possibility of visually fixing one's desirable identity, which until then had been reserved for those who could afford painted portraits, points to the socially constitutive power of images that become cultural sites of creating, viewing and contesting identities.

Interestingly, in Mexico even those individuals who did not seek to produce an image of themselves through the *tarjetas* found themselves being represented in them. Emperor Maximilian, the only monarch of the Second Mexican Empire, ordered the registration of prostitutes in 1864 and utilised *tarjetas* to identify them (Mraz 2009: 22). This modernising project was executed with the purpose of protecting the health of French soldiers (ibid.). Photographic records of prostitutes quickly formed part of an avant-garde socio-political project of using new technologies to identify people deemed a danger to the state (Debroise 2001: 41), which underpinned legislation. Thus, the camera became part of the state apparatus, used not just by individuals to express their individuality as well as their desire for social belonging, but also by the authorities to protect moral cohesion of the nation and its health. This process victimised those deemed a danger to the state and photographed as such, but such ethical concerns were not at the forefront of political or social agendas at the time. Nonetheless, it is worth noting at this point that Maya Goded's photographic work with prostitutes in La Merced historically forms a part of a long-standing and multi-faceted engagement between photography and prostitution.

Prostitutes were not the only individuals who were represented on the *tarjetas* with purposes significantly different from those of the Mexican bourgeoisie. The enormous popularity of the medium created new commercial possibilities, which were seized by a Mexico City photographic studio named Cruces y Campa (Mraz 2009: 24). Their *tarjetas*, which were available for purchase to the wider public, portrayed a variety of Mexican trades, identified only by their job (ibid.). Mraz argues that these *tarjetas* 'served in part to buttress bourgeois identity by representing that which they were not: the nameless masses engaged in manual labor' (Mraz 2009: 24). He also states that they inadvertently exposed the limits of what could be shown during the Porfiriato dictatorship, claiming that photographic representation presented a new problem for the ruling classes as a medium that could potentially expose the misery and abject poverty of the urban and rural poor (ibid.). Representing manual labourers as traditionally dressed, docile, and nameless embodiments of *mexicanidad* fuelled the aforementioned appetite for the picturesque at home and abroad. As much as the precise significance of the *tarjetas de visita* is difficult to determine, they are certainly part of the long European tradition of romantically representing rural and urban poor (Mraz 2009: 27). Moreover, they clearly influenced the subsequent fashion for postcards with renditions of picturesque representations of *costumbrista* Mexican types. In order to contextualise the nineteenth-century appeal of the picturesque, in the next part of this chapter I examine the role of foreign image-makers in the visual history of Mexico.

The Foreign Gaze and the Mexican Look

Due to colonial legacies in Mexico, foreign artists and photographers have always been active players in the country's visual field, contributing significantly to the way in which it was perceived from within and from without. Being seen through foreign eyes is part of the colonial and postcolonial paradigm. In the context of colonies or past colonies, one of the filters through which identity has to be expressed is that of the foreign gaze. That foreign gaze, however, is not entirely that of a stranger, since the colonial context necessitates a foreign filter of the hegemon. In other words, part of the colonial and postcolonial experience is the internalisation of the foreign gaze into the self, producing a fragmented and hybrid sense of identity, both on an individual and national level, of which Mexico provides plenty of visual examples.

This foreign gaze can be framed as oppressive continuing imposition of foreign expectations of exoticism on a nation with limited artistic and economic resources to resists such pressures. Nonetheless, it is more theoretically productive to frame the foreign gaze in Mexico as part of a multiplicity of gazes and expectations that create a national visual culture, albeit one that obscures the clear power imbalances behind it. The purpose of such a perspective is neither to dismiss the profound influence of foreign visual mediators on Mexico's visual culture and production and its reception abroad, nor to deny the post-colonial framework of such a visual hierarchy, where a de-colonised nation continues to be visually framed, produced, and reproduced by the hegemonic other. It is rather to show how meanings and assumptions produced within this hegemonic relationship are incorporated and challenged in the Mexican visual field, tracing the transfer of cultural agency from imperialistic gazes to a visual regard from within.

Mexico's appeal to image-makers at home and around the world is impossible to overstate. It is hardly a recent phenomenon either — ever since the invention of the first camera, the country attracted a plethora of explorers and photographers, becoming a compulsory fixture of the new exotic Grand Tour for many nineteenth- and early twentieth-century adventurers. Haddu traces the Mexican photographic legacy of one of the most famous documentary photographers, and contextualises his artistic presence and visual contribution within a historical framework of the country, which played host to and inspired the world's artistic and intellectual elites (Haddu 2008: 7). Mraz outlines Mexico's appeal as a unique mixture of cultures different from the 'developed world', striking geography, captivating ruins, and a fascinating combination of traditional and modern ways of living in very close proximity to the United States (Mraz 2009: 28). It provided opportunities for vast amounts of photographic works to be produced by foreigners, in the nineteenth century second only to Egypt (ibid.). Moreover, initially photography was a medium very much influenced by painting, which had already set conditions for representing Mexico as a 'picturesque land abounding in exotic types' (ibid.). As some of the artists who painted such scenes never visited Mexico before rendering it, photography played an important role in supplementing the imaginary with realist imagery, which, in turn, led to *costumbrismo* (ibid.).

Costumbrismo was a genre of imagery and literature adopted from Spain, which focused on representing traditional ways of life and folkloric customs, emphasising the variety of Mexico's local exoticisms. Importantly, it ignored the pervasive class differences that have been such a crucial element contributing to the exoticism of

Mexico, remaining politically uninvolved and palatable to the regime, which could not afford to show the grinding poverty many Mexicans endured (Mraz 2009: 28). The issues of exoticising indigenous communities in visual cultural production are the subject of an ongoing debate, which John Mraz in *Looking for Mexico* broadly outlines as a contrast between two modes of representation — picturesque and anti-picturesque (Mraz 2009: 77). The representatives of the former include Mexican photographers such as Luis Márquez and Rafael Carillo and foreigners such as Hugo Brehme, whom modern scholars of Mexican photography credit with constructing '"graphic system of *lo mexicano*", creating a "visual vocabulary" of *mexicanidad*, that constitutes "the base of today's national identity"' (Mraz 2012: Location 220). They chose romantic, idealised scenes modelled on nineteenth-century paintings that appeared beautiful and presented an unproblematic vision of rural Mexican life, following the *costumbrista* artist's lead established in the early nineteenth century by Humboldt's *Atlas Pintoresco* and the trend that ensued, which José Antonio Navarrete (2003: 34) credits with having a profound influence on developing nationalist imagery. The picturesque as a mode of representation remains a powerful tool in shaping expectations of Mexican photography at home and abroad to this day. Goded reports that her images are still viewed through the prism of picturesque expectations marked by a chiefly commercial search for a marketable attractiveness of 'Mexico lindo' (Goded 2013).

In terms of landscape, the pictorial conventions were initially underpinned by expansionist policies of the United States, whose government agencies sent out photographers with reconnaissance missions to explore the largely unknown territories west of the Appalachians (Debroise 2001: 57–58). Oliver Debroise claims that:

> [t]he photographers surpassed the expectations of the politicians in Washington and the scientists of New England, creating a mythology as well as an aesthetic. They [...] constructed a territorial conscience and a national pride. (Debroise 2001: 58)

While, on the one hand, this is of course testament to the natural beauty of Mexico, on the other hand it is seen through a governmental, powerful lens with an explicit economic agenda. The sublime beauty of the landscape is not photographed to celebrate the splendour of one's country, but rather as an attractive incentive produced by an expansionist probe. That these photographs were able to be appropriated as symbols of national pride and become models for generations of landscape photographers is testament to the medium's capacity to negotiate and incorporate conflicting interests, even if that capacity is not without internal paradoxes and contradictions. Again, Goded's landscape photography as part of her documentary work draws attention to the contrast between conventional picturesque depictions of space in Mexico and her representations that emphasise fractures and incongruities.

The first photographers who broke with picturesque conventions in Mexico were Edward Weston, Tina Modotti, and Manuel Álvarez Bravo, who rejected painterly aesthetic notions and sought to establish photography as a medium in its own right, with different possibilities and limitations (Tejada 2009: Location 1193). Particularly in the case of Modotti, her interest in photography went hand in hand with her political commitments, which is especially obvious when looking at her photographs of Mexican labourers. It was precisely this political potential of photography that emerged from the rejection of the picturesque, no longer representing people just for their pleasing appearance and their idyllic connotations, but linking them to their country in terms of their social, economic, and cultural agency as individuals capable of action, as opposed to static, docile representations of bourgeois fantasies about the popular classes.

The partial shift from the picturesque mode of representing the rural indigenous other towards the anti-picturesque occurred when the muralists were at the forefront of visually constructing *mexicanidad*. The connection between muralism and photography in Mexico is relevant to the study of changing visual landscapes, as muralists formed a cultural and political elite, which attracted photographers such as Edward Weston and Tina Modotti. She photographed the murals for sale to *Mexican Folkways* and the general public, until her expulsion from the country when the job was taken over by Manuel Álvarez Bravo (Tejada 2009: Location 1175). Before examining his very important contribution to Mexican photography, one must consider Modotti's, particularly in terms of the scholarly research into her life over the recent decades affirming her importance in the history of Mexican visual culture.

Andrea Noble, in her book entitled *Tina Modotti: Image, Texture, Photography* (2000), emphasises the photographer's appeal to feminist scholars, who seek to 'make good the erasures of the stories of women's lives and to reinsert them into the history of culture' (Noble 2000: xix). Tina Modotti was born in 1896 to a working-class family in Liguria, Italy and remained there until 1913, when she joined her father in California (Noble 2000: xii). Modotti's affair with the North American photographer Edward Weston started at the beginning of the 1920s when she was working as an actress in silent Hollywood films and married to the bohemian figure of painter and poet Roubaix de l'Abrie Richey (Robo) (Noble 2000: xiii). Robo travelled to Mexico at the invitation of Gómez Robelo and sent back enthusiastic letters about the country emerging from the 1910–20 revolution and the social and artistic possibilities it created (ibid.). Robo suddenly fell ill and died in 1922 while Modotti was on her way to him. A year later, Modotti and Weston travelled to Mexico and set up a studio there (ibid.). It was here that Modotti took up photography, and her legacy as a Mexican photographer is very often the main focus of scholarly research into her artistic output, despite the fact that she only spent seven years in Mexico.

Modotti's political commitments shaped her photographic career. She was deported from Mexico after being falsely accused of an assassination attempt on the president Pascual Ortiz Rubio and then refused entry to the United States because she would not renounce her political views (Noble 2000: xvii). Subsequently, her social involvement with the International Red Aid, an organisation founded by the Comintern to provide aid to political prisoners with communist sympathies, eclipsed her photographic activities. Despite the relatively short time she spent in Mexico, her contribution to Mexican photography is significant in terms of its political commitment and the influence it had on other photographers. John Mraz characterises Modotti's impact on national symbols as twofold, on the one hand 'filling Westonian forms with social content' and on the other hand historicising 'Mexican emblems by linking them to the international socialist movement' (Mraz 2009: 85). Her position within the pantheon of Mexican photographers was cemented through her inclusion in *Luces sobre Mexico* (2006), which is a photographic catalogue showcasing a selection of the most important archive photographs in the possession of the Fototeca Nacional del Instituto Nacional de Antropología e Historia [National Photography Archive at the National Institute of Anthopology and History]. Modotti's work is seamlessly nestled between works of other great photographers of Mexico, foreign and local, and she is the only woman with such a prominent position within the publication.

Modotti's legacy is historically and aesthetically linked with the work of Manuel Álvarez Bravo. He is often described as the most important Latin American photographer of the twentieth century who has influenced generations of Mexican image-makers, either through his photographs or because he was their mentor. His visual contribution is crucial to illustrating the cultural shift from the cult of the pictorial to the anti-picturesque. At this point, it is important to return to the division between the picturesque and the anti-picturesque and ways in which these visual trends shaped representations of *mexicanidad*. Before outlining Bravo's role in this shift, is it necessary to mention that he and his wife, who later became a photographer in her own right, inherited Tina Modotti's Graflex camera and her job as a muralist photographer (Debroise 2001: 226). Roberto Tejada asserts that recording the monumental murals made both Modotti and Bravo aware of photography's particular limitations in relation to those of other art forms (Tejada 2009: Location 1175). Despite being a medium capable of recording other forms of art in fine detail, it was also perceived as somewhat inferior to those art forms for its inability to represent the epic events of the past.

Manuel Álvarez Bravo's photography transformed this perception of the medium in Mexico. Mraz points out that often in order to visually comment critically upon the picturesque conventions, Álvarez Bravo had to present them in ironic terms, making his photographs both very articulate and ambiguous in their negation of the pictorial (Mraz 2009: 87). Esther Gabara in *Errant Modernism* points out that Álvarez Bravo saw the poetic and the documentary as complementary aesthetics, rather than opposing ones (Gabara 2008: 222), paving the way for photographers such as Goded whose documentary work straddles the genres of art and documentary photography. Moreover, such a view of his photography allows for a more nuanced attitude to the picturesque — anti-picturesque dichotomy in an effort to frame them not just as opposing approaches, but as creative reworking of visual symbols and tropes deemed politically impotent. Debroise indicates that it was Álvarez Bravo's contemplative but concerned approach to the people and situations he photographed that distinguished him from other photographers working in Mexico during the first half of the twentieth century, the majority of whom appeared distant or indifferent (Debroise 2001: 226). Goded's photography references that of Álvarez Bravo not just in terms of its shared aesthetic, but also in relation to the theme of absence, which is prevalent in the art of both. In Goded's works that probe the impossibilities and omissions of photographic representations one finds clear references to Álvarez Bravo's preoccupation with the unrepresentable (Gabara 2008: 224–25).

A very important aspect of Manuel Álvarez Bravo's social conscience and his political views was his involvement in education. In 1929, he started teaching photography at the Academia de San Carlos and later moved to the Mexican Institute of Cinematography and the Film Studies Centre of the Universidad Nacional Autónoma de México, teaching photographers who would become major players in Mexican visual culture, such as Nacho López, Héctor García, and Graciela Iturbide (Mraz 2009: 91). This is where Álvarez Bravo's influence gains practical importance for Maya Goded, who benefited from his tuition by proxy when she started working with Graciela Iturbide. More generally, in terms of the cultural landscape of Mexico, Gabara credits Álvarez Bravo with creating photography which 'maintains a relationship to social reality and promises a fictional alternative to documentary truth' (Gabara 2008: 228).

The country's appeal to many international photographers intertwines various representations of Mexican identity with the history of photography and its biggest names (Haddu 2008: 7). The exhibition *Mexico through Foreign Eyes* (1993) and its accompanying book by the same title both aim to display the extraordinary photographic attention the country has received from generations of artists. Both the travelling exhibition and the book were received with huge national and international interest. Although Mraz frames this reception as symptomatic of the privileging of foreign Mexican representations over the local ones (Mraz 2001: 194), it is important to acknowledge the way in which Mexicans have been seen by others in order to appreciate the influence of that foreign mediation on the construction of *mexicanidad.*

Mexico through Foreign Eyes (1993) is a compendium of foreign imagery of Mexico. Through its selection, it creates a canon of Mexican representations and affirms the significance of its representations in the history of the medium. Primarily, it draws on and actively constitutes the myth of Mexico as an exotic paradise, a place where one might find respite, particularly from the unrelentingly competitive US commercial society (Rosenblum 1993: 27). This sentiment is especially jarring when one considers Mexico's position of economic dependency underwritten by its northern neighbour through trade agreements. In that sense, escaping the United States into Mexico because of commercial pressure is not a movement away from commercial capitalism. On the contrary, it is a visual journey which showcases the consequences of twentieth-century capitalism. It is a veritable Grand Tour of its underbelly, and the proliferation of images of poverty taken by foreign photographers included in the album attests to that.

The album includes photographers such as Henri Cartier-Bresson, Robert Capa,

Hugo Brehme, Paul Strand, Carl Lumholtz, Mark Kozloff, and many others. Out of forty-nine photographers featured, thirty-seven are American. As such, the album betrays a clear US bias, but is useful in tracing the developments in photographic fashions, from Henri Cartier-Bresson's street photography, to the gritty realism of Kent Klich's images of children. It is also a catalogue of exoticism, from C. B. Waite's indigenous man in 'Hot Country Laborer' and Carl Lumholtz's indigenous women photographed at the end of the nineteenth century, to Abbas's 'Madona Chamulana' captured in 1983 (Naggar and Ritchin 1993: 171). Important as it may be in providing a trajectory of foreign photographic interests, *Mexico through Foreign Eyes* deals with a relatively small, if very significant, part of the visual heritage concerning the country. During and after the Revolution, the importance of home-grown representations of national character in Mexico gained a new urgency.

Ghosts of the Revolution

Oliver Debroise argues that the Mexican Revolution is one of the most intensively represented and intensely observed conflicts, which continues to excite imaginations (Debroise 2001: 174). John Mraz in *Looking for Mexico* explains the proliferation of images of the conflict by the flood of foreign reporters and photographers, who were attracted by the revolutionary social upheaval as well as the relative lack of censorship and control over the images, especially in comparison to strict visual restrictions of representations of Second World War (Mraz 2009: 59). Debroise acknowledges the importance of Mexican Revolution's photographic legacy, but he also questions its symbolic significance, by inquiring whether the importance of photographic records of the conflict may be a result of a retrospective gaze influenced by the state's desire to produce a fixed and comprehensible view of a 'chaotic situation' (Debroise 2001: 177). He also draws a comparison between the contradictory, chaotic, and incomprehensible nature of the conflict and attributes the same qualities to the imagery produced during the Revolution (ibid.), discursively strengthening the link between history and photography and stressing the latter's reliability as a record.

Indeed, Andrea Noble (2010: 15) argues for acknowledging the influence of nation-builders on consolidating the image of the war through photography. It was a conscious, politically motivated strategy to strengthen the gains of the revolution and to portray it as a homogeneous conflict with clearly defined factions, as opposed to a chaotic partisan struggle. However, Noble also emphasises the polysemic nature of photography by explaining that, despite their deployment as propaganda tools in order to consolidate budding national sentiments, these images were also open to different appropriations and reinterpretations (ibid.). In consolidating and archiving the photographic legacy of the Revolution, I outline the influence of the Casasola family whose photographic agency turned archive is a significant part of Mexico's visual history.

Augustín Víctor Casasola rose to prominence during the Porfiriato, first as a reporter and then as a press photographer. Daniel Escorza Rodríguez in his book

Casasola: el fotógrafo y su colección [Casasola: The Photographer and His Collection] provides an overview of Casasola's life and work (2010). He charts Casasola's career progression, from a reporter working for a number of Mexico City's newspapers such as *El Liberal*, *El Popular*, and *El Tiempo*, who began taking pictures to illustrate his articles, to a photojournalist courted by presidents and revolutionary leaders (Escorza Rodríguez 2010: unnumbered pages). In a shrewd business move, Casasola established the Agencia Mexicana de Información Gráfica [Mexican Visual Information Agency] just as demand for photographs of the armed struggle gathered momentum (Noble 2010: 27). Tellingly, its slogan read 'tengo o hago la fotografía que Ud. necesite' [I have or will take the photograph you need] (Escorza Rodríguez 2010: unnumbered pages), marketing the agency to those in need of visual narratives to support their stories and advertising the power of the new medium. Acting as a repository for the work of hundreds of photographers, whose authorship often went unacknowledged, the agency established the Casasola family as a dominant force within Mexican visual culture as they went on to photograph significant events in the life of the nation for some six decades after the Revolution (Noble 2010: 27).

Casasola's most significant and transformative publications are the *Historias gráficas*, which, for decades, have provided a publically available photographic record of historical events. Having bought the photographic archive of *El Imparcial* in 1917, he combined it with images he amassed between 1911 and 1920 which were edited together to form the first *Álbum histórico gráfico* [Illustrated Historical Album], published in 1921 (Debroise 2001: 186). The album did not enjoy the commercial success Augustín Víctor was hoping for and he only succeeded in publishing the first of six planned volumes (ibid.). Although it was designed to document a revolutionary decade in Mexican history, with Casasola being the main photographer of the struggle, Mraz argues that its composition suggests a Porfirian monumental narrative of national improvement led by a *caudillo*. Patriarchy is firmly entrenched in the album, with Great Men featuring in over 70 per cent of all the photographs, with 40 per cent of images devoted to the portrayal of various Mexican presidents (Mraz 2009: 73). Mraz tracks Augustín Víctor's commitment to Mexican leaders by pointing out his insertions of leaders' portraits into photographs that 'would otherwise be images of anonymous combatants or cityscapes', claiming that this crude adulatory visual practice supports the view that male leaders forge history and the new nation itself (Mraz 2009: 76).

Decades later, Gustavo Casasola Zapata realised his father's ambition of creating a visual historical narrative of the nation, which became hugely popular in Mexico (Mraz 2009: 192). John Mraz in *Looking for Mexico* and in *Photographing the Mexican Revolution* and Andrea Noble in *Photography and Memory in Mexico* argue against the assumption that the *Historias gráficas* provided an unbiased and objective account of the history of the nation, emphasising instead that they projected a particular perspective, one which was closely aligned with the interests of the regime of the day (Mraz 2009, 2012) and which, in turn, cemented Casasola's position as chronicles of the struggle and of the nation (Noble 2010: 27). Nonetheless, the importance of Casasola's *Historias gráficas* and their popularity is difficult to overstate when analysing the conjectures of national identity and photography. As late as in the 1980s, the regime headed by Miguel de la Madrid subsidised substantial reprintings of *Historia gráfica de la Revolución Mexicana* and *Seis siglos de historia gráfica de Mexico* (Mraz 2001: 196), attempting to legitimise one party dictatorship through their visual association with the history of Great Men.

Although Goded's photography is a clear thematic departure from the fawning presidentialism of Casasola's *Historias gráficas*, her artistic preference expressed in producing photographic books and photo-essays can be framed as part of the documentary tradition that emerged after the Revolution. Esther Gabara argues that:

> [p]hoto-essays were an integral part of a larger process of organizing representation following the Revolution, which included vast educational reforms from the elementary to the university level and the development of mass media from commercial magazines to cinema. (Gabara 2008: 148)

Not only does this statement contextualise Goded's aesthetic and formal choices, but it also helps to appreciate the role of photography in creating shared social imaginaries, which then have an important bearing on nation-building. This crucial function of photography was never lost on post-revolutionary leaders in Mexico.

The Revolution undoubtedly had a profound effect on Mexico and was one of the crucial moments of nation formation, which shaped its image abroad and still continues to play an incredibly important role in the national psyche, over time becoming a crucial historical tool in legitimising the PRI one-party regime. Although it hardly eradicated the profound differences between different fractions, it did help to forge a new vision of what Mexico as a nation should be, even if that vision was hardly uniform and homogeneous. Andrea Noble in her book on Modotti emphasises that in 1910 Mexico was a 'fragmented mosaic' (Noble 2000: 14) more than a nation, quoting Alan Knight's assertion that the contradictory revolutionary and conservative elements in Mexico at the beginning of the twentieth century continue to pose a significant problem for historians (Knight in Noble 2000: 14). As with any conflict viewed retrospectively, the question of identities in relation to armed struggle remains muddled, since they are forged in the process and can be as much a result of the fighting as of pre-existing political and social differences that led to it. Moreover, Noble underlines that Mexico's modernisation project was very problematic at the time, with an 80 per cent illiteracy rate and a tarnished reputation abroad, most crucially in the United States. Therefore, in the immediate aftermath of the revolution, the project of unifying the nation and incorporating hitherto shunned and socially and economically disadvantaged indigenous communities into a new idea of Mexican identity became of utmost importance.

This project of national unity had a crucial racial component, aiming to attempt discursively and visually incorporate Mexico's pre-Columbian and colonial past into a cohesive history of Mexican identity, which would underpin the nation's formation. The idea of *mestizaje* emerged and it became a bodily foundation of modern Mexican identity. Leopoldo Zea could not overstate its importance, when he claimed that:

> The *mestizo* is a flower and fruit of the union between the conqueror and the conquered. The *mestizo* and *mestizaje*, through which hateful racial

> discrimination disappears, are in one way or another made possible by the order inherited by Latin America, which is fortunately disappearing. (Zea in Oliver 2011: 254)

This romanticised view of national unity based on a racial and cultural synthesis does not acknowledge the exclusion and marginalisation of the indigenous community prior to the Revolution, when they were seen as obstacles to the processes of modernisation (Noble 2000: 15). Indeed, the post-revolutionary projects of sending educators into the countryside in order to teach its predominantly indigenous dwellers betrays a patronising attitude to non-metropolitan others (ibid.). Although Leopoldo Zea's view that *mestizaje* solved Mexico's racially underpinned inequalities by incorporating everyone into the idea of national identity (Oliver 2011: 257) gives one an insight into the idea's power and its importance to *mexicanidad*, it does not acknowledge the main problem stemming from it, which is important to recognise at this stage. Ofelia Schutte stresses that the Mexican concept of nationality is very much entrenched in European philosophy and social science (Schutte in Oliver 2011: 259). Therefore, the qualifying addition of an incorporated racial difference is not enough to allow indigenous communities access to ideas of community and nationality on their own terms (ibid.). The Chiapas rebellion is perhaps the strongest recent expression of indigenous discontent with the balance of power indigenous Mexicans symbolically underpin.

In a country with very high illiteracy rates, visual representations of new ideas of national unity were of crucial importance. Incorporating the *mestizo* into Mexican imagery became a cultural project with significant socio-political implications. One of the most important aspects of that project was Mexican muralism, which constituted a key part of the modernising zeal in symbolically revisioning national identity and was 'a colossal project that sought to elevate the nation's turbulent history, promote immediate social ideals, and determine a future political purpose' (Tejada 2009: Location 1176). Moreover, representations of indigenous communities were not just painted onto the walls of buildings such as the Escuela Nacional Preparatoria [National Preparatory School] or the Secretaría de Educación Pública [Ministry of Education]. Their participation in nationhood and their importance for *mexicanidad* were also symbolically incorporated into the visual narrative through photography. Indigenous communities were the subjects of photographic interest from abroad and within Mexico ever since the first daguerreotypes started arriving there. Although that interest is problematic from an ethical perspective and raises questions of subjugation and exoticisation, the photographic presence of the indigenous people does testify to their importance to national identity. The Instituto Nacional Indigenista had been commissioning photographic projects with a view to visually preserving and documenting the indigenous communities since its inception in the aftermath of the Revolution. In the early 1990s, Maya Goded was employed by the Instituto as one of its team of photographers, who travel from village to village throughout rural Mexico documenting the lives of people who are receiving subsidies from the Instituto precisely because of their symbolic racial status within the paradigm of *mexicanidad*. Indigenous communities have often interested female photographers, who sought out feminine representations of local and national identities that both conform to and contest expected photographic modes.

Gendered Perspectives

What can feminist criticism contribute to the gendered landscape of Mexican visual culture? The emphasis on Great Men in public imagery and their role in forging the country clearly marginalises women as historical participants and photographers to the advantage of their male counterparts. Examples of this privileging of images of men abound in Mexican visual culture, but perhaps one of the most striking case is that of the *Historia gráfica de México* where 'the participation of women, anonymous or identified, is extremely limited . . . [and] they appear in some 2 per cent of the photos' (Mraz 2009: 232). The lack of visibility of women is compounded by their reductive portrayal in images where they do appear, in *Historias gráficas* as 'archetypical camp follower[s]' (Mraz 2009: 232), on postcards as fetishised objects of beauty and non-threatening exotic female sexuality (Mraz 2009: 36), or as picturesque embodiments of folkloric ways of life. As Carlos Monsiváis attests in his 'Foreword' to *Sex in Revolution: Gender, Politics and Power in Modern Mexico* (2006):

> The Mexican Revolution has been unified in order to be understood as a whole [...] and has been characterized however the regime pleases, which prohibits understanding its complexity. Yet, [...] one thing is notorious: women . . . mean very little in political and social terms and practically nothing when set before the deity of those times: History, an exclusive masculine territory. . . . Although women's participation in the Revolution may have been influential in many ways, patriarchy is nothing if not an endless strategy of concealment. (Monsiváis 2006: 4–5)

Indeed, the patriarchal bias against visual production made by women or representing women is clear in connection with Mexican visual history and the photographic criticism relating to it. In spite of Graciela Iturbide being in the avant-garde of the country's artistic production, her position as a celebrated international artist having been cemented through her exhibition at the Tate Modern in 2014, scholarly engagement with her work has been limited, with a few notable exceptions, such as Roberto Tejada's analysis in his book *National Camera* (2009).

Recently, scholars have begun to address this lack of research on representations of women and by women, as B. Christine Arce's new book entitled *México's Nobodies: The Cultural Legacy of the Soldadera and Afro-Mexican Women* evidences (2018). In her study, Arce grapples with the paradox of the *soldaderas* and the Afro-Mexican women's erasure from official Mexican memory and history and ubiquity in popular culture. This intersectional, feminist study looks to the aesthetic realm to determine how songs, images, novels, murals, and other types of artistic production mediate the figures of *soldadera* and *Afro-mestiza* and how that intervention influences 'the construction of the social, political and cultural world' in challenging official exclusionary narratives (Arce 2018: Location 218). This is a crucial theoretical intervention that seeks to problematise the division between popular culture and official history by unravelling the latter's violent omissions. It works to undo the patriarchal strategy of concealing women's participation in public life by focusing on their neglected presence.

This strategy of concealment is clear not just in relation to images of women, such as those analysed by Arce in her book, but also in relation to images produced by women. Despite the odds being stacked against female photographers, Mexico produced a great number of them, but they usually receive less attention than men. A case in point is the first Mexican female photographer and wife of Manuel Álvarez Bravo — Lola Álvarez Bravo. She is rarely mentioned in studies of Manuel Álvarez Bravo, despite leaving an important mark on Mexican photography. In the first book dedicated to her work, entitled *Lola Álvarez Bravo* (2006), Elizabeth Ferrer argues that, even though becoming a professional photographer was an unlikely choice for a wealthy Mexican woman, Álvarez Bravo's intellectual ambition coupled with economic need and, most importantly, her husband's influence made her into the first woman photographer (Ferrer 2006: 9). She has never emerged from her husband's shadow, but Ferrer's account of her life at least allows a wider audience to see her as an artist in her own right, as opposed to the great photographer's wife. Even though her husband's influence on her visual production is difficult to overstate, Ferrer charts her development as an independent artist whose outlook on photography was driven less by 'technical virtuosity than by a reverence for the diversity of human expression' (Ferrer 2006: 20). For thirty years, Álvarez Bravo held the position of chief of photography at the Instituto Nacional de Bellas Artes y Literatura [National Institute of Fine Arts and Literature], which suited her interest in the arts and provided opportunities for some of 'the most memorable images of her career' (Ferrer 2006: 20–21). Although her work remains underappreciated and under-researched, Álvarez Bravo did pave the way for other women to take up the practice of photography and, in that sense, was a pioneer in the field.

Through his educational interest, Manuel Álvarez Bravo's influence on Mexican photography extended beyond his wife's photographic career. One of his most successful students is Graciela Iturbide, who became his assistant in 1969 (Iturbide in Carreras 2004: 127). In an interview with Claudi Carreras in *Conversaciones con fotógrafos mexicanos*, she recalls the years she spent learning from him with great affection and credits that time as being crucial in her decision to become a photographer (ibid.). Certainly, his influence is obvious in the way she talks about the political significance of her photography, on the one hand claiming that she photographs only because she likes to photograph, much like Manuel Álvarez Bravo (Debroise 2001: 226), and, on the other hand, citing her master's assertion that 'todo acto humano es político al final de cuentas' [in the end, every human act is political] (Iturbide in Carreras 2004: 129). This apparent contradiction is reflected in Goded's choice of projects that matter to her on a personal level, and are also socio-politically salient and indicative of widespread inequalities and prejudices.

Two characteristics distinguish Iturbide from other photographers. The first one is her desire to immerse herself in the world of people she chooses to photograph. Her most famous work in the state of Juchitán compiled in the book *Juchitán de las mujeres* [Women's Juchitán] (1989) was the result of 'ten years of work, countless trips to Tehuantepec, and long periods living with the people of the Isthmus' (Debroise 2001: 151). The second distinctive characteristic of her work is her experimental attitude to appearances, focusing on the ambiguities of the photographic medium (Debroise 2001: 150). Asked by Carreras about the relationship between photography and reality, she underlines the subjectivity of photography and the infinite multitude of different perspectives. She explains further:

> Esto se debe a que el resultado depende de quién es cada uno, de lo que ha visto, de lo que trae dentro. Por lo mismo, pienso que la fotografía jamás puede ser objetiva. Siempre existirá el factor subjetivo de cada fotógrafo. (Iturbide in Carreras 2004: 133)
>
> [That is because the resulting photograph depends on each individual, on what they saw and what they carry inside them. This is why I think photography can never be objective. There will always be a subjective factor to every photographer.]

Debroise traces Iturbide's subjectivity in her photographic reflections on 'how, when and why to make a photograph' (Debroise 2001: 152).

Graciela Iturbide is a very important presence in Maya Goded's photographic career. Goded confesses that, among Mexican photographers, she was most drawn to Iturbide's work (Goded in Carreras 2004: 92). Iturbide attests that Goded is the only photographer who could be considered her pupil (Iturbide in Carreras 2004: 136). Certainly, parallels can be found between their photography, since Goded's work is also often the result of many years of living with her subjects. Through their subjectivity, these women offer a glimpse of *mexicanidad*, which contests the visual narrative of patriarchal pictorial essentialism. Instead, through the combination of creatively reworking the picturesque tradition, and their intimate relationship with the communities they photograph, they create new visual presences and meanings, which question the hegemonic patriarchal viewpoint.

Iturbide and Goded evidently share a photographic interest in femininity and its relationship to Mexican society. Iturbide's *Juchitán de las mujeres* depicts a vision of a matriarchal society with women at its centre. Although Iturbide claims she never set out to make a political album, she does admit that it can be construed that way mainly because of Elena Poniatowska's accompanying text, which deals with the Juchitán political scene at the time (Carreras 2004: 132). Its reception as a feminist work has attracted some criticism. In an article seeking to give Zapotec women an opportunity to contest their representation through ethnographic study Edaena Saynes-Vázquez claims that Iturbide's and Poniatowska's view of the Juchitán society as matriarchal does not match the local women's self-perception (Saynes-Vázquez 1996: 189). Quite apart from the question of whether the photographer's representation matches the self-perception of her subjects, the Juchitán women have become emblematic in Iturbide's distinctive photographs. In particular, *Nuestra Señora de las iguanas* achieved an iconic status, especially amongst the Latino community in the United States (Iturbide in Carreras 2004: 133). Importantly, it is also celebrated in Juchitán where it was printed on posters and displayed on nearly every home to celebrate the tenth anniversary of the local Casa de la

Cultura [Cultural Centre] (Iturbide in Carreras 2004: 134). What is remarkable here is the gender reversal of the creation of emblematic imagery with nationalistic undertones. Iturbide creates a symbol in a way that mirrors the typical Mexican focus on visual historical narrative prominently featuring Great Men. That is not to suggest that through her exceptional gender status and her photographic practice she discovers an unproblematic way of representing national femininity. Rather, the ground-breaking value of this photograph, mediated through a female gaze, is its ability to create cultural meaning which goes beyond the conventional expectations of women and challenges them.

Similarly, Goded's work with the prostitutes of La Merced can be seen as a reframing of expectations. The photographer's focus on the bodily presence of the prostitutes has a surprisingly empowering effect, especially in a cultural context where feminine bodily presence is, all too often, erased into idealistic notions of virginity or degraded, should it fail to comply with those notions. Goded's portrayal of the prostitutes is far from idealistic, since she shows lives and bodies clearly marked by sexual violence. Taking and publishing these photographs is a form of protest against women's relegation to *zonas de tolerancia*, a space where their controversial presence cannot be ignored. Goded visually ignores the men involved with the women, whether as procurers or clients, choosing to focus on the women and their resilience in supporting the entire community around them. Such an approach is, of course, open to criticism similar in tone to that received by Iturbide for her representation of Juchitán women as independent people in charge of their own communities, because it glosses over the pervasive *machismo*, alive and well in Juchitán and in La Merced, where male pimps and clients enjoy much more freedom than the sex workers. Just as Iturbide reframes in *Juchitán de las mujeres* the symbolic power of the exotic indigenous woman, Goded in *Plaza de la soledad* reworks the myths of self-abnegating motherhood by focusing on its cultural antithesis, the whore. By providing a different perspective on women, who exercise agency over their own lives despite patriarchal constraints in which they function, Iturbide and Goded question the perception of disadvantaged women as weak and passive victims. Both women's photographs find an audience at home and abroad as they coin new cultural meanings, which pose an explicit challenge to patriarchy.

Goded attempts to expand the visible plurality of experience, so often slotted in Mexico into narrowly defined types. It is a challenge to preconceptions, but one that is rooted in a firm understanding of those preconceptions, seeing them not as deviations from the true form of people or phenomena, but rather as dominant forms of identifications and representations. By exploring and challenging the visual and conceptual tools necessary in order to categorise others, Goded's visual journey through socio-cultural ways of seeing demonstrates photography's ability to be actively constitutive of cultural horizons, which affect the way we see ourselves and others. The polysemic nature of photography underlines the dynamic and embodied qualities of human understanding, which, on the one hand, shifts with new information, but, on the other hand, is also capable of conjuring up new meanings.

Grounded in the personal and the historical contexts of Goded's photographic documentary, the next part of this book will focus on the conceptual framework underpinning the analysis of representation and subalternity in relation to Goded's photography.

CHAPTER 2

Subalternity, Representation and Photography

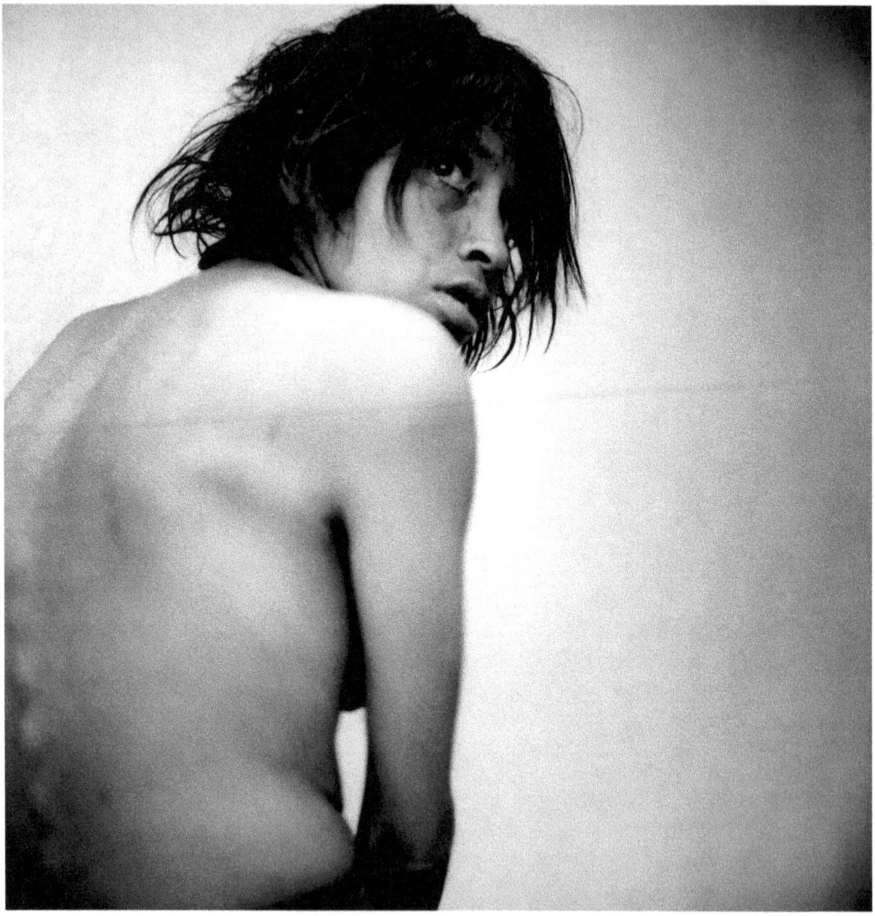

Fig. 2.1. M. Goded, *Good Girls* (2006).

A young woman in a photograph is anxiously looking up (Fig. 2.1). She is naked, her face is dirty and her hair dishevelled. She is wearily hunched over and looking up beyond the frame of the photograph, appearing vulnerable and defenceless. The image's composition is stark in its black and white colouring and austere simplicity. The woman's pose and her intense gaze directed at something or someone above her compels important questions of what is beyond the frame, both literally and figuratively. She appears frightened and her body looks mistreated and fragmented by the frame. Shot in a very tight frame, captured against a wall, and cast as a victim, she seems hounded. The formal ambivalence in the way Goded took this photograph, on the one hand framing it as a representation of the realities of the Mexican sex industry, and on the other hand capturing her subject in an uncompromisingly persecuting fashion, can be read as a metaphor for the well-documented ambivalence towards women in Mexican society. Revered in symbolic terms, but often significantly disadvantaged in comparison to men, they appear to be the ideal illustration for what David Levi Strauss (2005: 69) identifies as the tendency to denigrate and disregard in reality what is valued and cherished as an ideal. How can one approach and understand the palpable vulnerability of another human being represented in a photograph?

The concept of subalternity is an indispensable critical tool in theorising the multi-faceted vulnerability of people or groups excluded from socio-cultural hegemonies. Following on from the personal and the cultural context of Maya Goded's photography, this chapter anchors her art theoretically within critical paradigms of subalternity and representation. In order to account for the photographer's interest in representations of socio-economically disadvantaged people suffering exclusion from mainstream visual culture, this chapter maps out theoretical complexities of the triad of subalternity, representation and photography, and problematises them within the context of Goded's photo-documentary. In reference to Gayatri Spivak's and John Beverley's theories, I frame subalternity as a postcolonial category. Within the nexus of subalternity and representation, I argue for considering photography as a unique form of intervention into dominant regimes of representation, one with the capacity to transcend disciplinary and hierarchical divisions, albeit in problematic ways. This theoretical underpinning helps to examine photography's role in producing visual hegemony as well as its representative power in subverting such hegemony in relation to subaltern people and issues.

The term subalternity was first used outside military contexts by Italian Marxist thinker Antonio Gramsci to describe the subordinate and dispossessed nature of the Italian working classes and peasants (Gramsci in Beverley 1999: 7). The importance and originality of his contribution to Marxist thought lies in his holistic understanding of the impossibility of separation between the spheres of economic, social, cultural, educational and political influences (Ives 2004: 84, 91, 101). In Gramsci's conceptual framework, the notion of subalternity is inextricably linked to that of hegemony. The latter is not merely an issue of economic dominance. Hegemony has cultural, social and political aspects, which permeate value systems shared by those belonging to the hegemonic group, but also those who are excluded from it and disadvantaged by this exclusion (Gramsci 2000: 57). Gramsci underlines that those value systems are not spontaneous expressions of facts, but deliberate policies, which focus on preserving hegemony (Gramsci 2000: 210). As much as some account is taken of subaltern interests within hegemony in order to strengthen its influence, its main focus is on perpetuating the imbalance of power between different groups and preventing effective resistance of the subaltern.

One of the fundamental elements of dominance is the fragmenting and forgetting of subaltern histories out of the hegemonic historical perspective, which then forecloses their potential to foment resistance. Hegemony over history and language, therefore, enables power to operate in covert and insidious ways, blurring the boundaries between coercion and consent, direction and domination, and civil society and political society (Forgacs 2000: 423–24). In this context, photography that puts subaltern issues at the centre of its concerns, such as Goded's, becomes a tool in resisting the process of erasing subaltern lives from the hegemonic landscape, by clearly pointing to the existence of hitherto excluded subaltern histories.

Education plays an important role in Gramsci's understanding of hegemony as an organisation of consent (Ives 2004: 64). In colonial contexts, the educational relationship between the colonisers and the natives is structured to teach or civilise the latter. Such assumption not only erroneously designates the colonised as beings without history or education (Mignolo 2005: xii), but also gives the colonisers the ability to structure the world-view of the other in ways which benefit their own ends, even when such endeavours are framed as humanitarian or religious interventions. Postcolonial or de-colonised contexts arguably allow for a less polarised view of former colonisers and natives, but the sedimentation of cultural, social and educational effects should not be underestimated. Within the Mexican context, Octavio Paz in *El laberinto de la soledad* argues that the past never disappears from view and even the oldest wounds keep bleeding (Paz 2008: 45). Elsewhere, he remarks that 'the Creole is like the Native American, from here, and like the Spaniard, from there' (Paz in Rommens 2006: unnumbered pages), but that simple geographical distinction betrays the difficulty of encompassing these two contradictory identifications within one body and one consciousness, which is further confounded by an educational relationship which overwhelmingly favours one identification over the other. Indeed, it points to an inaccessible subaltern positionality emerging at the nexus of these two identifications, neither of which can properly address the shifting reference frame of 'here' and 'there' within the post-colonial Mexican context.

Gramsci's evident reluctance unambiguously to define the most essential concepts of his theory is, according to Ives, an exemplification of 'Wittgenstein's dictum, "the meaning of a word is in its use in the language"' (Ives 2004: 65). Anachronistically speaking, he displays a poststructuralist attitude before its time, making his ideas appealing to scholars working within the poststructuralist tradition. The notion of subalternity has been most notably adopted and redefined by the South Asian Subaltern Studies Group, for whom, as the name suggests, it has become a pivotal concept. This notion is here expanded to include complex relationships of power between nations, which used to be tied to one another by a colonial relationship of dominance. Edward Said in *Selected Subaltern Studies* (1988) outlines main concerns of the group, reappropriating many of Gramsci's theories in a different context. As such, subaltern studies are a hybrid phenomenon, which critically considers European influences alongside non-European strands, sharing and reconfiguring familiar paradigms (Said 1988: x).

This hybridity provides a fertile intellectual ground for analysing the conditions of post-colonialism across different disciplines. However, it also exposes subaltern scholars to criticism for their reliance on European or Western ideas, which create and sustain subalternity. A parallel argument can be made here about Goded's focus on subaltern issues in her photography, since she uses a medium implicit in creating hegemonic regimes of visibility in order to question their omissions and exclusions. Similar criticisms have been levelled at Gayarti Chakravorty Spivak's seminal essay entitled 'Can the Subaltern Speak?' where she examines issues of subalternity and representation (Spivak 1995).

The importance of Spivak's essay is difficult to overstate. One of her main arguments concerning representation is indispensable for theorising the role of documentary photography in shaping socio-cultural visibility. In the essay, she examines the difference between *vertreten* and *darstellen* in a passage from Karl Marx's *The Eighteenth Brumaire of Louis Bonaparte*. The former is understood as a proxy, or 'speaking for' in politics, and the latter is framed as representation in art or philosophy (Spivak 1995: 69). Although she concedes that there are similarities and convergences between the two, she also underlines that they cannot be run together. Her main critique of Marxism as well as Western post-Marxist debates lies in the astute observation that they all share in the persistent obliteration of the possibility of subaltern representation, which renders the domain of the subaltern inaccessible. Writing on the irretrievable heterogeneity of the other, Spivak states that to confront that heterogeneity 'is not to represent (*vertreten*) [it] but to learn to represent (*darstellen*) ourselves. This argument would take us into a critique of a disciplinary anthropology and the relationship between elementary pedagogy and disciplinary formation' (Spivak 1995: 84). Before analysing the implications of these statements for subaltern representation in Goded's photography, it is important to trace the trajectory of Spivak's and the South Asian Subaltern Studies Group's theories within the Latin American context.

Although Spivak warns that the issue of subalternity in India 'cannot be taken as representative of all countries, nations, cultures and the like that may be invoked as the Other of Europe as Self' (Spivak 1995: 76), her contributions to the debate and, more generally, the work of the South Asian Subaltern Studies Group have far-reaching theoretical implications for scholars around the world, European or otherwise. The intellectual exchanges between the South Asian scholars and their literary and cultural counterparts working within the field of Latin American studies led to the creation of the Latin American Subaltern Studies Group in 1992 (Legrás 2004: 126). Its 'Founding Statement' published in 1993 declared a need for 'new ways of thinking and acting politically' (Latin American Subaltern Studies Group 1993: 110) and referenced the work of the South Asian Group in relation to the necessity of re-examining Latin American historiography and its exclusions. The Group disbanded after nearly a decade due to political and disciplinary differences (Rodríguez 2001: 29), but its work continues to have an impact on scholars working within the field of Latin American studies and still foments debates for and against the application of the term 'subalternity' to that particular discipline.

One of the group's founders, John Beverley, engages with Spivak's theory on the impossibility of subaltern representation inasmuch as it helps him to expose the paradox within subaltern studies (Beverley 1999: 2–5). In terms of academic representation, he argues, the subaltern will remain elusive, not unlike Jacques Lacan's category of the Real, and will always remain a 'gap-in-knowledge', logically inaccessible to discourse, which is complicit in constructing the conditions of its invisibility and silence (Beverley 1999: 2). Therefore, to Beverley, a productive theoretical and political engagement with subalternity does not consist of paternalistically rescuing the subaltern from its historical silence, but in examining the dividing line that produces dominance and subordination, historically as well as in the present (Beverley 1999: 7). This relates to the concept of power, which within subaltern studies is the legacy of the French thinker Michel Foucault. Spivak problematises that concept by referring to 'Edward W. Said's critique of power in Foucault as a captivating and mystifying category that allows him "to obliterate the role of classes, the role of economics, the role of insurgency and rebellion"' (Spivak 1995: 75). She adds to that critique by underlining yet again the transparency of the Western intellectual in his totalising concept of power and his inability to conceptualise '*the kind of Power* [...] that would inhabit the unnamed subject of the Other of Europe' (ibid.). Invariably, the subaltern and its power remain elusive.

Ileana Rodríguez, who was one of the founding members of the Latin American Subaltern Studies Group, declares that the inaccessibility of the subaltern is not as problematic and theoretically paralysing as it would first appear (Rodríguez 2001: 9). In 'Reading Subalterns across Texts, Disciplines, and Theories: From Representation to Recognition' she asserts that subaltern studies is not a study of subalterns (ibid.). In her view,

> Subaltern studies are postmodern and postrevolutionary attempts to understand the limits of previous hermeneutics by challenging culture to think of itself from the point of view of its own negations. Another goal is to recognize that in the history and culture of 'societies' Others' we can find, paradoxically, new ways of approaching some of the riddles created by the incapacity of bourgeois culture to think about its own conditions of discursive production. (ibid.)

Rodríguez explains that questioning culture from the point of view of its negation by references to Ranajit Guha's book *Dominance without Hegemony: History and Power in Colonial India* (1988). He declares that a radical critique of any culture is impossible if the ideological parameters of the critic coincide with those of the culture they are aiming to analyse. Therefore, in his view, a distance between object and its agency is necessary in order to critique the structural limitations of a hegemonic relationship (Guha in Rodríguez 2001: 9–10). Rodríguez describes the necessity for this distance as the paradox of knowledge; the productive negation, which opens up the possibility of speaking against the grain of the dominant culture and from a variety of subject positions (Rodríguez 2001: 8), thereby circumventing the constitutive silence of the subaltern.

Subaltern studies, both in Latin America and internationally, attracted criticisms that necessitate analytical engagement. First of all, Spivak's seminal article on the subaltern is sometimes framed as 'imperialistic in spirit' (Rabasa 2010: 4) mainly because of her explicit focus and conceptual reliance on Western philosophy. In response to that frequent challenge, it is crucial to stress that the value of the subaltern project does not lie in the elusive possibility of uncovering the voice of the subaltern and filling in the gaps of hegemonic historiography — that would indeed make it an imperialistic project in its positivist zeal and implicit belief in pure forms of consciousness. The task at hand is more nuanced. In the absences and gaps of historical narratives, which determine present outcomes, it seeks spaces for the revolutionary possibilities of thinking otherwise. The subaltern studies scholars often self-consciously recognise their own Western bias as part of the historically constitutive nature of subaltern studies in particular and academic knowledge in general — after all, academia is highly hierarchical and very much complicit in the epistemological violence essential to building coherent world-views and informing policy and education. This recognition, although always incomplete and opaque, at least opens up possibilities of questioning dominant representations from positionalities outside hegemonic structures.

The question of the (im)possibility of subaltern representation is one which is at the very core of subaltern studies. Spivak's apparent foreclosure of that possibility in 'Can the Subaltern Speak?' and her tracking of the figure of 'native informant' within the field of postcolonial studies in her book *A Critique of Postcolonial Reason* (1999) is far from a straightforward denial of the possibility of representation. It rather points to the difficulties or impossibilities of subaltern representation within certain imperialistic paradigms. Those paradigms, however, are not impervious to a poststructuralist critical analysis, which has the potential of turning silence and absence into a conceivable site of resistance against being rendered mute by discourse. Spivak's work on subalternity is centred on that productive absence (Spivak 1995: 89). However, in order to engage with that absence at all, one must necessarily also engage with hegemonic representations and historical narratives. From that perspective, it is easy to anticipate Spivak's critics, who label her contribution imperialistic (Rabasa 2010: 4). In her own words, '[t]he postcolonial intellectuals learn that their privilege is their loss' (Spivak 1995: 82).

Predictably, a similar accusation has been levelled at the members of the Latin American Subaltern Studies Group. Their productive engagements with the South Asian Subaltern Studies Group have been criticised by some in the United States and Latin America as an attempt to transpose an imperialistic and foreign concept onto a different place where it remains inapplicable (Rabasa 2010: 4). Although some scholars, such as Horacio Legrás, dismiss this accusation as 'puerile' (Legrás 2004: 127), it is a criticism which requires examination. John Beverley discusses these concerns in his 'Introduction' to *Subalternity and Representation*. First of all, he acknowledges his own hegemonic position versus that of his Latin American counterparts, especially in the light of the power and prestige of US academia against the underfunded intellectual life of Latin America, decimated by neo-liberal policies directly linked to the economic hegemony of the United States (Beverley 1999: 18). Alluding to shared concerns but not specifying them, he then proceeds to explain that Latin American intellectuals' resistance to subaltern studies is 'itself symptomatic of a kind of subalternity — the unequal position of Latin American culture, states, economies and intellectual work in the current world system' (ibid.). However eloquent, this statement simply deepens the divide between the two perspectives and locks them into a theoretically unproductive stalemate. He then claims that Hugo Achugar and Mabel Moraña risk misrepresenting history in representing the nations they claim to speak for by rejecting subaltern positionalities (Beverley 1999: 19). In that statement, he is in fact extremely close to his critics, as both the argument for and against subaltern studies is here underpinned by the implicit belief in the pure form of consciousness, which can be accessed and represented through theory. Presenting the arguments in this way, where two elitist viewpoints compete for a hegemonic position, forecloses the potential for subaltern studies to forge a space for exploring absences and silences within dominant discourses.

The criticisms presented by Achugar and Moraña are not without validity. Moraña's charge of neo-exoticism (in Beverley 1999: 19 n. 26) is particularly difficult to refute, when Spivak's entire argument in 'Can the Subaltern Speak?' relies on defining subalternity as difference (Spivak 1995: 80). However, these two seemingly irreconcilable viewpoints need not be seen as exclusionary binary oppositions. On the contrary, subaltern scholars' engagement with subaltern and non-subaltern histories or themes, interpreting them against the grain, should be subject to a persistent and rigorous critique from without as a useful reminder of the ever-present opacity of theory. In other words, it is important to remember that as subaltern studies deal with the absence of historical representation, they also, by definition, unwittingly create more absences in their wake. Similarly, regardless of how many hitherto invisible phenomena and people Maya Goded succeeds in bringing to a wider audience through her photography, her work will always be necessarily exclusive in its choice of subjects, leaving some groups unrepresented.

At this point, it is important to return to the criticism that subaltern studies, as a discipline, is reliant on importation of hegemonic theories from Europe and the West. Ileana Rodríguez engages with this criticism by citing Latin American scholars' long-standing interest and engagement with Western theory (Rodríguez 2001: 7). That is not to proclaim the need for continuous Western dominance over academic discourses in Latin America, but to underline the history of dialogue. Subaltern studies continue to provide a productive theoretical platform for scholarly investigations that engage with local particularities in Latin America. Within the area of Mexican studies alone, two recent major publications engage with issues surrounding subalternity, namely *Without History: Subaltern Studies, the Zapatista Insurgency, and the Specter of History* (2010) by José Rabasa and *Trans-Americanity: Subaltern Modernities, Global Coloniality, and the Cultures of Greater Mexico* (2012) by José David Saldívar, both exploring hegemonic history and its implications on Mexico's cultural and socio-political realities in the twenty-first century from radically different perspectives.

For José Rabasa, framing Mexican history and the Zapatista insurgency from the perspective of subaltern studies is a way of engaging past concepts and analysing their influence on the present (Rabasa 2010: Location 199). 'In critiquing the writing of Lenin or Gramsci, I treat them [...] as texts that we must engage in imagining our present. The past is not something that happened a long time ago but a presence that *faces* us in its immediacy' (Rabasa 2010: Location 199). Rabasa understands history as a multitude of objects and events that exceeds human consciousness while shaping it simultaneously (Rabasa 2010: Locations 200–02), as well as an academic discipline that produces hegemonic accounts of the past, as one of the discourses legitimising the state. For the latter understanding of history, he sees in subaltern studies a promise of interrupting the single-voice history as well as a mode of effective resistance to the hegemony of the state by bypassing its institutions and enabling existence wholly outside of the state apparatus (Rabasa 2010: Location 90).

For her part, Spivak places a moral imperative on her engagement with subaltern studies when she declares that 'to ignore the subaltern today is [...] to continue the imperialist project' (Spivak 1995: 94). It is not within the scope of this project to summarise the intellectual dialogue between different subaltern scholars across the globe, but the discussions summarised above demonstrate that subaltern studies is an idiosyncratic area, encompassing a variety of views, and incorporating many paradoxes in theory as well as in practice. It is important to acknowledge here that for some subaltern scholars, such as John Beverley or Ileana Rodríguez, subaltern studies is a leftist project, which is in alignment with their political persuasion and is also, at least to some extent, a tool of political resistance against neo-liberalism (Beverley 1999: 21, Rodríguez 2001: 3). Such associations, although expected, especially when one considers Beverley's declaration that subaltern studies is a 'project of Marxism' (Beverley 1999: 21), do indicate a possible convergence between two types of representation specified by Spivak, one concerning politics and the state, the other concerning art and theory. Subaltern scholars' openly declared political bias is a deliberate break with the implicit idea of the transparency of the intellectual.

Subalternity as a postmodern, postcolonial and interdisciplinary category produces relevant intellectual implications for the concept of hegemony itself. Suspending one's belief in pure consciousness means that no position and no identity can be considered as wholly hegemonic. That is, naturally, not to deny that power imbalances do exist and that hegemonic representations are much more influential than subaltern ones, which remain silent and absent. It is merely to underline that fractures within hegemony are a prerequisite for a subaltern silence to occupy them. Moreover, in semantic terms, the very possibility of subaltern studies points to the idiosyncratic nature of hegemony, which is rarely a cohesive phenomenon in itself. It is only in a simplistic and misleading contrast to the subaltern and its absence that the hegemonic presence appears all encompassing. This is, again, one of the productive paradoxes of subaltern studies.

Consequently, hegemony and subalternity are not to be thought of as binary opposites, but rather as phenomena that remain permeable and dependent on one another. The subaltern studies scholars' preoccupation with history can be framed as a concern with time understood as one of constitutive concepts within Western philosophy. Particularly debates surrounding modernity are inextricably linked to the problem of a linear and transparent understanding of time and progress. José Rabasa's preference for the use of the term 'nonmodern' as opposed to 'pre-modern' (Rabasa 2010: Location 2209) exemplifies this concern as the latter notion is already loaded with teleology that constructs modernity as a historical necessity. As such, he sees no contradiction in modern and non-modern life forms coexisting in the same subject or society, 'as has been the case in Amerindian societies from the first contact with Europe to the Zapatistas today' (Rabasa 2010: Location 2173).

The coexistence and co-dependence of hegemony and subalternity can be examined through the specificity of the medium of photography. Just as the concept of subalternity has its origins in Western philosophical thought and is dependent on the same theoretical system it sets out to question, so too photography as a medium is implicated in creating hegemonic representations that produce and sustain dominant discourses of vision. Goded's photography of subaltern subjects is therefore affected by a similar productive paradox to that marking subaltern studies, whereby representations and meanings are made and remade in relation to hitherto invisible people or phenomena, but with inevitable references to representational practices, which had been excluding subaltern representations. Her artistic practice is not free of ambiguities that stem from placing the subaltern at its centre through the use of a medium complicit in its exclusion. Despite this strong link between hegemony and photography, Goded's persistent attempts at including subaltern subjects in her documentary both expand horizons of vision and provide a visual point of reference for questioning such horizons. The following analysis focuses on the triad of subalternity, photography and representation and their role in creating alternative histories within hegemonic narratives.

Photographing the Subaltern, or the Ethics of Seeing

Although hegemony is intertwined with subalternity and the respective meanings of these two concepts can only become clear in relation to each another, the issues of subaltern invisibility and muteness remain a pivotal element in sustaining the imbalance of power in favour of the hegemonic. Photography can intervene within this power dynamic, allowing the hitherto unseen subaltern to gain visibility and therefore challenge visual hegemony with their representation. This intervention demands a thorough critical analysis. As a starting point, it is helpful to return to Spivak's detailed discussion on the difference between two different types of representation, namely representation as proxy, or political representation (*vertreten*), and re-presentation in art or philosophy (*darstellen*) (Spivak 1995: 69). She concedes that the former cannot exist without the latter but resists conflating them, as that would not confront the challenge of addressing the heterogeneity of the other (Spivak 1995: 84). According to Spivak, a proper response to that heterogeneity is not an attempt at portraying it (*darstellen*), but rather an effort at finding means of politically addressing it, which would constitute a political representation (*vertreten*) in one's own name, and not in the name of others. In other words, an adequate political response to the subaltern other is a step toward recognising their heterogeneity, instead of just picturing it reductively through Western bias. The task of looking at and representing the subaltern has to include an examination of the hegemonic Western perspective from within which such representations emerge. The critical awareness of one's own visual and theoretical perspectives, even if it is necessarily partial, is an integral step in working to diminish their reductive potential in viewing and representing subalternity. Therein lies the challenge of subaltern representation in photography. It is tasked with providing an image as a re-presentation (*darstellen*), but it operates within a structure where that image may help to form a context for political representation (*vertreten*). In order to examine that process, I begin with an analysis of the medium of photography itself and ways in which it functions within hegemonic and subaltern contexts.

In the hegemonic context of market capitalism, photography forms a very important part of its structure. Susan Sontag in *On Photography* argues that the importance of images in capitalism is twofold (Sontag 2005 [1973]: 140). They are used as entertainment for the masses, anaesthetising the injuries of class, gender and race. They also help rulers collect vital information, which then can be used in order to exploit resources, keep order and control people (ibid.). More than four decades on from the publication of Sontag's *On Photography* in 1973, the saturation of images in the West and in the rest of the world has been increasing steadily, aided by technological advances in terms of digital photography and digital distribution of images. This context, which David Levi Strauss describes as pandaemonic, where publicity replaces and trumps democratic rights and obscures local and global injustices (Berger in Levi Strauss 2005: 39), has two crucial implications for the subaltern. First of all, lack of visibility becomes the most ostracising of social conditions, one that precludes one's access to political representation. Secondly, Levi Strauss emphasises the change in the politics of images, whereby 'the way [the images] are organized has changed, and this has acted to erode their effectiveness, and their power to elicit action' (Levi Strauss 2005: 81–82), thereby preventing photography's potential from becoming a tool for moving on from re-presentation (*darstellen*) to representation (*vertreten*). Therefore, it is important to consider the role of social photo-documentary in capturing the subaltern in the context of a visual pandaemonium, where the subaltern is either completely invisible or only visible in ways which are socio-culturally insignificant. Within such a framework, Goded's work appears to exploit its subaltern subjects in producing a documentary whose scope does not extend beyond it being a form of visual entertainment, working to reinforce its subjects' lack of agency.

This nihilistic view of photography and its power to represent others constitutes only one, if very significant, perspective on photography. Sontag's (2005 [1973]: 140) claim to images as tools for anaesthetising and invigilating the masses cannot be exhaustive. Photography remains a politically significant way of engaging with others, as 'what you show people, day in and day out, is political. [...] And the most politically indoctrinating thing you can do to a human being is to show him, every day, that there can be no change' (Wenders in Levi Strauss 2005: 101). Photography as a process embodies change. To photograph is to intervene and, despite the continual erosion of context within the visual pandaemonium, Brazilian photographer Sebastião Salgado underlines that 'you photograph with all your ideology' (Salgado in Levi Strauss 2005: 45). Maya Goded echoes that sentiment when she states, 'cuando estoy tomando fotos, traigo todo el bagaje' [when I take pictures I carry all my baggage with me] (2013). As Levi Strauss argues in response to Ingrid Sischy's criticism of Salgado,

> [t]o represent is to aestheticize, that is, to transform. It presents a vast field of choices but it does not include the choice *not* to transform, not to change or alter whatever is being represented. It cannot be a pure process, in practice. (Levi Strauss 2005: 9–10)

Therefore such intervention can never be neutral or objective, although its meaning is not determined by the intentions of the photographer, and remains open to reviewing and reinterpretation due to the fugacious nature of images. Therein lies the creative potential of Goded's photography to question its subjects' subaltern position, which cannot be critically foreclosed by arguing that her photography atrophies or aestheticises the people and phenomena it represents.

John Berger in his essay 'Uses of Photography' in *Selected Essays* (Berger 2001: 286–94) postulates that a photograph torn from its context becomes a dead object, which can lend itself to any use (Berger 2001: 291) and carries no meaning in itself. That is not to suggest that Berger renders photography intrinsically meaningless, rather that he insists that photographs rely on their context for meaning. This issue of context is the main distinction he makes between private and public uses of photography; the former is steeped in it, whereas the latter demands continuous contextualisation in order to ward off vacuity (ibid.). In his argument the emphasis on context is linked to the comparison between photography and memory, as he suggests that before photography the only way in which one could revisit the past was through the process of reflection (Berger 2001: 287). Reflection, however, lacks the photographic ability to freeze a moment in time and always remains a subjective experience, which is impossible to share with someone else with the same ease, or effect, as a photograph. However, the comparison between the faculty of memory and the medium of photography illustrates the relevance of the latter as a tool of historicising its subjects, saving them from oblivion. That quality is crucial in analysing Goded's photographs of subaltern people, as it turns their historic absence into a presence, which is an essential first step in gaining social and cultural visibility and overcoming the discriminatory hegemonic order of seeing. Nonetheless, it also separates and fragments the events that it immobilises, removing them from their temporal and contextual attachments. As such, it always carries a risk of atrophy and disposability, which turns its witnessing into a mere exercise of externalising memory and affect. Consciously responding to those risks, according to Berger, 'is to incorporate photography into social and political memory instead of using it as a substitute which encourages the atrophy of any such memory' (Berger 2001: 292).

In his view, that incorporation can be achieved through the recovery of context in photographic representation, which then invests photographs of others with social and political significance and assimilates them into their own continuity, however guilty and tragic (ibid.). It is only through the epistemic process of building knowledge of the world outside the frame that photographs can become agents in transforming one's understanding of oneself and others through representation. Although such a response seemingly goes against the grain of the fragmentary nature of the medium itself, it is indispensable in analysing its ability to historicise people and events.

Numerous scholars have answered Berger's call for photography and photography criticism, which focus on the recovery of such contexts. Susie Linfield argues that seeing photographs as products of particular historical times and circumstances requires an effort that does not come naturally (Linfield 2010). The context to such images does not occur spontaneously — it has to be consciously created, or re-created (Linfield 2010: 50). Although Linfield admits to the existence of 'fatal gaps' between seeing, understanding and acting when faced with images of suffering, she also argues that the way in which one uses the images of cruelty is a question of an ethical response to seeing (2010: 60). Jay Prosser stakes a similar claim, by writing that '[p]utting the photograph back in its context can restore a complex frame and narrative to the photograph, and so [...] offer points of reference to the photographs and circumstances that surround the single image' (Prosser 2010: 8). Ariella Azoulay takes further the issue of responsibility in relation to photography by arguing that it lies not just in taking pictures, but also in making them speak (Azoulay 2008: 122). At this point, it is important to determine what lies at the core of photography's ability to influence the social and historical memory. In view of fleeting contexts and singular arrested frames, how does photography's fragmentary nature figure within the historical?

In order to answer these questions, I examine the unique nature of photography in relation to the people or objects it captures, in order to analyse the specific and sometimes paradoxical ways in which photography intervenes in historical discourses. Berger claims that photography's ability to capture and preserve the appearance of a person or an event closely links it to the idea of the historical (Berger 2001: 59). Moreover, the historical moment in the West when photography was invented, in the first decades of the nineteenth century, coincided with the belief in the judgement of history in the name of progress, accompanied by the agents of democracy and science (Berger 2001: 290). Photography, considered at the time an aid to these agents, owes its reputation as truth to this historical moment (ibid.). Although technological advances have transformed it in the twentieth and twenty-first centuries, at its core photography remains a medium capable of recording reality through the writing of light.

In *Words of Light* (1997) Eduardo Cadava cites William Henry Fox Talbot's description of photography as words of light and uses that reference to illustrate the citational nature of both history and photography (Cadava 1997: xvii). Although both language and photography are 'haunted by history' (ibid.), photography is not bound by what can be expressed by the discursive. On the one hand, it is precisely this freedom that leads to a fleeting nature of its context, but, on the other hand, it also offers subjects who are discursively shunned a way of accessing representation. Moreover, that representation is, according to Berger, different from all other forms of visual image, since it is a trace of its subject and not its interpretation, or rendering (Berger 2001: 287). This view of a photograph as a trace, which belongs to its subject unlike any other image (ibid.), is one of Cadava's main concerns in analysing Walter Benjamin's understanding of history and photography. The conceptual proximity of history and photography is partly founded on the fact that 'historical thinking involves "not only the flow of thoughts, but their arrest as well"' (Benjamin in Cadava 1997: xx). Hence photography, which immobilises the flow of time and of history, can be a model for the understanding of the latter (Cadava 1997: xx). Indeed, Berger claims that 'the ideal of photography, aesthetics apart, is to seize an "historic" moment' (Berger 2001: 51).

This demand for photography to write is a consequence of Cadava's concept of a rapport between photography and philosophy consisting in their common reliance on light (Cadava 1997: 5). Photography, the writing of light, relies on the latter to capture a historical trace. The indispensability of light for photography draws one's attention to light's importance for cognition more generally. In philosophy, it coincides with conditions for the possibility of lucidity, reflection and clarity, 'that is — for knowledge in general' (ibid.). The quote from Walter Benjamin's *Passagen-Werk* Casava uses to illustrate the importance of light is crucial here: '"knowledge comes only in flashes" [...], in a moment of simultaneous illumination and blindness' (Cadava 1997: 5). That statement broadens one's understanding of a subaltern position within hegemonic discourses, inasmuch as it strengthens the aforementioned thesis that subaltern studies, while illuminating some aspects of subalternity, by necessity leave other absences in their wake. Moreover, this focus on omissions and invisibilities in relation to Goded's photography shows her documentary work and practice as a contextualised cultural intervention, which is capable of representing only small aspects of its subjects' subalternity. Knowledge is, therefore, always an incomplete and unfinished experience, and photography, through its momentary illumination and record of a moment, underlines that incompleteness through its paradoxical oscillation between absence and presence.

Photography's importance to knowledge and history in the twentieth century leads Cadava to claim that politics and history can no longer be understood in separation from technology, or as prior to it (Cadava 1997: xxiii). The way in which they are mediated, and the growing appetite for instantaneous communications, makes them 'derivative forms of telecommunications' (ibid.). Furthermore, photography's influence is compounded by the seemingly insatiable appetite for images, supported by the communication and technology revolution of the past decades, which demands a constant expansion of the saturated field of vision. The resulting loss of context and indifference to what the omnipresent and ever-changing images signify are some of the recurring themes in scholarly debates surrounding photography. Importantly, the explanation for this expansive consumption of imagery is not exhausted by Sontag's view of images within capitalism as tools for entertaining and controlling the masses. The unyielding demand for images can be conceptualised as a way of familiarising and glossing over that which is least familiar about a photograph, namely its uncanny ability to halt time. The rapid saturation of one's field of vision, apart from the loss of meaning, also furnishes a sense of continuum, or at least conceals the opportunity for reflecting on mortality inherent in every image. Cadava echoes Berger's concern with the photographic externalisation of memory and its consequences for meaning in his discussion of Siegfried Kracauer's concern with 'the historical blinding amnesia at the heart of photographic technicalization' (Cadava 1997: xxvii). Risks of meaninglessness and disposability notwithstanding, Cadava underlines that critical theory cannot exist without an understanding of photography and ways in which it interacts and transforms social tradition (Cadava 1997: xxx). He lauds Walter Benjamin's and László Moholy-Nagy's shared insight that the ability to read photography is as important as literacy (ibid.).

At this point, it is important to reflect on how Cadava's understanding of the crucial role of photography in history and in critical theory is reflected in the twenty-first-century market economy. The connection between wealth, imagery and the writing of history, although hardly new, does take on a different dimension when one considers a short 'Image-Text', published at the end of David Levi Strauss's book *Between the Eyes* (2005), entitled 'Pennsylvania, U.S.A., April 15, 2001'. It briefly describes Bill Gates's purchase of the Bettman and United Press International photographic archives and their subsequent move from New York to a climate-controlled and virtually inaccessible storage vault buried in a mountain in Pennsylvania (Levi Strauss 2005: 189). In 2001, Bill Gates's private company Corbis owned the rights to more than 65 million images (ibid.). At the time when the images were purchased Bettman claimed that Gates 'now owns the history of everything' (Bettman in Snow 2001: unnumbered pages). Since then, Corbis has purchased numerous national archives and press agencies and set up its digital business buying photographs and selling them in fifty different countries around the world (Corbis Corporate 2012). Ownership of such a large proportion of archive and commercially available photographs illustrates how economic power creates visual hegemony, for it is the Corbis editorial teams in different countries that determine the availability of images on the global market, and decide which archival photographs are available in electronic form, and which are confined to Corbis's climate-controlled vaults. In light of such domination, or, perhaps more accurately, in its shadow, analysing photography's ability to deliver a meaningful message about subalternity acquires a new urgency.

A photographic encounter with subalternity in Goded's work is necessarily an encounter with exclusion and suffering. Consequently, the risk of decontextualising that image and rendering it meaningless takes on an ethical dimension. Although photography always involves a power imbalance between the subject and the photographer, that inequality is especially stark in an encounter with subalternity. Levi Strauss in 'The Documentary Debate: Aesthetic or Anaesthetic?' stresses that to represent another person, be it through discursive or visual means, means always to encounter a minefield of political problems (2005: 8). As such, any act of representation is an act of communication and negotiation, one which has a slim chance of succeeding in its attempt to represent (ibid.). It is pivotal to ask what such success in representation would mean from the perspective of an intersubjective social gaze. That question exposes the fact that representational veracity is a positivist ideal, which obscures the tensions inherent in and indispensable to the practice of documentary photography. According to Levi Strauss, these tensions are precisely the constituents of documentary practice (ibid.).

The representational dilemmas of photographing the subaltern are intensified through the way in which such images are distributed and viewed. Berger notes that the public use of photography suppresses the social function of subjectivity through the focus on the medium's veracity (Berger in Levi Strauss 2005: 16).

> From this simplification, [...] it follows that what a photograph tells about a door or a volcano belongs to the same order of truth as what it tells about a man weeping or a woman's body. (ibid.)

The lack of theoretical distinction between photography as communication and photography as evidence is, according to Berger, a deliberate strategy (ibid.). It allows rendering the medium transparent, in much the same way that Western thought, and academic convention for that matter, renders the Western intellectual transparent. In photography, the belief in such transparency is perhaps one explanation for the opposition to documentary photographers, who have a distinctive visual style and thus deny the genre its illusion of objectivity. For it is that tension between the aesthetic and the ethical which presents the biggest challenge in finding an appropriate response to analysing subaltern photography such as Goded's. Levi Strauss addresses the burden of such a response in his essay on the photographs of the Rwandan genocide, starting it by quoting Aimé Césaire:

> Most of all beware, even in thought, of assuming the sterile attitude of a spectator, for life is not a spectacle, a sea of griefs is not a proscenium, a man who wails is not a dancing bear. (Césaire in Levi Strauss 2005: 79)

Can documentary photography be a resistance to treating the suffering of others as a spectacle? On the one hand, such a demand seems in conflict with photo-documentaries' contribution to the saturation of one's field of vision. Documentary photography cannot escape the market economy any more than other photography genres and, in certain contexts, can contribute and solidify the divisions it makes apparent. Martha Rosler in her essay 'In, Around, and Afterthoughts (on Documentary Photography)' implies that it is made on the backs of the exploited, carrying old information from a subaltern group of people to a different group 'addressed as socially powerful' (Rosler 2003: 262–67). Similarly, when Levi Strauss analyses the indifference surrounding the shocking images of Rwanda's genocide, he emphasises the change in the politics of images, whereby 'the way [the images] are organized has changed, and this has acted to erode their effectiveness, and their power to elicit action' (Levi Strauss 2005: 81). Separated from their historical context, they serve to conceal viewers' complicity in the captured events, and as a commercially useful contrast between Western prosperity and relative security against the misery and war raging elsewhere (Levi Strauss 2005: 82). Indeed, Eduardo

Galeano in his essay 'Salgado, 17 times' (1990) remarks that 'poverty is a commodity which fetches a high price on the luxury market' (Galeano in Levi Strauss 2005: 45), adding an economic dimension to the inequality between the subjects of the photographic gaze, the photographer and spectators. Levi Strauss argues that most European and North American documentaries stem from a hegemonic assumption of consumerist capitalism that poverty is the greatest ill, which can be remedied by replacing the culture of the poorer classes with that of the rich (2005: 45). Images captured from such a perspective can never galvanise change, as they serve as a mere pictorial contrast, reinforcing the gulf between the centre and the periphery (ibid.), the hegemonic and the subaltern.

On the other hand, it is crucial to remember that there is another side to the contemporary saturated field of vision, namely its giving a false impression that everything of importance is recorded. In the age when the camera is omnipresent and means of distributing images have become more widely accessible than ever through social networking, the illusion that one can picture and see everything is compelling. In this context, subaltern invisibility is a particularly limiting ostracism, one which is perhaps clearer to see from outside of photography scholarship. After all, one's representation can only be contested providing it exists. Simon Blackburn in *A Very Short Introduction to Ethics* (2001) frames the question of ethically witnessing the suffering of others in a wider context of the possibility of moral knowledge.

> So is there such a thing as moral knowledge? Is there moral progress? These questions are not answered by science, or religion, or metaphysics, or logic. They have to be answered from within our own moral perspective. Then, fortunately, there are countless small, unpretentious things that we know with perfect certainty. Happiness is preferable to misery, and dignity is better than humiliation. It is bad that people suffer and *worse if a culture turns a blind eye to their suffering*. Death is worse than life; the attempt to find a common point of view is better than manipulative contempt for it. (Blackburn 2001: 115, emphasis added)

The photographic encounter with the subaltern mediated by Goded can become a site of moral as well as intellectual enquiry. A documentary photographer can be a concerned witness and not a detached voyeur. Finally, documentary photography can play a part in reshaping social tradition, and not just furnishing highbrow entertainment for the luxury market. Given the right context, it can become an active element of change, instead of a passive emblem of the loss of meaning. Berger calls for 'a radial system [that] has to be constructed around the photograph so that it may be seen in terms which are simultaneously personal, political, economic, dramatic, everyday and historic' (Berger 2001: 293). Photography of the subaltern in particular has an important role of shifting the horizons of vision and inviting the possibility of turning an artistic representation into a political one. In order to prevent Goded's documentary from being viewed as a mere spectacle, establishing contexts for people and phenomena hitherto invisible is a way of understanding the interconnectedness of photography and epistemology.

Ariella Azoulay (2008) offers a new way of conceptualising photography, especially documentary photography, as a social activity with specific rules. Her understanding of the medium is not centred on any one agent within its apparatus, reframing the significance of the trace of the other in photography as a trace of a meeting (Azoulay 2008: 11). The significance of that meeting cannot be determined by one person alone and is always a result of negotiation. As Maya Goded describes it in relation to her own photographic practice,

> Siempre hay alguien que quiere ser mirado. Es una cosa de los dos lados. Es un acuerdo — tu quieres contar la historia, y el quiere que la cuentes. El acuerdo es lo más importante. (Goded 2013)
>
> [There is always someone who wants to be looked at. It works both ways. It is an agreement — you want to tell someone's story and they want you to tell it. This agreement is of utmost importance.]

In order to gain new theoretical perspectives on the circumstances and outcomes of such meetings preserved in photographs, Azoulay invents a civil political space which photographers as well as subjects and viewers of photography imagine every day (Azoulay 2008: 12). Put in the simplest of terms, Azoulay looks to photography as a way of addressing injustice. She underlines that photographed subjects may see photography as a way of addressing the hegemonic structures that injure them and deny responsibility for causing that injury (Azoulay 2008: 18). In the social imaginary space created by the intersubjective plurality of gazes in photography, subaltern subjects can find an alternative, however weak, to the hegemonic denial of the legitimacy of their claims. Azoulay's argument hinges on the importance of photography as a way of looking back at the state or other political or social structures, which discriminate against individuals or whole groups. If the camera is a tool of controlling the masses, as Susan Sontag and John Tagg, among others, argue, Azoulay reclaims its ability to look back at that mechanism of control from within a social plurality.

Azoulay's organisation of the photographic gaze around the concept of a civil contract was guided by her attempt to move beyond guilt and compassion and outside of 'the merely psychological framework of empathy' (Azoulay 2008: 89) in order to view the photographed subjects as citizens within photography, who are equal to her as a viewer of their representation (Azoulay 2008: 17). Although this plurality does not neutralise inequalities between different parties, its very existence does undermine the 'apparently stable conditions' of hegemony (Azoulay 2008: 142). Azoulay's resistance to sentimentality bears an intention to ethically address the claim of the other made through a photograph not just within her own moral perspective, but also within an imagined photographic community. Nonetheless, it is important to note that empathy or compassion for the other does have a place in viewing photo-documentaries that address subalternity, because of the importance of an affective response for ethics. As Simon Blackburn states, 'when it comes to ethics we are in the domain of preference and choice [...] [where] reason is silent' (Blackburn 2001: 95). Indeed, Azoulay clearly states that she developed the concept of a civil contract as a way of considering her response to the 'unbearable sights presented in the photographs from the Occupied Territories [...] and enduring the difficulty of facing them day after day' (Azoulay 2008: 16). As such, the subjective gaze and one's affective reaction to it has to be at the root of any response to photography, because it guides the ethics of looking at others.

> Mute at its inception, the photograph maintained its silence. Such silence, which can sometimes scream to the heavens, attests to the fact that it is our historic responsibility not only to produce photos, but to make them speak. (Azoulay 2008: 122)

Photographs demand a socio-political structure in which their existence can have a social and historical meaning beyond visual distraction and escapism.

Within the social plurality of gazes, Azoulay labels a certain type of demand made through photography as an emergency claim. It refers to an image of horror, one which can be a result of war, catastrophe or massacre, but also an effect of grinding poverty, abuse or humiliation (Azoulay 2008: 197). However, not every image of horror becomes an emergency claim, which is a demand for action (Azoulay 2008: 198). Particularly in the case of photographing subalterns, i.e. people whose civic status is already impaired by their disadvantageous position within hegemony, an emergency claim is difficult to make. An attempt to understand what such an emergency claim involves means, at least to some extent, accepting responsibility for producing a response to it.

Azoulay's approach to photography and its ability to stake claims of emergency is innovative and liberating in a field that has been for years dominated by sceptical suspicion of the power of photography. However, Azoulay's theory's biggest strength is also its weakness — the rigour and coherence of her arguments make them somewhat inflexible. It is true that Azoulay's aim was not to find a universal way of analysing photography that could be applied to any context, but rather to find a way of incorporating images into the civic space of her own socio-political context and making them resonate within that space. In order to examine the self-imposed limitations of her theory, it is crucial to return to Azoulay's argument for her employment of vocabulary normally associated with politics or business, such as her use of the term 'contract', in the context of photography. As stated above, it is a deliberate strategy to move beyond an affective response to photography, one which Azoulay scorns as 'merely psychological' (2008: 89). This dismissal is curious, since it creates a contrast between Azoulay as a photography critic and the autobiographical information included in the book that describes in affective terms her first encounters with photography and images (Azoulay 2008: 11–14). Nonetheless, such attitudes are common in photography criticism, where, as Susie Linfield claims, the fear of sentimentality (2010: 10) and the outright denial of emotional responses to photography (2010: 22) are expected and often perceived as a sign of intellectual prowess. Azoulay's dismissal of affect in favour of a critical framework derived from ideas on citizenship and politics deserves an analysis as a prevalent theoretical stratagem in photography criticism.

Susie Linfield underlines the importance of context in analysing the theoretical contributions of the Frankfurt School critics. She argues against their revered status within photographic theory and, while valuing their critical insight, she contextualises them within their own historic time from her twenty-first-century perspective (Linfield 2010: 23). The implicit aim of such recontextualisation is twofold. Firstly, it emphasises the volatile political background of the Weimar Republic and analyses its impact on the Frankfurt School's criticism of photography. Secondly, it justifies Linfield's own quest in finding a way of theoretically approaching photography that is suited to her particular historic and political context. In other words, Linfield reinterprets the Frankfurt School's photographic criticism against the entrenched and ossified reading of it in order to find new theoretical ways of approaching the medium. In doing so, she radically disagrees with the denial of affect in relation to photography, explaining it as an entrenched prejudice against emotions that grew out of the Frankfurt School criticism (Linfield 2010: 24). Even though she acknowledges parallels between the darkness of Weimar Germany and our contemporary context, rife with exploitation, inequality and violence, she is also careful to pinpoint the differences between these two distinct historic moments, which call for a reframing of photography criticism (ibid.).

Linfield argues that this denial and distrust of affect in relation to photography hinders one's ability to engage with images and respond to them 'as citizens who seek to learn something useful from them and connect to others through them' (ibid.). By emphasising the status of viewers of photographs as citizens, Linfield places photography in the context of social responsibility, as does Azoulay. The widespread distrust of photography in critical theory can be framed within a parallel between the desire for emotional transparency of the photography critic and Spivak's critique of the apparent intellectual transparency of Western thinkers (Spivak 1995: 70). Just as the latter renders the intellectual unaware of their own bias and unable to conceptualise the plurality of the other, so the former distorts the affective lens through which images are viewed, but cannot do away with it. Jay Prosser reminds his readers that viewing photographs is always a sensory experience (Prosser 2010: 9) and an argument has to be made for it to be viewed as an emotional experience as well. Linfield states categorically that: '[t]here is no doubt that we approach photographs, first and foremost, through emotions' (Prosser 2010: 22). What is worth noting, however, is that pitting politics against affect (Azoulay 2008: 89) in the context of photography criticism appears similarly futile to pitting ethics against aesthetics. Theory that could incorporate affect without derision would enrich one's understanding of photography. Indeed, Linfield quotes film critic Pauline Kael's argument that a suitably extensive and mature way to experience the visual is to combine one's affective reactions to the material with a probing analysis of them (Kael in Linfield 2010: 12). It is not a matter of framing new criticism of photography through an exclusively affective lens, but rather finding ways of theoretically conceptualising emotional responses to photography and incorporating them into one's critical horizon. Insights resulting from a holistic engagement with photography would enhance and enrich, rather than undermine, critical thinking (Kael 1969: unnumbered pages).

Incorporating affect into critical analysis of photography opens up a new field in terms of engagement with images and their subaltern subjects. The recognition of the other, and their suffering or subjugation in a photograph, is an intrinsically emotional endeavour which need not denigrate subjects, viewers or photographers for being so. The way in which photography can garner compassion for the plight of its subaltern subjects has perhaps been better understood and acted upon outside photography scholarship, although recent studies are noticeably committed to evidencing the power of photography to alter the ethical climate in which it operates. Namely, Susie Linfield and Jay Prosser both remind their readers of the links between photography and human rights and humanitarian organisations' reliance on photographs to make the subaltern situation of others known to a wider audience (Linfield 2010: 46–47, Prosser 2010: 8). Goded's own involvement with human rights organisations in Mexico City is testament to the interrelatedness of her documentary practice and humanitarian work aimed at improving the lives of subaltern subjects. Linfield stresses the role of Don McCullin's photographs of the Biafran starving children during the Nigerian–Biafran war of 1967–70 in inspiring the rethinking of humanitarian aid that led to the founding of Doctors Without Borders in 1971 (Linfield 2010: 50). This is precisely where photographic representation paves the way to political representation, and, without conflating the two, where it is most obvious that the latter could never come to be had it not been for the former.

Naturally, it would be naïve and anachronistic to suggest that the road from photographic to political representation, or from *darstellen* to *vertreten*, is a straightforward one. Indeed, it is the difficulty that subaltern subjects have in entering the realm of the political, even if they do have a visual presence, which often lies at the core of condemnation of documentary photography as an exploitative practice that compounds subjugation. If picturing the plight of subalterns does not alter their abjection, how can documentary photography possibly defend its interest in the destitute? In other words, if one remains sceptical concerning the socio-culturally transformative potential of documentary photography, what is there to be gained from making a spectacle out of other people's subalternity? Although Linfield acknowledges the gaps between seeing, understanding and acting (2010: 60), she also argues that to expect photography to put an end to atrocities is an unrealistic demand. As a medium, it cannot be expected to change the inequalities and barbarities that have been part of human society for centuries. Critics such as Sontag, Berger, Levi Strauss and many others attributed this inability to act upon seeing images of atrocity to our saturated field of vision, which desensitises viewers to the horror they witness through somebody else's lens. Linfield has a radically different perspective.

> [T]he desensitization argument is exactly wrong. For most of history most people have known little, and cared less, about the suffering of those who are unknown and alien. [...] [T]oday, in a few parts of the world, those outside one's immediate circle of concern sometimes matter too. [...] And it is the camera [...] that has done so much to globalize our consciences; it is the camera that brought us the twentieth century's bad news. Today it is [...] impossible to say, 'I did not know': photography has robbed us of the alibi of ignorance. (Linfield: 2010: 46)

Linfield argues that learning of the suffering of others through photography is almost inescapable in the twenty-first century. It may also go some way to explain the resentment, mistrust and anger towards photography that Linfield identifies in photography criticism and against which she argues (Linfield 2010: 40–45). Despite the declaration of human rights many decades ago and political commitments to peace declared by the vast majority of nations around the globe, documentary photographs keep showing images of suffering and pain. They constitute a damning body of evidence that creates a cognitive dissonance between what one would like to believe of oneself and one's place in the world and the reality as captured by somebody else's lens. As Linfield puts it in a creative reworking of Walter Benjamin's quote, '[e]very image of barbarism [...] embraces its opposite, though sometimes unknowingly. Every image of suffering says not only, "This is so", but also, by implication: "This must not be"' (Linfield 2010: 33). The 'globalised conscience' (Linfield 2010: 46), courtesy of cameras, is far from clear and has to face up to its glaringly undeniable inadequacies that are evident from documentary photographs. Addressing that social cognitive dissonance is one of the biggest challenges of twenty-first-century photography theory.

Importantly, Linfield's refutation of the scepticism and mistrust of photography that dominates photography criticism has to be questioned. Although it is true that always viewing photography with suspicion will render limited theoretical conclusions, Linfield's opposition between engagement with photography and postmodern mistrust towards it (Linfield 2010: 11) creates a binary between a positive and a negative engagement with the medium. More productively, it is possible to engage with photography and embrace photographs without dismissing their exploitative potential. A medium that relies on imbalance of power in the very act of taking a photograph should be subject to an analysis which can acknowledge that inequality, especially in cases when subaltern subjects are being represented. Such analysis can productively question current practices of documentary photography and need not proclaim a moral value judgement. It can instead examine how photographic representation alters regimes of visibility and changes horizons, and how these changes affect the ethical climate of our times and our opinion of others as well as ourselves. Photography can provide a space where the subaltern gains historical representation, but that process is always a negotiation across different power dynamics, ethical questions and visual regimes.

How do Maya Goded's photographs challenge the Mexican and international visual hegemonies? What claims, if any, do they make for the subaltern groups they represent? In order to answer these questions, I contextualize her art within three main theoretical concepts — liminality, the body, and the issues of visibility and invisibility. The analysis of photographic representations in Goded's art is undertaken through the focus on liminal spaces occupied by the subaltern, as well as the specificities concerning subaltern embodiment, and issues of visibility and invisibility in relation to subalternity. Although these notions are interrelated in the following analysis of Goded's photographic documentary, a separate focus on liminality helps to establish a sense of space in her art, which is then followed by concentrating on embodiment that, in turn, leads to questions of vision.

CHAPTER 3

Liminality: Picturing Subaltern Spaces

Following the analysis of subalternity as an absence of historical representation in the previous chapter, it is important to examine how the concept of liminality can illuminate Maya Goded's photographic representations of subaltern spaces in her work, which visually forge a new symbolic territory for her hitherto invisible subjects. This chapter will focus on liminality in the framework of post-colonial Mexico. After historically situating this concept, it will help to weave Goded's photography into a web of theoretical and social references in analysing photographic representations of space and their relationship to the notion of subalternity. Such a socio-visual analysis, which will mostly focus on Goded's photographs from *La vida oculta* and *Tierra de brujas*, with references to her other photo-essays, expands the understanding of subaltern positions and their relationship to the rest of Mexican society. In addition to aiding the examination of the liminal aspects of subaltern representations and their loci, the concept of liminality is also useful in analysing the medium of photography itself as a social and cultural phenomenon between and betwixt its subjects and the viewers of the photographs. Therefore, I posit the medium's materiality in relation to the spatio-temporal materialities it captures and the impact they have on the socially constitutive visual horizons in Mexico. Moreover, I consider the liminal position of the photographer in relation to the characteristics of their photographic intervention.

Bjørn Thomassen (2009: 7) claims that liminality is one of few anthropological notions with legitimate claims to universality. The concept has been gaining significant popularity since the 1960s, when anthropologist Victor Turner rediscovered Arnold van Gennep's book entitled *Rites of Passage*, first published in 1908. The volume was a study of ritual in small-scale, primitive societies, based on van Gennep's extensive ethnographic research, and rooted in the experiences he witnessed in the field. Indeed, this approach was indicative of his wider ambition to create a social science methodology inspired by biology, particularly in terms of its reliance on empirical data instead of *a priori* frameworks (Thomassen 2009: 9). Van Gennep was the first anthropologist to describe the importance of rituals and their role in shaping how societies and individuals approach significant changes. Before moving on to expanding on van Gennep's and Turner's ideas, it is worth mentioning that a photograph today forms an inextricable part of many rituals and rites of passage and can be seen as such in and of itself. Goded's photographic focus on rituals such as weddings, first communions and funerals symbolically emphasises their social and individual importance, which brings her subaltern subjects into the hegemonic symbolic order.

Van Gennep was aware at the time that his insight into the importance of rituals, their structure, and the way in which they shape individuals and societies was a breakthrough in anthropological research. In 'Conclusions' to *Rites of Passage* he clearly frames liminal rituals as important milestones in the lives of individuals and societies, processes which not only mark important occasions but play a crucial role in constituting them (van Gennep 1960: 189, Location 2846–2855). Therefore, rites of passage are framed as indispensable tools in making sense of time and change, as well as making meaning. Given van Gennep's clarity in realising the importance of his insight into liminal rituals and the ever wider application of the term 'liminality' in different disciplines since the 1960s, it is important to analyse why van Gennep's research was not appreciated by his contemporaries. Such a focus will help to examine the importance of the concept of liminality for the possibility of revolutionary potential in Goded's photographic representations of subaltern subjects.

Bjørn Thomassen outlines that van Gennep's approach was revolutionary because of its break with neo-Kantian reliance on *a priori* principles. He argues that van Gennep's interest in putting experience of liminality at the heart of social research was revolutionary, because it opened a pathway for a different way of thinking about the foundation of society, where primacy is not given to categories and classification external to the individual, but where the point of departure is firmly rooted in the experience of the individual (Thomassen 2009: 12). He states that in order to break away from the neo-Kantian tradition and explore the potential of the concept of liminality, one would have to move beyond that tradition, and not 'simply solve the problem as posed from within it' (ibid.). This revolutionary potential of the concept of liminality is useful in illuminating the concept of subalternity. *A priori* knowledge is by definition reductive and selective in its relationship to its referents, which are only relevant inasmuch as they support its categories and can be universalised. Using an epistemological paradigm that allows for experience to shape knowledge, such as the one proposed by van Gennep in his study of liminality, allows at least the possibility of subaltern knowledge and experience to be acknowledged.

Examining van Gennep's epistemological framework has an important impact on the understanding of the revolutionary potential of photography as a liminal medium in relation to representing subalternity. Conceptualised within the neo-Kantian context, photography's potential to intervene visually in hegemonic power structures and their representational regimes is limited. If analytical distinctions of social structures and meanings are fixed and refer to *a priori* categories independent of experience, then photography cannot challenge them. Instead it is reduced to a medium through which difference and otherness are produced, and through which hegemonic epistemic violence is reflected by visually fixing subaltern identities as a constitutive border of acceptable identifications. Indeed, photography criticism anchored in neo-Kantian thinking is often critical of photographing subaltern subjects because of the way in which the medium can visually fix their identities and compound their stigmatisation as others.

It is through the departure from the neo-Kantian epistemic framework that the concept of liminality, understood as a spatio-temporal break from the social structure, questions its fixed and seemingly unchanging character. Photography conceptualised as a liminal medium, apart from being necessarily transformative through representation, can intervene and mediate between different social strata, without necessarily automatically reaffirming the hegemonic visual horizon. That is not to deny the medium's links with hegemonic power structures, but to emphasise that its liminal characteristics provide at least a possibility to question that hegemony by working against the epistemic violence that produces subalternity. Maya Goded's interest in communities which have very little social agency and a minimal or non-existent visual presence, and her ability to represent them photographically, creates a visual space that resists the hegemonic epistemic violence and questions the status of subaltern subjects as an epistemic border, relevant only as a negative constitutive referent of the hegemonic.

The potential of liminality to challenge the neo-Kantian epistemic framework was developed when Victor Turner came across van Gennep's *Rites of Passage*. Turner (2008) expands van Gennep's notion of liminality beyond its original meaning and use. He focuses on the process of the ritual itself and is most interested in the exploration of the liminal period within a ritual, where everyday norms are suspended and the ritual subject is removed from the ordinary notions of time and space. He claims that the symbolic detachment of the individual or group from their 'earlier fixed point in the social structure', or from their previous state results in an acquisition of ambiguous characteristics (Turner 2008: 94). Turner often resorts to metaphor in describing liminality and links it to 'death, to being in the womb, to invisibility, to darkness, to bisexuality, to the wilderness, and to an eclipse of the sun or moon' (Turner 2008: 95). This difficulty in categorising liminal processes and their flexibility in absorbing and reflecting meaning to some extent explain the appeal of this terminology. Its specific usefulness to understanding subalternity, however, lies in its potentially disruptive qualities.

The problematic and disconcerting aspects of liminality are particularly relevant in contexts where a liminal state becomes fixed. Firstly, it is important to acknowledge that conceptualising liminality as a fixed and permanent state is paradoxical. As Thomassen argues, in anthropological usage, 'the liminal state is always clearly defined, temporally and spatially: there is a way into liminality and there is a way out of it' (Thomassen 2009: 21). Nonetheless, this is where the methodological approach of allowing events to shape theories bears critical fruit, which would be inconceivable within the neo-Kantian framework. Although seemingly against van Gennep's definition of liminal state as a limited phenomenon occurring in a particular context, the idea of fixed liminality can be applied to a whole host of minorities: gender, sexual, ethnic, political, etc. (Thomassen 2009: 19). In such a context, Goded's photographic representations depict elements of fixed liminality within the subalternity of her subjects, both in terms of visually arresting them within the frame of an image and therefore fixing them, but also in hinting at the socio-cultural difficulties of changing one's subaltern position within hegemonic structures of power. The concept of fixed liminality can become a vantage point for expressing liminal positions that function in the interstices of structure and hierarchies, and provide a space for positive identifications (ibid.). Thomassen recognises the strategy of writing 'from the in-between' as a postcolonial strategy used by writers such as Homi Bhabha, who find positive identifications in their liminal position, which allows him to express difference without succumbing to a discriminating social structure (Thomassen 2009: 18). In the 'Introduction' to *The Location of Culture* (1994) Homi Bhabha draws on the legacy of postmodern and postcolonial discourses that destabilise the singularity of class or gender as homogeneous identifying categories and introduces a variety of subject positions, which allow for new identifications and for renegotiations of one's place within socio-cultural contexts. In his own words, 'It is in the emergence of the interstices — the overlap and displacements of domains of difference — that the intersubjective and collective experience of *nationness*, community interest or cultural value are negotiated' (Bhabha 1994: 2, original emphasis). The idea of alternative identifications being created and performed in the interstices of dominant cultural contexts is crucial to Bhabha's concept of cultural hybridity (ibid.), which provides a template for theorising de-colonised societies. It prevents normative binary identifications from becoming fixed and allows for an element of negotiation between them, which is instrumental in creating a socio-cultural environment which can accommodate difference without an 'assumed or imposed hierarchy' (ibid.). As such, the similarities and convergences between subaltern and liminal positions become ever more obvious, although the definition of the former hinges on its inferiority within hegemonic structures, which cannot be said of liminality.

Bhabha's concept of border merits more analysis in relation to Maya Goded's photographic work on Mexico's borders and borderlands. He points out that the wider epistemological significance of postmodern and postcolonial self-conscious fragmentation rests in the rediscovery of the limits of ethnocentric identifications as places of origin and possibility (Bhabha 1994: 4). The border is simultaneously a limit and a place of origin, depending on the position of the subject, and this fractioning of a single concept into two distinct roles is one of the founding principles of theorising culture as an intersubjective phenomenon. More importantly, this apparent binary can be further problematised by framing borders as sites that invite crossings and transgressions, as well as flows of people, goods and capital. Borders become, literally and figuratively, sites where alternative identifications become possible. The border, therefore, becomes a liminal space, not just a limit as such, but also a new beginning, challenging the very structure of which it forms a part. Particularly in relation to Mexico, where borders provide a plethora of socio-geographical phenomena emerging at the nexus of coloniality, capitalism, and epistemic and systemic violence, problematising the apparent peripheries leads to a better understanding of the centres and relationships between them.

Walter Mignolo explores the liminal potential of borders and border thinking in his book entitled *Local Histories/Global Designs: Coloniality, Subaltern Knowledges, and Border Thinking* (Mignolo 2012b). One of the most important theses in the book is the idea that modernity is inextricably linked to colonialism, the latter being the former's constituent rather than its consequence (Mignolo 2012b: Location 75). Therefore, the internal logic of modernity hinges on Western culture's power to subordinate and exploit other cultures, universalising a local history into a narrative of development and progress through epistemic violence. The main argument within the book is for a new way of thinking, not just in terms of conceptualising borders, but, more importantly, also in terms of 'border thinking' (Mignolo 2012b: Location 250). Border thinking is crucial to Mignolo's concept of a new epistemological order based in resistance to the hegemony of Western modernity, history and capitalism.

> Engaging in border thinking is tantamount to engaging in decoloniality; that is, in thinking and doing decolonially. Why? Because the main thrust of border thinking is not directed toward 'improving' the disciplines, but toward 'using' the disciplines beyond the disciplines themselves, aiming and building a world without modernity/coloniality. (Mignolo 2012b: Location 250)

Mignolo argues that it is through differently embodied epistemological positions that occupy geographical and social borderlands that Western hegemony can be challenged, and the decentralisation of knowledge can begin (2012b: Location 282). It is important to note that the arguments in the book problematise Western culture as a heterogeneous phenomenon, and do not argue for an epistemic break with Western hegemony. Instead, Mignolo postulates epistemic disobedience anchored in an attempt to provide responses to challenges of Western hegemony, which cannot be answered from within (2012b: Location 304). Such dialogic engagement resultant from border thinking is, according to Mignolo, a decolonising project which uncouples epistemology from Western hegemony, therefore building a pluriversal epistemology (2012b: Location 338). It is precisely through occupying the liminal borderland — an area demarcated by hegemonic discourses of coloniality and modernity — that embodied knowledge can challenge epistemic structures that relegate it to the betwixt and between. Within such a framework, Goded's subaltern representations can be framed as visual testimonies to the material effects of epistemic violence.

The concept of liminality is also useful in illuminating Mexico's subaltern position on the world stage. Classed as one of the developing countries through a hierarchy originating from hegemonic powers which deem themselves developed, Mexico is epistemologically reduced to a status of constantly becoming, but never quite arriving. Its vulnerable economic position is full of ambiguities characteristic of liminal states, especially in relation to its northern neighbour. It is at once indispensable for its supply of cheap labour, tax-free sweatshops and preferential trade deals, and deemed dangerous for illegal immigration (itself a liminal phenomenon), drug trafficking, crime, as well as endemic violence. The pervasive influence of the Chicano culture in the United States is an apt illustration of the liminal immigrant presence emerging through the interstices of a hegemonic cultural landscape, particularly in creative industries. The liminal status of the country is most keenly felt through the experiences of the vulnerable sectors of its population, who are at the mercy of economic and cultural forces outside their control and the control of their government. It is in the experiences of marginalised people, whose lives Maya Goded documents, that subalternity and liminality converge and compound each other's effects.

Liminality, Marginality and Subaltern Photography

Following the detailed discussion of the concept of subalternity and its application to Goded's photography in the previous chapter, it is useful to underline the distinctions between subalternity and liminality. Liminality is a useful concept in understanding subalternity, since the liminal can be framed as gaps in the social structure. Social structure, on the other hand, is a product of hegemonic powers, or at least a product of negotiations between the hegemonic powers and other forces, which are acknowledged within the structure in the interests of necessary flexibility and social cohesion. Although subalternity and liminality share their interstitial position within wider structures, the former has a crucial element of inferiority, which is lacking in the definition of the latter. In other words, although liminality as a phenomenon is unstructured and ambiguous, its existence within a wider context does not imply that an external force dominates it. Therefore, the experience of subalternity is necessarily a liminal one, but liminality is not automatically a subaltern phenomenon.

Another important distinction to make, particularly since this chapter's aim is to analyse liminal spaces in Maya Goded's photography, is the relationship between the liminal and the marginal. Arpad Szakolczai explains that in any situation with strongly demarcated centres and boundary lines, such as the Western definition of a modern nation-state for example, there is a clear distinction between the centre and the border or margin, where the latter is 'irrelevant, local [and] backward' (Szakolczai 2009: 152). However, when the emphasis shifts to a relationship between the centres, the border zones that used to be marginal become liminal in their position between and betwixt the two centres, 'thus mediating them' (ibid.). It is a role so important that it may decentralise the system and draw attention to the liminal mediators between the centres, as is the case whenever the issues of the US and Mexican border is raised. As such, the shift from marginality to liminality is symptomatic of a cultural landscape, which has undergone digital and social revolution, where the flow of people and of information necessitates a redefinition of the positions of the centre and the periphery. Liminality, therefore, is posed as a question of position.

How can the concept of liminality, posed as an issue of position, help to enrich critical analysis of photography? It affords a way of conceptualising the medium, adding a new dimension to the critical understanding of the way in which it affects environments and relationships. Photography is a liminal medium par excellence, inasmuch as it is always a mediation in time and space between the representation, its referent, the photographer and the viewer. Yet in and of itself photography more often than not escapes definition. Its ontological status remains fluid and undefined partly because it is impossible to conceive of it without considering the people or phenomena it represents. As such, it is always between and betwixt its referent and its representation — its symbols and meanings are never fixed, however rooted they may be in concrete reality. Photography is situated between the world it captures and reproduces and the visual effects of that reproduction, namely the oft-cited image saturation of twenty-first-century public and private spaces. It is a medium situated at the threshold of reality, reproducing and historicising it, but also potentially threatening to change it. Its ambivalence as a liminal medium consists in its simultaneously threatening and impotent position vis-à-vis the people and events it documents, their reception and their meaning. On the one hand, the power of photographic representation is always transformative, and, on the other hand, its effects are independent of the realities they depict and by definition remain open to new interpretations and perspectives.

Such ambivalence produces specific theoretical effects. The elusive nature of photography and its paradoxically tenuous relationship across time to the reality it represents led critics such as Siegfried Kracauer to claim nihilistically, in his 1927 essay entitled 'Photography', that '[w]e are contained in nothing and photography assembles fragments around a nothing' (Kracauer 1993: 431). That is not to say, however, that in his view photography is therefore meaningless. On the contrary, it is meaningful but not in relation to the world it represents, but rather in creating a world of appearances which, instead of approximating viewers of the photographs to their subjects, isolate them further from the world in which they live (Kracauer 1993: 432). According to Kracauer, that separation's primary attraction is to ally one's fear of death, but it does so through presenting images frozen in time, in itself already a premonition of death (Kracauer 1993: 433). While photographic presence is 'seemingly ripped from the clutch of death, in reality it has succumbed to it all the more' (ibid.). As such, there is a paradox at the very heart of Kracauer's theory of photography, a circular game to be played with the human experience of time, where an attempt to stop time and preserve a phenomenon or a person in a given moment simultaneously immortalises that instance, while also making the passage of time, and therefore death, ever more apparent.

This phenomenon of temporary separation from the lived experience in the here and now in favour of vicarious experiences through images can be compared to Turner's description of liminoid experiences which, he argues, replace liminal states in large-scale societies (Turner 1974: 65). Owing to the decline of traditional rituals in such societies, the potentially risky and transformative liminal state of a ritual is replaced by a liminoid experience (Turner 1974: 65–66), where a subject can temporarily gain a similar feeling of being in and out of time, and suspended from social structure through art, entertainment or play. Framed as a liminoid experience, photography loses some of its ambivalence, since it becomes a spectacle that separates instead of connecting. Kracauer's notion of photography, as a medium that isolates through its ability to create a world of appearances separate from the reality which they represent, is one that was shared by many of his contemporaries within the Frankfurt School. Linfield argues that this approach has a substantial legacy in photography criticism leading to photography being viewed as a suspicious and, at the same time, impotent medium. She argues that:

> In approaching photographs with relentless suspicion critics have made it easy for us to deconstruct images, but almost impossible to see them; they have crippled our capacity to grasp what John Berger called 'the *thereness* of the world.' And it is just that — the texture, the fullness of the world outside ourselves — into which we need to delve. Photographs can help us do that. (Linfield 2010: 30)

Arguing against the notion of photography as a mere simulacrum focused on distancing individuals from themselves and from one another, Linfield attempts to circumvent the legacy of the Frankfurt School in photography criticism. Although she does not call it such, *The Cruel Radiance* can be considered an argument for photography as a liminal, and therefore transformative, medium. She searches for a way to analyse photography in relation to the world, not in isolation from it, to view it as a 'connective tissue' between different people and cultures (Linfield 2010: 31).

The difference between seeing photography as a liminal and not a liminoid medium has important implications for its political resonance. In relation to Goded's visual engagement with her subaltern subjects, framing the effects of her practice as liminoid would reduce them to their entertainment value, produced on the backs of the exploited and disadvantaged subjects for the benefit of the socio-culturally powerful. It is useful to return here to Thomassen's discussion of Turner's theories, particularly his point that equating liminal experiences in small-scale societies to liminoid ones in large-scale societies is problematic (Thomassen 2009: 15). Thomassen's main concerns are threefold; they relate to Turner's oversimplification of differences between 'traditional' and 'modern' societies, overlooking the dangerous and unsettling aspects of liminality in the definition of the liminoid, and ignoring the key transitory feature of liminality (ibid.). Furthermore, Thomassen argues that this 'delimination of liminality' in Turner's theory leads him to exclude ways in which liminal experiences play a role in political or social transformations (ibid.). This discussion is of particular importance for photography, since when it is framed as a liminoid cultural phenomenon, it becomes little more than ethically dubious entertainment underpinned by hegemonic power structures and invested in keeping the status quo by transforming it through representation and obscuring it. It is precisely this view that photography critics such as Linfield argue against, pointing to photography's connective and transformative aspects.

Conceptualising photography as a liminal medium is a productive critical approach to analysing its pervasive socio-cultural influence. Furthermore, it allows for Goded's photographic representations of subalternity to be seen as potentially transformative cultural texts, which have the capacity to foment social change. First of all, placing the emphasis on the transitory aspects of photography centres the discussion on the connections between subjects, viewers and makers of photographs. The focus is, therefore, not on separations, but on networks between people who are differently affected by the medium of photography, underlying its cultural importance through a web of social connections. The photographer becomes not the master of the image, but an intermediary between different moments in time and different people and phenomena. Secondly, the concept of liminality helps theoretical questioning of the transformative nature of photography, without necessarily reducing it to a medium that atrophies people and experiences to produce a substitute reality. Instead, the focus is on representation as a transformative act of crucial socio-cultural significance, whose consequences can never be fully predicted, and which influences the process of historicising events and making cultural meanings. Finally, conceptualising photography as a liminal medium is a move towards forging a more complex understanding of the effects of living in the era saturated by images and of remoulding notions to fit the visual as well as the socio-cultural horizons of the twenty-first century.

At this point, it is important to mention Jacques Rancière's approach to images where he searches, in principle not dissimilarly from Susie Linfield, for a theoretical approach to photographs, which circumvents the 'disenchanted knowledge of the reign of the commodity and the spectacle, of the equivalence between everything and everything else and everything and its own image' (Rancière 2009: 32). Rancière proposes 'unreasonable hypotheses' which consist in reconfiguring and reframing every situation from the inside as a 'scene of dissensus' without reference to 'a reality concealed behind appearances nor a single regime of representation and interpretation' (Rancière 2009: 49). Indeed, his proposal is unreasonable because a self-conscious contradiction in terms forms its very premise, namely the fact that dissent is necessarily a response to external structures. Nonetheless, his proposal can be productive precisely because of its similarities to the concept of liminality. Rancière stresses the potential of dissensus as a tool, which can reconfigure what is seen and what is thought and therefore 'alter the field of the possible and the redistribution of capacities and incapacities' (2009: 49). Certainly, framing photography as a liminal medium allows for seeing its revolutionary potential of having the ability to alter current horizons of vision meaningfully.

Photographers such as Goded, who deliberately seek out invisible phenomena and people, work on the threshold of what is and what is not seen. They are an intermediary between realities they witness and the way in which these realities enter into regimes of visibility. The focus on the places and environments photographed by Goded in this chapter is an attempt to anchor the subaltern geographically in her art and emphasise the influence of the physical environment on her subjects. The function of such a focus is twofold. First of all, it is to contest the idea of a global village, which is often shorthand for the cultural and societal effects of accelerated globalised telecommunications, and which overlooks the fact that, geographically speaking, the global village is relatively small, and the vast majority of people who populate the Earth reside outside it. Secondly, it is to analyse the relationship between the representations of liminal spaces to the representations of people who occupy them, and the discernible influence that they have on one another. Such an approach will provide a way to analyse Goded's snapshots of the global south in relation to its international framework, but also allow for a focus on its local particularities rooting it in a concrete geographical and socio-cultural context.

Imprisoned Liminality and the Missing Subaltern

Maya Goded's focus on marginalised and disenfranchised groups makes apparent different aspects of their physical, social and cultural vulnerability, as well as their disposability. Photographing the subaltern is, therefore, not just a historical act of documenting their ignored and marginalised presence, it also necessarily attests to their absence. In focusing on the space in which her subjects live or used to live, Goded is able to mark this telling absence. On the one hand, it evidences their erasure from the dominant regimes of visibility and history, and yet, on the other hand, it also references concrete circumstances in which they live and die. As such, Goded uses the medium of photography to provide irrefutable evidence of the existence of the subaltern, through its unique ability to provide a material, be it digital or chemical, trace of what is before the lens. Her presence and the presence of her camera transform the liminal spaces inhabited by subalterns in Mexico into visual evidence of their historical erasure and marginalisation. In order to analyse the liminal spaces of Goded's photography, I examine a number of her images from a variety of her photographic projects. *La vida oculta* (2010), which is a series of photographs from prisons, will be compared to *Tierra de brujas* (2008), a photographic essay documenting sorcery in northern Mexico. In addition, the liminal space of the missing subaltern will be examined through a focus on a number of images from *Plaza de la soledad* (2006) and from Goded's work for *Justicia para nuestres hijas* (2007), which deals with violence in and around Ciudad Juárez. These photographic juxtapositions will evidence the precariousness of liminal spaces in Mexico and emphasise the role of photography as a 'connective tissue' between different cultural and social contexts.

Analysing photographic representations of prisons as liminal environments allows for a reflection on their role in society and the function they fulfil. In *Simulacra and Simulation* (1994) Jean Baudrillard (1994: 14) claims that the main function of a prison is to obscure the carceral nature of the social, drawing on Michel Foucault's comparisons between prisons and other social institutions in *Discipline and Punish: The Birth of the Prison* (1995). Crucially, Foucault describes the principle of visibility in Bentham's architectural figure of the Panopticon as a trap, for it is through constant internalised supervision that the totalising power of the state operates on an individual level. As much as Foucault's theory on the operations of power within penitentiary institutions is important to acknowledge, its usefulness in examining Mexican prisons is limited, because of the differences between the French and the Mexican contexts. The Western hegemonic idea of a perfect power apparatus at the service of the all-seeing state does not fit the context of the Mexican state and its underfunded prisons.

There is a paradox at the very heart of the concept of a prison, since it usually forms part of a normative legal apparatus, but it also necessarily stands outside it. That is not to suggest that prisons are unregulated, but to emphasise that their regulations always differ from those applied outside prisons. This difference in regulatory systems between the world inside and outside a penal institution is both a founding element of every prison and the very reason why, in developed as well as developing countries, prisons are often sites of abuses of power and rife with violence between inmates. As part of the state apparatus, prisons are underpinned by hegemonic principles and supported by legal frameworks that stem from them. Consequently prison populations reflect the biases of hegemonic power systems, of which they form an integral part. Members of subaltern groups, therefore, are much more likely to be imprisoned than those who fit into normative hegemonic standards. Ethnic minorities, people from the poorest strata of society, as well as those with no formal qualifications or even basic literacy skills, form a disproportionately large segment of the prison population the world over, be it in developed countries such as the United States or Britain (Berman 2012: unnumbered pages) or in Latin America.

The difficulties of writing about Mexican prisons stem partly from the fact that little is known about the way in which the penal system functions on a day-to-day basis because of a lack of central statistics, woeful underfunding and overcrowding (Azaola and Bergman 2007: 74). The Mexican government and its agencies are aware that their penitentiary system is in crisis, as is evident from the official government website where *Cámara: Revista de los Centros de Estudios de la Cámara de Diputados* [Chamber: Institute of the Chamber of Representatives Journal] is published. There, Centro de Estudios Sociales y de Opinión Pública [Centre for Social Studies and Public Opinion] published a statement entitled 'La crisis penitenciaria en México' [The Penitentiary Crisis in Mexico], emphasising that this phenomenon is not exclusively Mexican or new, for that matter, and outlining long-term centralised plans for the necessary reforms (Trejo 2013). Meanwhile, over 200,000 inmates live in overcrowded prisons (International Centre for Prison Studies 2013), where they often have to rely on their families to provide necessities such as food and clothing (Azaola and Bergman 2007: 83) and have little access to proper legal representation before or after the trial (Azaola and Bergman 2007: 85). The Mexican government's capacity to deal with that problem effectively remains uncertain not only due to the current economic crisis but also because of its poor record on corruption. Transparency International ranks Mexico's public sector at 34 on a scale of 0 (highly corrupt) to 100 (very clean), and the majority of Mexican prisoners report having to bribe officials (Azaola and Bergman 2007: 83, 85). Moreover, a recent report into human rights in Mexican prisons issued a rather damning verdict on the state's record of dealing with the penal system.

> Poco o nada han importado a la administración penitenciaria mexicana las condiciones de vida infrahumana que perduran en las cárceles. La autoridad penitenciaria menos que procurar la efectiva readaptación social como lo ordena la Constitución, no han logrado siquiera el mínimo de las condiciones requeridas para hacer de las cárceles sitios decorosos en donde se desenvuelva la comunidad carcelaria. El adjetivo de humanas o humanitarias está muy lejos de aplicarsele a los establecimientos penitenciarios mexicanos. (Peláez Ferrusca 2011)

> [The inhuman conditions of life in prisons have mattered little or nothing to the administrators of the Mexican penitentiary system. The penitentiary authorities cannot even provide the minimum requirements for making prisons decent places with a sense of community, not to mention their inability to provide constitutionally demanded rehabilitation and social readaptation. Words such as 'humane' or 'humanitarian' cannot be applied to Mexican penitentiary establishments.]

The situation of Mexican prisoners, who are both incarcerated and effectively abandoned by the state, is certain to worsen due to the growing drug trafficking and violent crime. Moreover, during an economic crisis and in the context of a national budget already stretched beyond its capacity, public sympathy for those labelled as dangerous enough to become imprisoned will be in short supply. Therefore, rather than examining the Foucauldian trap of visibility in the Mexican context, it is more productive to focus on the trap of invisibility, where the gaze of the state is averted from prisons.

Mexican prisons can therefore be seen as sites suspended in their liminality. Having been devised by a penal system rooted in Western tradition, where they are designed to have a punitive as well as redemptive role, prisons are liminal in principle, inasmuch as they are meant to be sites where people who have committed crimes can be rehabilitated and transformed into law-abiding citizens. According to the article entitled 'Cárceles en México: Cuadros de una Crisis' [Prisons in Mexico: Charting a Crisis], '[de] acuerdo a la constitución mexicana y a la perspectiva oficial, los reclusorios son centros de readaptación social' [according to the Mexican Constitution, prisons are centres for rehabilitation] (Azaola, Bergman 2007: 83). Although this overt aim is a failure documented by high reoffending rates, in Mexico the liminal nature of prisons can also be understood as a convergence of different elements. Due to the state's lack of resources, prisons become an intermediary space produced by corrupt government, normalised brutalisation, human rights abuses, inadequate resources and endemic violence. They offer material, concrete evidence of the consequences of the somewhat elusive flow of neo-liberal capital through Mexico's geographical terrain, particularly in terms of drug and human trafficking.

Maya Goded's photographic series taken in Ignacio Allende prison in Veracruz in 2010 is unusual in comparison to her other work. Through her husband's film industry links, she found out that Mel Gibson was going to make a film in a prison located close to the harbour in Veracruz.[1] Despite the protests of prisoners and their families, the authorities decided to move the inmates to a different prison, which was under construction at the time, because of the fees the filming crew was willing to pay for the use of the prison (Goded 2013). Maya Goded received permission to photograph the prison just as the inmates were moved out, but before the film crews arrived. During the liminal time when the prison ceased to perform its official function, but had not yet become a setting for a fictional narrative, Goded spent three days and nights photographing the virtually empty building. She also came across an inmate who was left behind, whose hands captured in some of her photographs are the only human presence within the series.

La vida oculta contains no photographs of people — it is a study of a building and its walls. Such a choice can be read as a protest vote against the inhuman conditions in which the prisoners are forced to live, suspended in a liminal space of being at the mercy of an absent state. Walls become a symbolic site of resistance as well as a way of engaging with the material reality of the absent state. As Julie Peteet (1996: 139) notes in her work focusing on cultural meanings of graffiti in the context of the occupied West Bank towards the end of the twentieth century, marking walls is an intervention in the relationship of power. In the context of repressive situations where walls are a means of physical containment of people, reappropriating them as communication channels, which carry polysemic messages from subaltern voices, is a practice of cultural resistance (Peteet 1996: 140–41). Indeed, it is only the marks and inscriptions on the prison walls of Ignacio Allende prison that testify to the marginalised presence of the inmates. The walls are used for marking the passage of time, and therefore symbolically claiming control over it. They mark memories, bear witness to declarations of love, and play host to devotional images. In particular, the latter category of images transforms the walls from a constant physical reminder of punishment into a promise of redemption. They also evidence experiences and aspirations, referencing the world outside prison, and thus symbolically questioning the aims and effects of physical divisions between the inmates and the rest of society.

Instead of photographing prisoners Goded's focus on the building helps her to circumvent the persistent link between the legal system and photography, where the latter becomes an apparatus of the state focused on identifying and categorising its subaltern and dangerous elements. Her focus on the details of the prison environment and the traces left there by people who occupy this liminal space force viewers to analyse the frame in a way not dissimilar from someone who is forced to look at the same walls every day. Taking advantage of photography's ability to capture and preserve detail in a way in which memory cannot, Goded's photographs of prison walls produce a curious effect of aligning the gaze of a viewer with that of an inmate through tightly cropped images.

Despite its lack of representations of people, *La vida oculta* is compelling through its visual references to their presence. One of the photographs of this series depicts a corner of a room with two flip-flops discarded close to the edges of the wall (Figure 3.1). The frame is relatively tight, allowing only for a narrow view of the floor, two walls and the shoes, mimicking the extreme narrowing of the visual horizon, which forms part of the daily experience of prisoners. The photograph's colour palette is muted and ranges from dark greys to dirty whites, adding to its rather heavy and oppressive atmosphere. The liminal space of the prison, sustained by the letter of the law, but standing outside it, appears small and contrived. The walls are white and very dirty and look to be made of the same concrete as the floor. The white paint is coming away from the walls, revealing layers of other colours buried underneath, physical evidence of the prison's permanence, but also of the past labour of its inmates. Hinting at somebody's nearby presence, a couple of very worn-out flip-flops lie on the ground. Their soles are discoloured and worn to the ground at the

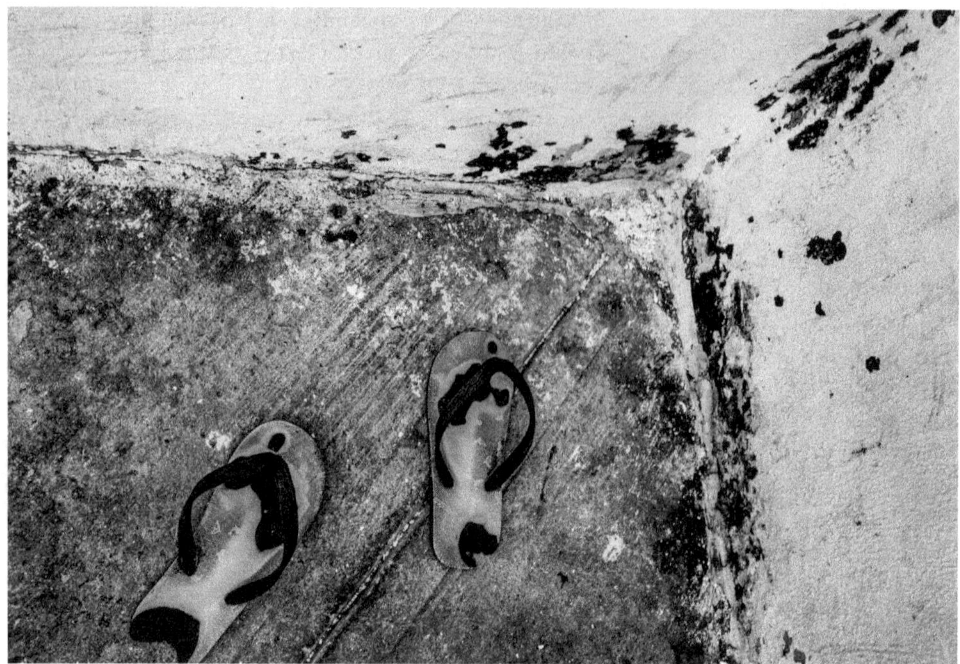

FIG. 3.1. M. Goded, *La vida oculta* (2010).

heel, evidence of many an hour spent pacing the concrete floor. If their owner was wearing them in the exact position in which they were photographed, they would have their legs crossed and they would be facing the corner between the two walls. The evident poor quality of the shoes serves as a reminder of the prisoners' invariably difficult economic situation of being held within a prison, which provides very little even in terms of essentials. Their positioning in the corner facing the walls serves as a visual metaphor for the impossible situation of the prisoner, trapped within a system which cannot support him or set him free.

The missing owner of the flip-flops is significant not only because it helps Goded's work to avoid an alignment with the state apparatus. It is also a silent tribute to the men and women who are victims of violence in Mexican prisons every year. Although central statistics are scarce or non-existent and few reports are able to provide reliable numbers, violence is understood to be an endemic problem within the Mexican penal system (Peláez Ferrusca 2011). The absence of the owner of the flip-flops is therefore not just a visual comment on the extreme vulnerability of Mexican prisoners, but also evidence of their long-standing subalternity and invisibility. With nobody to substantiate the claims of endemic violence, viewers are left to examine the worn-out soles against the concrete.

The flip-flops themselves can be framed here as a poignant visual comment on the idea of the global village. They are the preferred choice of footwear for millions of tourists every year, often appearing in holiday advertisements, as they are now a visual trope instantly associated with relaxation and good weather. It is that familiarity of footwear associated with holidays that sets the scene for the political reading of this photograph. Flip-flops are not just the tourists' footwear of choice; they are also extremely popular in many parts of the developing world due to their very simple manufacturing process and low cost. In that sense, the flip-flop can be framed as an element of life in the global village where people living on different continents and occupying different social and cultural positions find themselves united by their consumer choices, and uniform in their preference for simple footwear. Viewers are therefore likely to have a pair of flip-flops not dissimilar to that captured against a prison wall by Goded, yet their very freedom to look at the photograph sets them apart from the imprisoned owner of the shoes.

The link between the casual beach footwear, and its relationship to the flow of capital and goods throughout the world, merits further analysis especially in relation to subaltern groups. The flip-flops' popularity and availability has unintended consequences for many seaside communities, as the plastic shoes wash up on the shores of the Indian Ocean (Ryan et al. 2009: 1999), creating an environmental threat, and evidencing the dangers of irresponsible attitudes to marine debris. Although there are numerous art and commerce-based initiatives which attempt to turn this particular type of waste into commercially viable ornaments,[2] it is also acknowledged that the mounting plastic debris in the seas is not monitored very well and its impact, as well as its trajectories, are not fully understood (Ryan et al. 2009: 1999). What is clear, nonetheless, is that this environmental issue disproportionately affects subaltern groups, who are reliant on the sea for their livelihood. The proliferation of consumer choices in capitalist societies, in this example embodied in the colourful plastic waste floating in the oceans, does not make for a more equal global village, where fashions and styles of footwear are shared the world over. Instead, the photograph of the flip-flops against the concrete floor of a Mexican prison makes apparent that it is one's positioning, geographical, social as well as economic, that determines one's choices more than the worldwide availability of similar fashions. Tightly framed, the plastic shoes become Rancière's scene of dissensus, where an apparently innocuous everyday item serves to underline both similarities and differences between the absent, figurative subaltern owner of the shoes and the viewer of the photograph. Goded's *mise en scène* succeeds in becoming a liminal site of encounter, which pictures the extremely limited choices of the owner of the flip-flops, revealing yet another similarity between the absent subaltern and the viewers of the photograph — namely a universal reliance on larger economic and social forces beyond the control of any one individual. Nonetheless, the flip-flops' worn-out state and extreme spatial confinement prevent a sentimental identification between their absent owner and the viewers, instead producing an uncomfortable encounter with the uncanny.

The vast majority of the photographs that form *La vida oculta* depict walls, which is clearly a visual reference to confinement as an intrinsic part of every prison. Through tracing changes on the poorly maintained walls, Goded's photographs aim to offer viewers a similar view to those experienced by the absent inmates. Despite not being depicted in any of the published photographs, the prisoners' presence is obvious in the signs they leave on their surroundings, of which some are deliberate

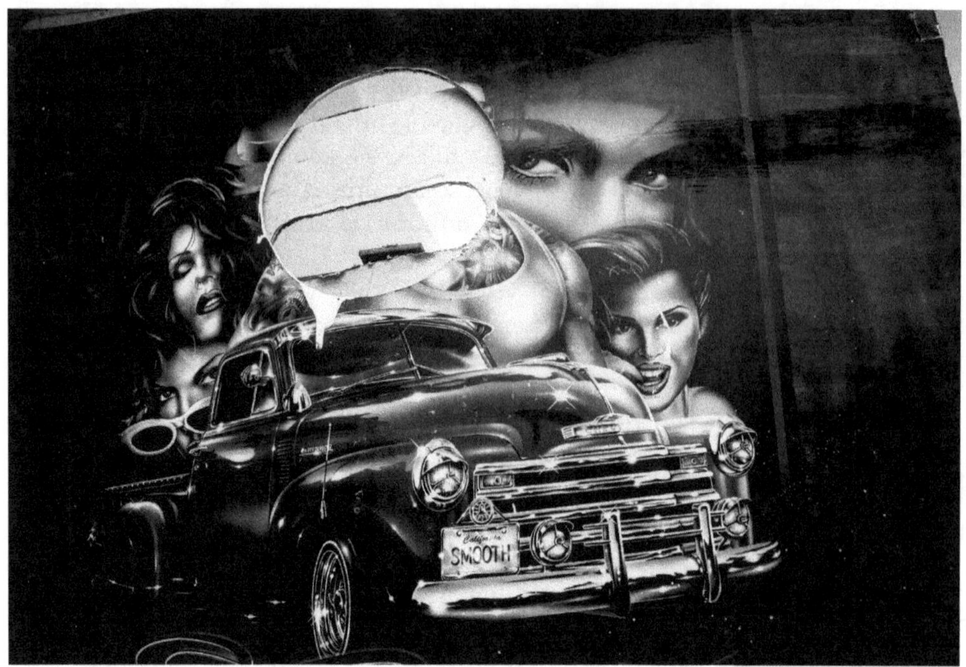

FIG. 3.2. M. Goded, *La vida oculta* (2010).

and others appear to be the effect of poor maintenance and overcrowding. Goded's focus on the walls, apart from emphasising the confinement of the absent subaltern, also showcases them as canvas for self-expression. In that sense, her photographic focus on the physical limits imposed on the prisoners becomes Bhabha's interstitial site where the possibility of an alternative identification emerges through representation.

One of the images from the series is a photograph of a prison wall with a poster, which is placed against a wall thinly painted with brown paint (Figure 3.2). The shot is taken from below and its main focus is a classic 1950s blue Chevrolet pickup truck surrounded by a sea of attractive, idealised female faces that are orbiting above the car. The car's number plate, characteristically placed on the left-hand side of the shiny front grill, reads 'smooth'. The dominant colours on the posters are blue, black as well as different shades of grey; red is used on the lips of some of the women pictured around the car to emphasise their attractiveness. Right above the car, in the centre of the poster, a bust of a man emerges from behind the shiny roof, heavily tattooed and dressed in a white vest. The area of the poster where his face would have been has been removed; the photograph only shows a circular hole where the man's head used to be. The hole exposes part of a cardboard backing and a fragment of the wall, which is painted a different colour from the surroundings of the poster. Because of the way in which the poster has been defaced, the main focus of the photograph is the missing man, who would have been the main protagonist of the static drama of this image, his status reflected in the car pictured below him and the women surrounding him.

This photograph offers a wealth of interpretative possibilities, largely because of its focus on a damaged poster and the hole where the face of the main character should be. Firstly, it can be read as a self-conscious meta-photograph referring viewers to other images in *La vida oculta*, which focus on spaces as opposed to people. Although, at first view, this emphasis seems seamless and aesthetically consistent, this photograph demonstrates the photographic violence of omitting human subjects in the context of an overcrowded Mexican prison. The man with the missing head is a stand-in for the missing men of the series. Secondly, the hole where the man's face should be can be read as a visual metaphor for the figurative hole the prisoners leave in the lives of their families and communities when they are incarcerated. Finally, it is a reference to the wider context of endemic violence and impunity, of which the crisis in Mexican prisons is only one symptom. International NGOs report a sharp rise in violent crime linked to the operation of drug cartels supplying narcotics from and through Mexico to the United States (Sosa 2010: unnumbered pages), resulting in thousands of men being killed with impunity every year. It is a photograph of loss documenting an aesthetic defacement, which bears witness to life within the prison walls.

The missing part of the poster competes for attention with the meticulously represented classic car. The vehicle is at the forefront of the composition taking centre stage. This particular model, a 1950s Chevrolet pick-up truck, is a cultural trope of freedom and independence, emblematic of the idea of the American dream. Apart from implying freedom, it is also a clear status symbol, closely linked to traditional patriarchal ideas of masculinity defined through a man's material possessions and perceived wealth. The fact that the car is American underlines the pervasive influence of US cultural symbols and ideas on aspirations and ambitions in Mexico, especially among young men. This particular poster is, therefore, a representation of a culturally syncretic version of Mexican *machismo*, a fantasy of freedom and wealth placed against a prison wall. Women represented within this image are not there to signify the importance of relationships or community links; disembodied and suspended around his figure they are symbols of the sexual prowess of the owner of the car. Their facial expressions are suggestive and their attractiveness is emphasised by the selective use of red. They are clearly modelled on the photographs of women in magazines and pornographic publications. Peeking from behind the missing man, their beauty is a commodity devised to underline his status, in a way not dissimilar from the car. Although this image is clearly demeaning from a feminist perspective, framing women as satellites orbiting around the central figure of the *macho*, it is more productive here to focus on the insight it offers into the fantasy of *machismo* from within the boundary of a prison.

Patriarchy as a normative cultural construct shapes the expectations and experiences of both men and women and even though, by definition, the latter are in a subordinate position to the former, it is important to acknowledge the limited identifications available to both genders. The photograph of the defaced poster throws into sharp relief the contrast between the *macho* fantasy and the reality lived by the majority of the prisoners. The overcrowded and chronically underfunded prisons are full of men rejected by their society and oppressed by the underfunded penal system, yet if this poster can be seen as a symbolic representation of their aspirations, they fit into the accepted norms of masculine ambitions, centred on expensive vehicles and objectified women. In most patriarchal societies, mainstream cultural products construct masculinity around economics of desire centred on expensive cars and objectified, beautiful women. Particularly in the case of the pervasive cultural exchanges between Mexico and the United States, the northern neighbour plays a crucial role in providing an aspirational template for *machismo* through films, photographs and other publications. The dominant economic position of the United States and its prolific cultural output is a difficult combination to resist in an environment where few alternatives are offered.

The poster in question is a reworking of that masculine fantasy, but the fact that it has been photographed in prison leads to questions over the ways in which capitalist aspirations influence choices. Here, it is important to return to Kracauer's assertion that images have the capacity to isolate subjects from the world in which they live by providing an alternative simulacrum, which seems more attractive than their lived experience (Kracauer 1993: 432). The poster provides evidence of the power of the visual horizons — the car is a classic model, the women are conventionally attractive, and the man's body is portrayed in stereotypically masculine terms, covered in tattoos, very muscular and disproportionately bigger than the car and the women surrounding it. This fantasy of stereotypical masculine success is all the more poignant by being stuck to a prison wall, where even the most basic commodities such as bedding or toiletries are out of reach, not to mention the paraphernalia of masculine success. To dismiss it as an escapist fantasy, however, is to fail to understand the possibility of a scene of an alternative identification emerging from the interstitial space within the hegemonic discourses of *machismo* in capitalist contexts.

Kracauer's aforementioned notion of photography as an alienating medium fails to account for its power to be a tool in identity building, which helps individuals to assert their own position within socio-cultural contexts in relation to their own representation as well as those of others. It is Linfield's notion of photography as a connective tissue (Kracauer 2010: 31) that sheds more light on the role of images in creating new economics of desire and providing opportunities for positive identifications. Bearing in mind the importance of visual representations of Great Men for *mexicanidad* and the saturation of the Mexican visual horizon with imagery originating in the United States, it is reasonable to propose that the majority of Mexican men experience a dissonance between what they can see in the media, and the aspirations it creates, and what is their daily experience. Although such dissonance is part of the rich fabric of living in an era of accelerated telecommunications, it is important to underline once again that the idea of a global village ignores the significant differences between the standards of living between its different inhabitants. As the example with the flip-flops has shown, the uniformity of consumer choices does not translate into the uniformity of experience. Similarly, the reception of similar images will depend on the socio-cultural positioning of their viewers, and not just their visual content. For Mexican men, the contrast between the images of *macho* success they see and their own lives will be stark. On the one hand, their cultural context provides plenty of identification templates, and on the other hand, it provides few legitimate opportunities for satisfying the desires it creates. In that sense, the young man with his head removed does not belong within the image, of which he is the protagonist. Moreover, the contrast between the standards of living within the global village, especially between countries in such close proximity as Mexico and the United States, provides alternative routes that promise to deliver the possibility of narrowing the gap between aspirations and experience. The violence and crime of Mexican drug cartels is, after all, fuelled by demand in the United States and the rest of the developed countries. Although the state's lack of ability to deal effectively with the rising crime rates is part of the problem, fundamentally Mexico is reduced to passively managing the consequences of rising demand for drugs with its limited resources. The US economic and cultural hegemonic influence is twofold here; it provides both the dream of prosperity and the means to achieve that dream. Although the creation and buoyant development of Mexican violent drug trafficking business may not have been its explicit aim, it is undoubtedly one of its consequences.

That is not to claim that regimes of visibility and their influence on one's choices are to blame for the criminal activity of individuals, as that would be a condescending oversimplification. Nonetheless, the aim here is to show how a piece of seemingly conventional prison art does point to the wider dynamic at play, where men fall victims to endemic violence, which they help to create in the absence of state provision and lack of the state's constructive response to their violence. In that sense, the poster reinstates the men's position at the centre of that dynamic, despite the fact that it is issued from a place of subalternity, confinement and virtual invisibility. Goded's photographic mediation of the defaced poster allows it to become a liminal encounter between the similarities of masculine capitalist aspirations in different social and cultural contexts.

The only two photographs from *La vida oculta* that contain a glimpse of the bodily presence of the inmates are staged against a whitewashed wall. One of them depicts two hands holding basic tattooing tools and the other (Figure 3.3) pictures one hand holding up a flat wooden bat with the words 'asuntos internos' [internal affairs] carved on the front of it. The two photographs are very similar in terms of their composition; they are arranged against the same wall and they are held by the same person. The hand holding up the bat is dirty and a layer of grime surrounds the visible fingernails. The index finger appears to have its top part missing. The wooden bat, positioned in the centre of the composition, is a clear visual reference to the endemic violence suffered by many Mexican prisoners. The overcrowding, as well as lack of resources and qualified personnel, contributes to an atmosphere of intimidation and impunity, which make any claims for prisons as places of rehabilitation seem unrealistic. In 'Cárceles en México: Cuadros de una Crisis', Azaola and Bergman (2010: 83) stress that the self-confessed sense of fear amongst many prisoners is actually one of the obstacles in obtaining reliable data relating to their experience. The words carved on the bat, 'asuntos internos' [internal affairs], clearly hint at its use as a weapon within the prison, exposing the institutionalised brutality of the Mexican penitentiary system, but without stigmatising individual

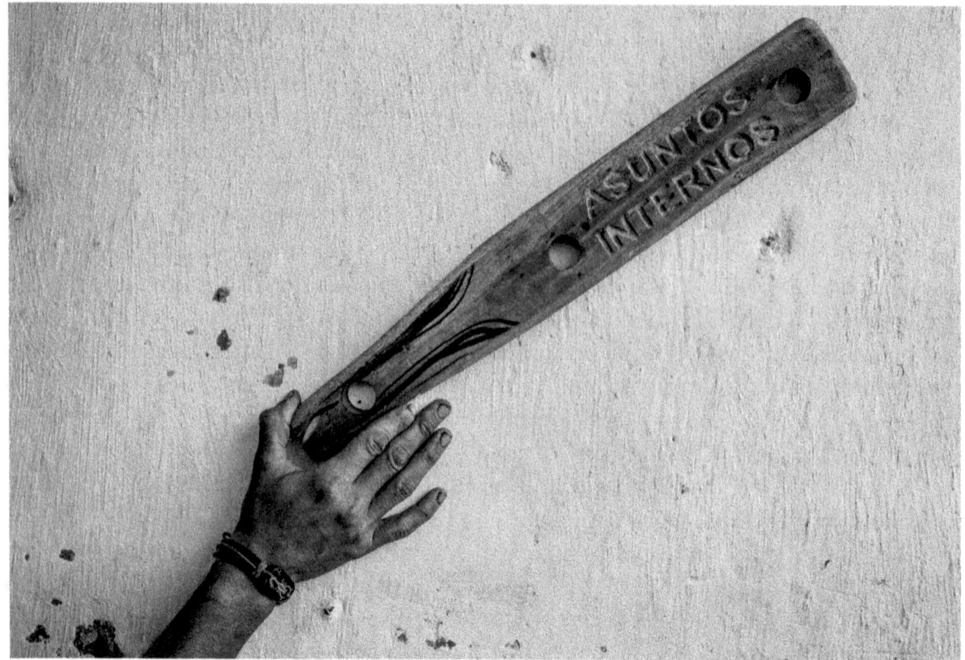

Fig. 3.3. M. Goded, *La vida oculta* (2010).

prisoners or guards through photographic representation. The closeness of the composition and its precise arrangement contribute to a sense of entrapment within a cycle of violence, exposing the prisoners' vulnerability. The photograph is not staged as a plea for sympathy, but rather as a comment on the institutionalised violence within Mexican prisons, hence its static composition. Nonetheless, its shocking quality lies precisely in the unremarkable regularity of using a wooden bat to intimidate and control other human beings, especially those who are already confined and reliant on others for their basic needs.

Prisons are not the only site of impunity and violence photographed by Goded. Her earlier project entitled *Plaza de la soledad*, featuring photographs of prostitutes in La Merced, is thematically different from *La vida oculta* as it encompasses plenty of images of people and their bodies, which will be the focus of the next chapter. Nonetheless, in *Plaza de la soledad* Goded's interest in the liminal space occupied by her subaltern subjects is evident in her photographs of the environments in which her subjects work and live. Moreover, it is important here to point to the similarity between the confinement of inmates in Mexican prisons and the virtual imprisonment of prostitutes in legally sanctioned *zonas de tolerancia*. Both prostitutes and prisoners are subaltern; ostracised, confined, vulnerable and largely absent from the dominant visual and literary discourses, except as a limit of acceptable identifications. A comparison of photographs from the two projects reveals similarities between the liminal spaces they inhabit.

In terms of the formal qualities of *La vida oculta* and *Plaza de la soledad*, both projects lack any photographs of open spaces and mostly focus on tightly framed

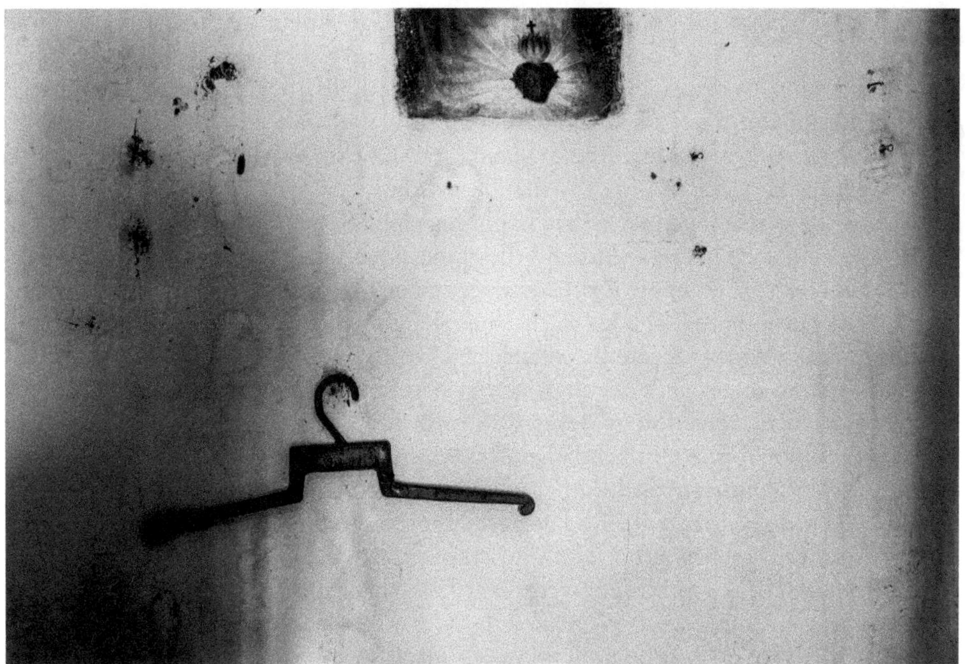

FIG. 3.4. M. Goded, *La vida oculta* (2010).

walls and courtyards, underlining the confinement of people who live between them. The walls often become canvases for self-expression, where visual clues are displayed as to the hopes and aspirations of the subaltern subjects, who are sometimes absent themselves, their presence discernible only through the mark they have left behind. Through Goded's lens, the spaces where people are forced to live are very similar and similarly portrayed in La Merced and in Ignacio Allende prison. Walls are cracked and dirty with layers of old paint, rooms are small, windows barred, and exits nowhere to be seen. Moreover, one of the most significant similarities between *La vida oculta* and *Plaza de la soledad* is the presence of religious imagery on the walls. On the one hand, such images should be expected in a largely Catholic country, where religious beliefs play an important role. On the other hand, seeing them in places inhabited by prostitutes and prisoners, who are normally labelled as sinners and serve as an antithesis of desirable Christian behaviour, demands further investigation.

In *La vida oculta* religious imagery is displayed alongside posters of women and cars. Among twenty-three photographs published on Maya Goded's website, three contain images of Christ with a further three showing images of women. It is clear that in the absence of a properly functioning penitentiary structure, religious beliefs play an important part in providing a hope for redemption. The Catholic Church is actively involved in the vast majority of Mexican prisons, where priests visit at least once a week to celebrate mass for the inmates and offer their counsel. The website of the Pontifica Comisión para América Latina [Papal Commission for Latin America] cites examples of priests falling out with local authorities due to their criticism of the conditions within the penal system and injustices suffered by the inmates (Centro Nacional de Servicios de la Pastoral Penitenciaria Católica [Pastoral Prison Services National Centre] 2012). Bearing in mind the pivotal importance of the ideas of sin and redemption within Catholic discourse, it is imperative to analyse the material evidence of the prisoners' worship photographed by Goded on the walls of Ignacio Allende prison.

Within the series, an image that is photographed twice is the Sacred Heart of Jesus (Figure 3.4). This repetition of the same devotional picture, previously seen in *La vida oculta* in compositional recurrences in the photographs of the wooden bat and the tattooing tools, adds to the sense of confinement and being confronted with the same images repeatedly, which is a liminal photographic mirroring of an everyday prison experience through the eyes of an inmate. Moreover, the choice of this particular depiction of Jesus is significant because it is one of the most popular devotional images in the Catholic Church the world over, also commonly worshipped by Anglicans and Lutherans. The image of the Sacred Heart of Jesus is typically a bust of Christ with his hand touching or holding a burning human heart emphasising two aspects crucial to Christianity, namely the concept of embodied divinity and Christ's willingness to sacrifice that human body in redemptive suffering. As an image that focuses on Jesus' endless compassion and forgiveness, its appeal to prisoners can be understood in terms of offering comfort and worship that does not condemn them, instead offering the possibility of redemption. Additionally, using such a popular image is a visual attempt at creating connections between the absent subaltern and potential viewers of the photographs, who may recognise the missing prisoners as people who share similar visual landscapes, and perhaps even the same faith.

Goded's photograph of the Sacred Heart of Jesus (Figure 3.5) is unsettling due to its somewhat surprising composition. The image of Christ is not centre stage; in fact, the framing of the photograph cuts it in half, leaving only the bottom part of the religious depiction hovering at the top of the photograph. This framing forces viewers to focus on the fragment of the wall below the image, a grey area of painted concrete with rusty hooks and nails protruding from it in different places. Below the cropped image of the Sacred Heart of Jesus, there is a black empty clothes hanger placed on one of the rusty nails. There are faint water marks scattered around the wall fragment, but the two main focal points are the cropped devotional image and the empty hanger. The wall has a slight blue-grey tinge to it, which contrasts with the image of Jesus' heart, glowing against a darker background and painted a vivid red colour. The heart itself is surrounded by a crown of thorns, which signifies suffering in Catholic imagery and refers to Jesus' passion. The flames painted on top of it, just below a small cross, are a visual reference to the redemptive nature of Christ's suffering and symbolise the purifying fire of his divine love. This image of Jesus' heart, very small yet pregnant with redemptive symbolism, is set against the cold, aesthetically unappealing wall. For all its symbolic meaning, it is cropped to form just a small part of the prison environment. Furthermore, its framing is significant, as by only showing the bottom part of the image Goded visually decapitates Christ, fragmenting the Christian god. The empty hanger below, on

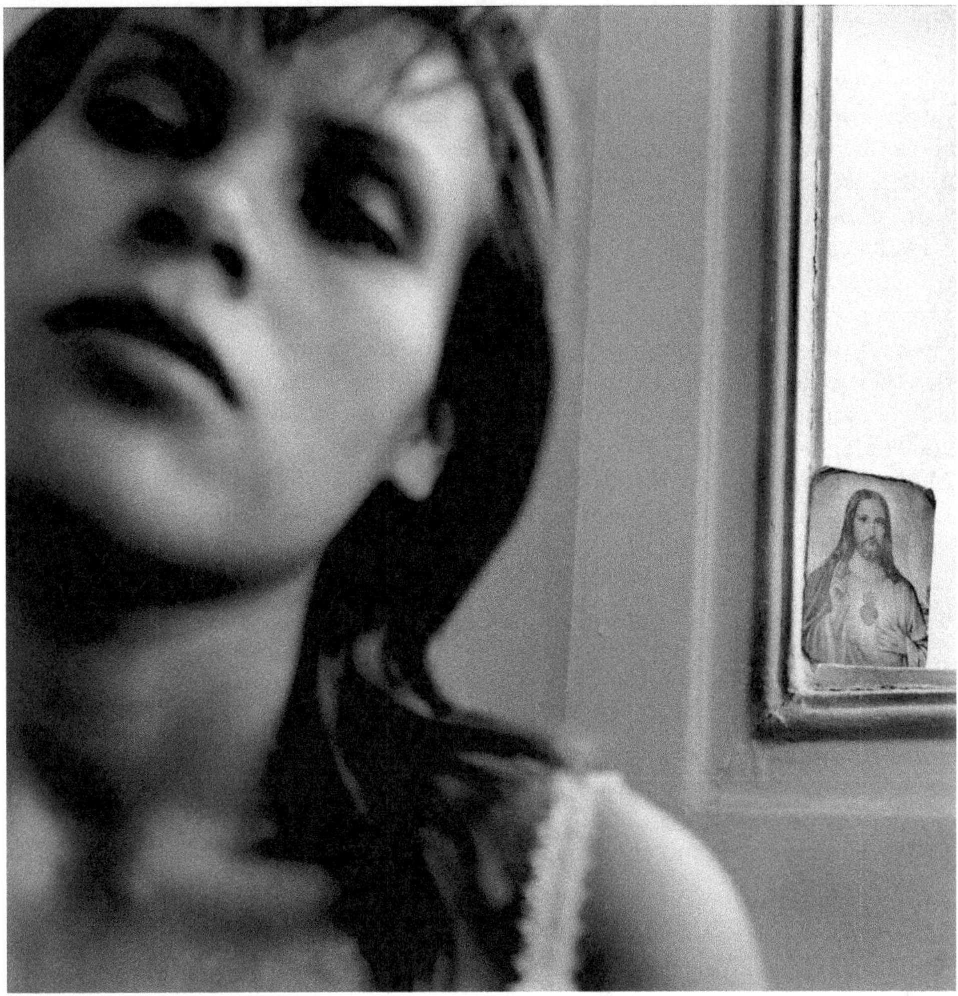

FIG. 3.5. M. Goded, *Good Girls* (2006).

the other hand, is compositionally intact. Such a contrast between the two different focal points of this photograph is a visual comment on the desperate situation of Mexican prisoners. As much as faith may offer the hope of redemption, missing entirely from the underfunded and corrupt penal system, the desperate poverty of incarcerated men and women is their lived economic reality, symbolised here by an empty hanger.

The popularity of the image of the Sacred Heart of Jesus is evident in *Plaza de la soledad*. On page 58 of the album, a small devotional image is tucked into a window frame (Figure 3.5). Its corners are worn and flaky, but the face of Jesus and his heart are in sharp focus, in contrast to the woman at the forefront of the composition, whose face is blurred. Although the composition here is different from Goded's later work in Ignacio Allende prison, the tight faming achieved through deliberate cropping bears a resemblance to her photographs taken in prisons. Including devotional images in her photographs of rooms used by prostitutes, Goded attempts to give a picture of their religious beliefs in order to counteract their one-dimensional identification as a border of acceptable behaviour, a boundary of respectable morality. Just as with the image of the Sacred Heart in prison analysed above, here viewers can again find a liminal connection through a community of experience and of faith or, at the very least, appreciate the subjects' beliefs.

In aesthetic terms, Goded's project on the missing women of Ciudad Juárez, undertaken in cooperation with Justicia para nuestras hijas [Justice for our daughters], bears resemblance to her work in prisons through her focus on walls and empty spaces. Apart from the aesthetic link which will be explored through a close reading of her photographs, there is also a clear political connection between the two projects, as Goded photographs the spaces inhabited by the victims as well as convicted perpetrators of violent crimes. Her photography forges a liminal connection between the two different groups situated at different ends of the Mexican penal system, both suffering injustices through their subaltern position within the hegemonic structures of power. Although Goded's project on the missing women does contain some photographs of the families left behind, as well as images within images of the victims, her focus on the haunted, empty spaces left by the women who used to inhabit them points to the formal difficulties of representing suffering, and to the photographer's self-confessed struggle with the gravity of the subject. In contrast to Goded's work in Ignacio Allende prison, the non-appearance of the women in her photographs taken around the northern border of Mexico has not been staged to enact absence metaphorically, but constitutes its document instead.

Liminal Landscapes and the Absent Subaltern

Goded's experience of photographing the disappearances and murders in Ciudad Juárez affected her deeply on a personal level and formed a basis for her next photographic series. In an introduction to her project, *Tierra de brujas*, published in the *International Review of Photographs: Private*, she confesses to needing to heal from the violence and impunity she witnessed on the Mexico–US border (Goded 2011a). This statement emphasises the liminal and transformative aspects of photography not just in relation to its subjects and viewers, but also in relation to the photographer, who is changed by what they witness and photograph. In an attempt to refresh her outlook, Goded takes fewer tightly framed photographs and captures more sweeping vistas instead. Both her work for *Justicia para nuestras hijas* and *Tierra de brujas* contain several landscapes, providing an opportunity for analysing the absence of her subaltern subjects in liminal spaces and areas that are different from the concrete walls of prisons, narrow streets of La Merced or abandoned rooms in Ciudad Juárez. In order to examine the relationship between subaltern subjects and landscape, it is pivotal to analyse first the notion of landscape in photography.

Liz Wells (2011) traces the history of pictorial depictions of nature in painting and in photography, analysing the conventions and ways of seeing which constitute landscape photography. She emphasises that there are few regions in the world that are untouched by human presence and that the vast majority of people live in environments that are a product of culture, understood in its widest sense, as opposed to nature (Wells 2011: Location 647). Moreover, Wells also examines the binary opposition between nature and culture and links it to the Cartesian separation between body and mind (Wells 2011: Location 383). Analysing the relationship between epistemology and its influence in structuring visual horizons, Wells questions the binary opposition between nature and culture in Western philosophy, stating that the two are intertwined with one another, explaining that Cartesian and Christian insistence on singular subjectivity obscures our existential reliance on environment and the impossibility of thinking outside it (Wells 2011: Location 393). She emphasises that '[n]ature is both "internal", fundamental to what constitutes us as human, and "out there" in that we experience the external world through the senses, including sight' (ibid.). It is in the lack of clearly designated boundaries between nature and culture that the liminal potential of landscape in photography is revealed, since it becomes a way of constructing new meanings and a potential to unsettle old ones. 'Human action contours the landscape, and stories told give meaning to it' (Wells 2011: Location 647).

The epistemological separation between nature and culture in Western philosophical tradition is significant because of its relationship to capitalism. Wells in her discussion of Mark Dorrian's and Gillian Rose's collection of essays *Landscape and Politics* emphasises that 'historical separation from land, and its constitution as *landscape*, was concomitant with early modernity and the emergence of Capitalism' (Wells 2011: Location 695, original emphasis). The need for pictorial depictions of land, therefore, only emerged in response to the separation between communities and the land as a primary mode of sustenance (ibid.), producing an alienating effect. Therefore, from its very inception in Western tradition, picturing the land was not a politically neutral activity. On the contrary, it was often employed to show the land in an aesthetically pleasing, pastoral way while obscuring the people and the work that had shaped it (Wells 2011). The landscape tradition is a specific relationship to land visually articulated in patriarchal and capitalist terms. Particularly in terms of the relationship between colonisers and colonies, seeing understood as a form of possession (Berger 1972 in Wells 2011: Location 789) helps us to appreciate the objectification of colonial landscapes, which became an exotic visual confirmation of status and entrepreneurial success (Wells 2011: 789). When photography first emerged as a new medium of picturing the environment, the old conventions of landscape remained in place. Nonetheless, bearing in mind that it is histories and perspectives that give specific meaning to landscapes, picturing the land is always a liminal, transformative activity that is open to interpretation.

If, as Wells argues, 'the act of naming is the act of taming' (Wells 2011: Location 353) then the act of framing is also an act of taming. Although the landscape tradition in Mexico is undoubtedly rooted in colonial legacies, and the lens through which the country's geography is viewed is often foreign, photography as a liminal medium offers an opportunity to question and destabilise these legacies without obliterating them. One of the ways in which this can be achieved is through emphasising links between people and the land, as opposed to concealing them. Graciela Iturbide's famous photograph *Mujer Ángel* [Angel Woman] is a good example of a conscious play on pictorial conventions. On the one hand, the composition of the photograph follows a classical template for a sweeping vista. On the other hand, the figure of an indigenous woman in traditional dress climbing the path with a portable music player in her hand offers an idiosyncratic contrast that unsettles the convention. It offers a seemingly romantic image with an element of disconcerting surprise, which posits questions of land ownership as well as technological transformations. Moreover, especially within a country which relatively recently fought for its independence, and where territorial losses from the war with the United States are still mourned, picturing the land from within is a way of trying to understand the shape of the national character.

Maya Goded's interest in the relationship between land and people is evident in the fact that two of her projects contain the word 'tierra' — *Tierra Negra* and *Tierra de brujas*. In *Tierra Negra*, she photographs the black communities on the Costa Chica who are so culturally and socially marginalised and invisible that many Mexicans are unaware of their existence. The project is a conscious effort in using the relationship between the coastal regions and the people inhabiting them as a way of legitimising their claim to *mexicanidad*. *Tierra de brujas* is Goded's project on sorcery in northern Mexico, mostly undertaken in the state of San Luis Potosí, where landscape plays a role almost as important as the witches she sets out to photograph. Goded's expressed desire to recover her way of seeing after witnessing the impunity and the violence in Ciudad Juárez and surrounding area is in *Tierra de brujas* visualised in terms of reframing *mexicanidad*. The photographer sets out to rediscover her country and in landscape seeks the antidote to injustice and suffering, looking for alternative meanings. The desolate, otherworldly images of dry, foggy landscapes evoke some of the atmosphere of Juan Rulfo's *El llano en llamas* (1953), a book of short stories set during the Mexican Revolution and the Cristero Rebellion. The harshness of the landscape and the suffering of its inhabitants are intertwined in Rulfo's stories, which are one of the most important works of Mexican literature and world literature, constituting a cultural canon that is instrumental in creating a sense of national identity. Goded's choice of landscapes is a reference to magic realism and its importance to *mexicanidad*. In critically combining landscape conventions and symbols of Mexican identity, Goded's photographs are a way of forging new meanings through interstitial cultural spaces between them, from a position of a woman photographer.

One of the photographs in the series *Tierra de brujas* is a classically composed landscape at sunset or sunrise, during the transition between day and night (Figure 3.6). The land takes up approximately two-thirds of the composition and the sky occupies the rest, in accordance with the classic compositional conventions, but in contrast to many of Goded's photographs of people and urban spaces that are often deliberately framed off-centre or extremely close up. The compositional regularity of the photograph is also at odds with its rather unusual content. In the foreground, a young white lamb is standing on grey gravel; on closer inspection, it is clear that she is held in a very small cage, but because of the colour of the wire cage the

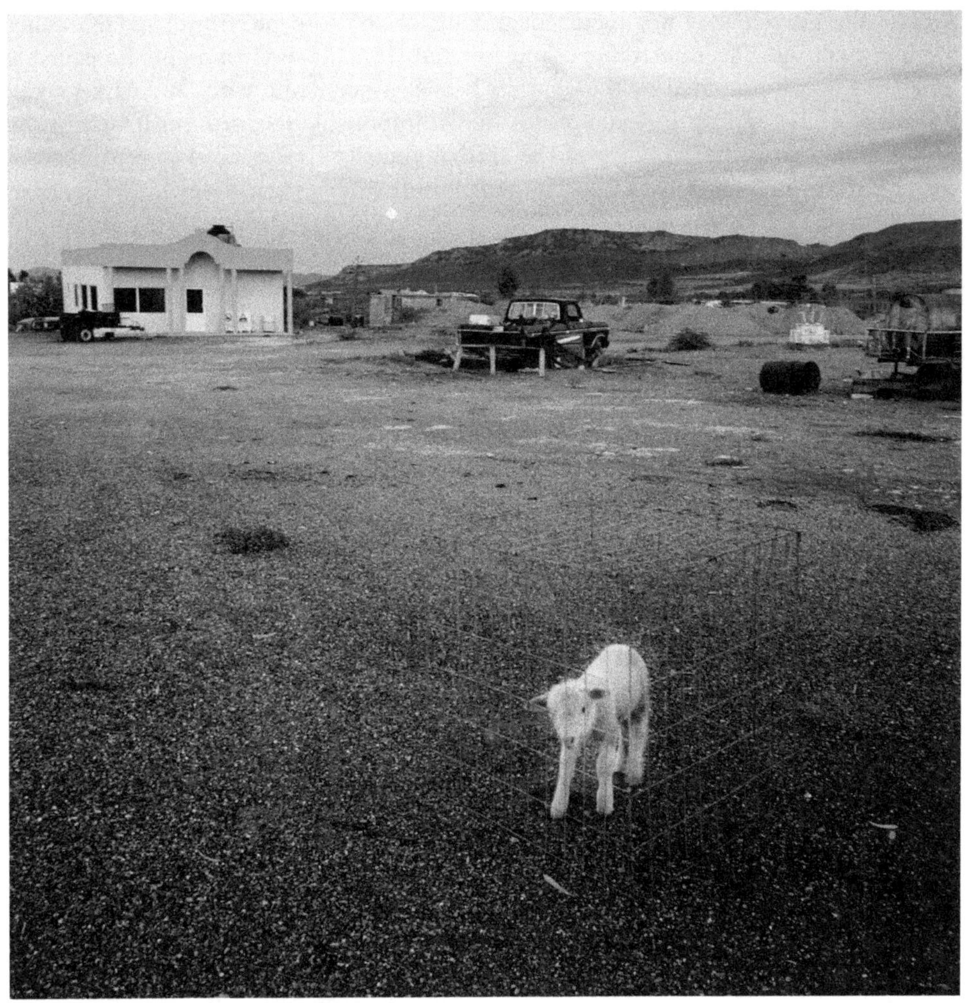

FIG. 3.6. M. Goded, *Tierra de brujas* (2008).

animal's captivity is almost indiscernible at first glance. Behind the lamb in the middle of the photograph there is an abandoned pick-up truck with wooden blocks instead of wheels. To the left of the car, there is a small house freshly painted in pink, and to the right there are two rusty old barrels. Behind the mountains on the horizon, a faint moon is either rising or setting. In this photograph, the subversion of pictorial landscape convention relies on the inclusion of all the typical elements, which often feature in landscapes, namely domestic animals, small dwellings, and forms of transport set against a sweeping background, and on arranging them in such a way that, instead of producing a familiar picturesque effect, they become unsettling. Indeed, if this photograph borrows from pictorial landscape conventions, it also employs some surrealist strategies, especially in capturing the pickup truck on wooden block instead of wheels, which are a visual reference to surrealist use of stilts in paintings. Similarly, the lamb in the foreground cuts a lonely figure against the gravel; it is not pictured grazing or in close proximity to any other animal, making it seem estranged and isolated from its environment. Its palpable loneliness is compounded by the contrast between her white wool and dark gravel; the edges of its cage are in some places almost impossible to distinguish against the background. Both the captivity of the animal and the conspicuous disrepair of the car contribute to the sense of entrapment within the image, despite the apparent feel of space.

The unsettling nature of this landscape can be seen as a reference to a typical response to sorcery in modern Mexico, which is one of disconcertation and mistrust, mixed with curiosity. In an interview with ASX TV, Goded (2011b) describes the witches she set out to photograph as living on the edges of communities, feared and ostracised, but also trusted with people's health because of their connection to the land. These women occupy a liminal position between the villages and the open countryside, feared and trusted in equal measure in the absence of other methods of treating illnesses. They are subaltern inasmuch as they occupy a position outside the villages and use healing methods that are both feared and respected, but certainly not recognised as legitimate by any authorities, suspended in legal and social limbo. Goded compares their social position to that of prostitutes; they are rejected and ostracised by their communities and live marginal lives (Goded 2013), but their enduring presence is testament to the important functions they play within their communities, even if they are shrouded in taboo. Their practice is an effect of cultural and religious syncretism, a fusion between indigenous beliefs and Catholic rituals. Despite the fact that one of the definitions of *mexicanidad* is that of fusion between indigenous and Spanish elements, of which shamanism and Catholicism are major exponents, sorcery that combines the two is seen as transgressive and marked as dangerous. In that context, Goded's unsettling play with pictorial conventions, where all the seemingly familiar elements produce a deep unease through their juxtaposition, is a visual metaphor for the socio-cultural situation of the witches of northern Mexico. Their subalternity is metaphorically represented in the liminal arid landscape, during the liminal time of transition between night and day.

Just as in *La vida oculta* Goded photographed the same walls several times in order to compound the impression of entrapment and confinement, so too in *Tierra de brujas* the same tropes haunt different images, increasing the familiarity of the viewers with the landscape. The pickup truck suspended on stilts in the image described above (Figure 3.6) comes back centre stage in another photograph in the series (Figure 3.7). The composition of the image is relatively conservative, with the grey-blue sky taking up a little over half of the photograph and the ground taking up the rest, the two meeting at the horizon line softened by mist. The photograph is in focus, but the fine milky mist reduces the sharpness of its details gradually towards the centre of the photograph and makes some elements of the horizon virtually imperceptible. The immobilised vehicle languishes in the middle of the image, propped on thick grey stilts — its condition and the items surrounding it and piled in its bed are the same as in the previous image (Figure 7). Made for movement and symbolising freedom, the car without its wheels faces towards an

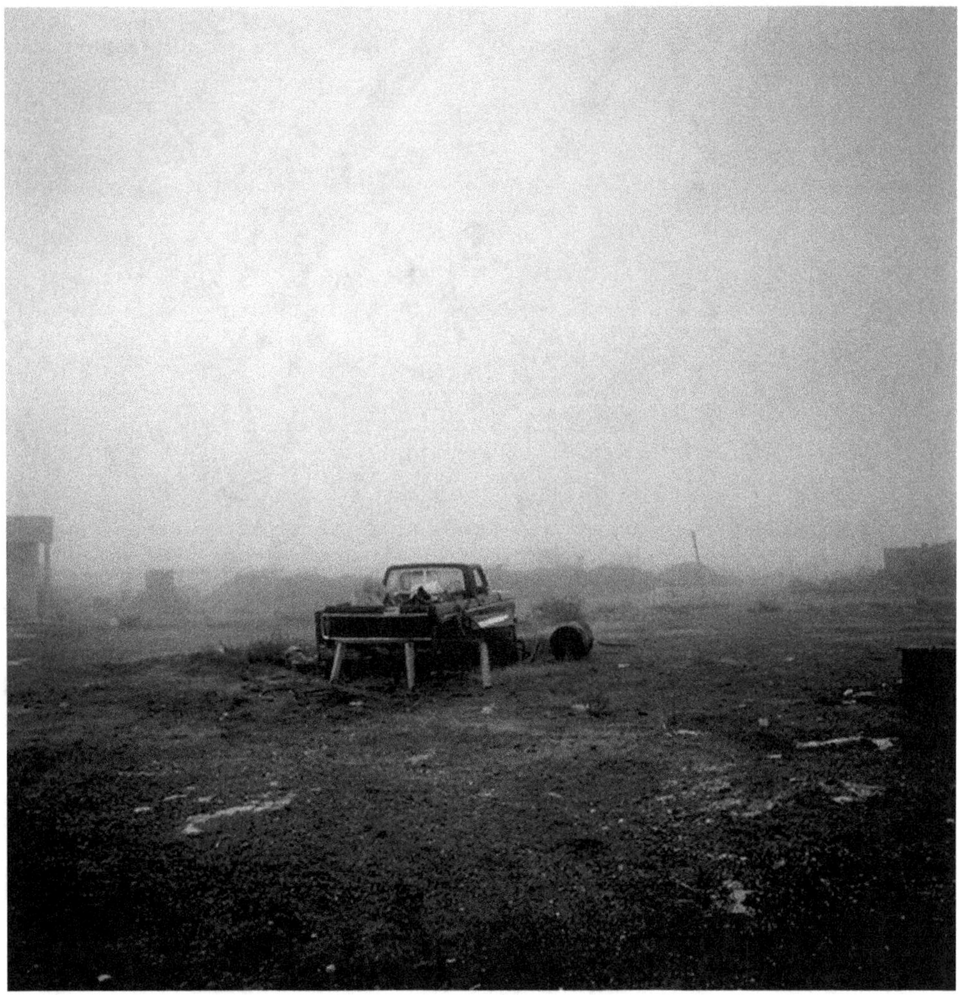

FIG. 3.7. M. Goded *Tierra de brujas* (2008).

empty horizon, a grey nothingness. Its presence is liminal, since it has ceased to function as a vehicle, but has not disintegrated, suspended on stilts and static in its uselessness.

The pickup truck's appearance in *Tierra de brujas* is very different from its idealised image captured on the poster in *La vida oculta* (Figure 3.2) analysed before. The contrast between these two representations is a visual comment on the dissonance between hegemonic idealised imagery and the lived experience that tries to emulate it. The dilapidated car in *Tierra de brujas* is not only liminal in its function, suspended in between usefulness and nothingness, but also suspended in this liminality. Slowly disintegrating in the countryside of San Luis Potosí, a trope of freedom becomes a reminder of how hegemonic aspirations come to pass within subaltern contexts. The car's presence also alters the landscape, making the liminal space of Mexican

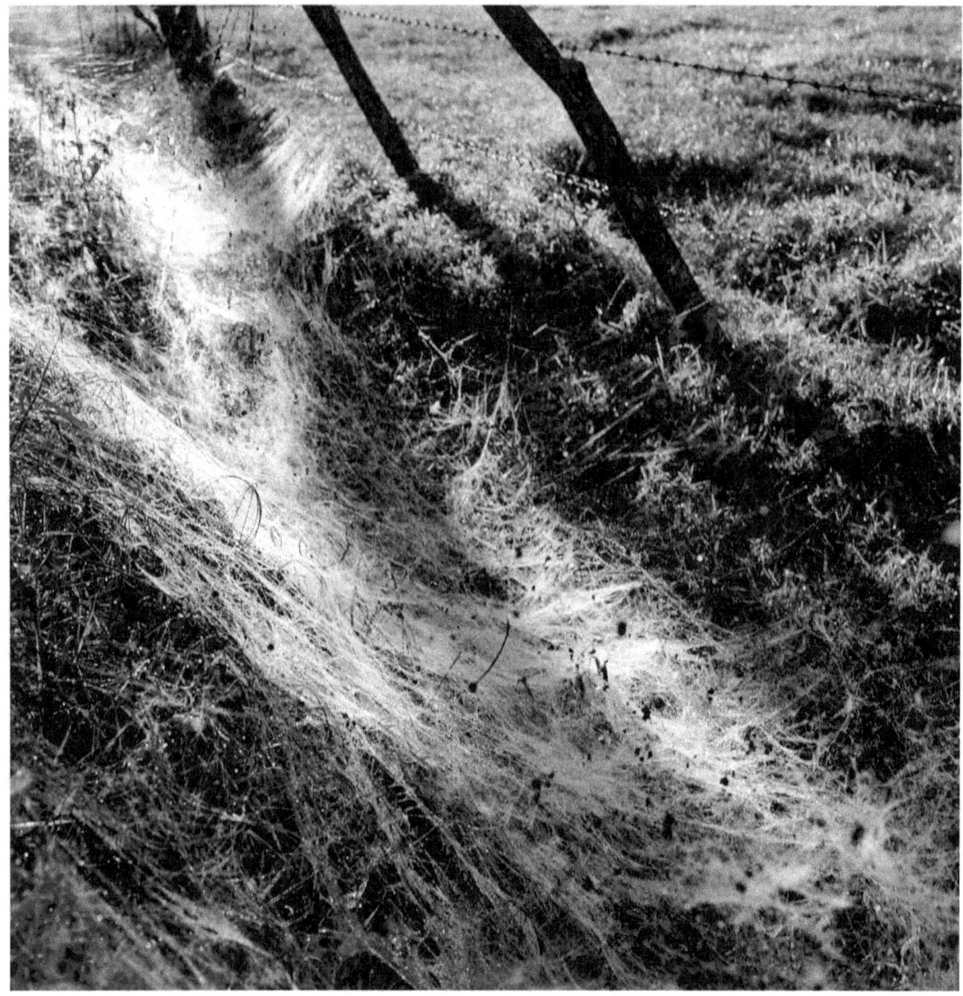

Fig. 3.8. M. Goded, *Tierra de brujas* (2008).

plains a repository for discarded symbols of the American dream. The image is clearly dystopian in its atmosphere, which is made even more apparent through the inevitable slowness of the process of disintegration. The photographic instance capturing a single frame of its decay hints at the long process of degeneration that looms ahead, not dissimilarly to the milky fog that eventually fades into the horizon with the apparent promise of erasing it all.

The changing context of the rural landscape of San Luis Potosí in terms of the relationship between Mexico and the United States is all the more poignant when one considers the spread of drug-related violence throughout the region. After completing her work on femicides in Ciudad Juárez and her work on prostitution on the border between Mexico and the United States, Goded travelled through San Luis Potosí as a way of escaping the endemic violence against women, and finding alternative ways of healing. In the absence of justice for victims, she photographically mirrors the journey of grieving mothers, who often seek solace in traditional *brujerías* after their daughters disappear (Goded 2013). At the time, San Luis Potosí was relatively safe to travel through and Goded completed the series alone driving her car through the countryside. Yet despite the fact that some of the photographs in the series were taken as late as 2009, Goded claims that the region is no longer safe to travel through on one's own because it has been swept up in drug-related violence and is now used as part of a drug-trafficking route leading to the US border. The liminal landscape preserved in her images and its changing socio-political context underline the vulnerability of subaltern spaces, which, in this case, have since become a backdrop for the international drug trade.

Goded's conscious visual play with conventions of portraying landscapes is most apparent in her photograph of a ditch covered in spider webs (Figure 3.8). The trench is the main focus of the image, photographed from above and bathed in natural sunlight. The barbed wire fence to the right of the ditch casts a long shadow on the grass covered in spider webs. The precise focus and the chiaroscuro effect emphasise the shadows of the fence making patterns of light through the intricate, fine cobwebs layered on top of one another. The trench itself is a place in between different areas of land, or perhaps a border between the road and the countryside, a designated liminal area. Its function as a boundary is further emphasised by the barbed wire fence. The image is the opposite of picturesque, with its focus on cobwebs and fences, but despite its unusual subject matter it is a very aesthetically compelling composition. Within the liminal space of the ditch, scores of small spiders have made their webs in between the sloping ground and the large fence, covering the ground in a fine white blanket.

This photograph can be read as a visual metaphor of Goded's photographic interests more generally, for she is interested in subaltern phenomena that are pushed to the margins of visual horizons, sometimes to the point of being completely absent. Her wider socio-political interests as a documentary photographer inform her framing of the trench. By focusing on the unexpected beauty in the potentially unappealing combination of cobwebs draped over barbed wire, she showcases the liminal space as a site of potential and transformation. The spiders, negotiating their webs between man-made attempts to control and own landscape, are anthropomorphised through the similarity of their interstitial presence to that of Goded's human subjects. On the one hand, the arachnids in this photograph are clearly limited by the physical boundaries put onto the landscape by human activity. On the other hand, however, they are also changing and reappropriating those boundaries by using them as starting points for building their webs. In that sense, this photograph is also evidence for the impossibility of separating nature from culture (Wells 2011: Location 393) in its portrayal of animal life incorporating marks of human presence.

Liminality as a concept allows for a wider understanding of the way in which socio-cultural meanings are made through photography in relation to subaltern subjects. It aids in the analysis of visual material through the subversions, gaps and omissions of dominant social structures. Goded's photography of the liminal spaces, in which the subaltern subjects of her projects dwell, opens up the possibilities of interrogating their position, placing the responsibility for finding meaning through gaps in understanding on the viewer. Goded's surprising compositions, which often break conventions, are an aesthetic invitation to a political interrogation of the situation of her subjects and its wider context. As such, her photography becomes a liminal space in documenting the subalterns' lives and thus an antidote to their historical absence. Moreover, through photography's privileged relationship to the material reality of lived experience, Goded's work anchors the invisible and often displaced subalterns within their geographical space, evidencing their existence through the mark they make on their environment. By altering horizons of vision to include the liminal spaces in which her subjects live, Goded creates an environment where their existence and its representations may be considered from other vantage points, such as that of the body, which is the focus of the next chapter.

Notes to Chapter 3

1. It is the 2012 action thriller entitled *Get the Gringo* directed by Adrian Gutenberg.
2. Flip-flotsam is a documentary filmed in the Lamu Archipelago of Kenya detailing ways in which local inhabitants deal with this particular type of waste <http://www.flipflotsam.pwp.blueyonder.co.uk/about.htm> [accessed 17 March 2013].

CHAPTER 4

Abject Bodies and Embodied Subalternity

The spaces represented in Maya Goded's photographs and analysed as liminal provide concrete geographical settings for framing subaltern bodies. Her works of landscape and urban photography specify a context for the subaltern subjects she wants to represent through her lens, framing their physical environments as fragmented and disjointed experiences of space. Subaltern protagonists of Goded's photographs occupy marginal positions within the city and the country from which they are discursively and, to a significant extent, physically excluded. For example, prostitutes from La Merced, although physically located in the heart of Mexico City, are legally bound to stay within their exclusion zone or *zona de tolerancia*. Goded's other projects focus on people living on the border with the United States or within the coastal areas. This physical relegation constitutes and reinforces the social and cultural invisibility of the subaltern. Photographic representation intervenes here tracing their embodied presence in liminal spaces and redressing their relegation through imagery that makes their existence apparent.

This chapter will analyse the representation of marginal bodies within Maya Goded's documentary photography in order to examine the visual and epistemological tensions that stem from representing embodied otherness. The visual analysis will examine issues of race, body commoditisation and death as markers of difference that constitute aspects of subaltern embodiment. Goded's *Tierra Negra*, *Plaza de la soledad* and her photographic project on the missing women in Ciudad Juárez will constitute the main corpus for analysing bodily abjection in the context of shunned ethnic communities, prostitutes and murder victims killed with impunity in Mexico. The analysis of Goded's photographs will focus on examining the tension between engagement and exploitation, which is central to documentary work that visually exposes groups vulnerable in their subalternity. In order to link theoretically that photographic tension to social normativity in Mexico, Judith Butler's theory of embodiment and Julia Kristeva's theory of abjection will be used as critical tools to examine Goded's visual representations of embodied marginal femininities. Butler's theories on the discursive limits of the body in *Bodies that Matter* (1993) and Julia Kristeva's insights on the abject from *Powers of Horror* (1982) help to problematise the issues of representing the marginal. Although their theoretical routes examine the subject–abject distinction within epistemology, they are also applicable to the study of images, and help to examine how the discursive limits of embodiment affect the way images of bodies are produced and received, particularly in relation to subaltern people. Through its power to influence discourse, photographic representation will be considered as socially constitutive in itself. Moreover, the visual domain of photo-documentary will be construed as a system of signs in its own right, quite apart from discourse, despite their inevitable and necessary convergences.

Theorising embodiment in order to analyse its photographic representations is a challenge that demands a re-examination of the relationship between materiality and meaning. First and foremost, there is a fundamental contrast between the tangible materiality of the body and the abstract thought processes, which are needed to make it intelligible at all. This is not to posit the body's temporal or material precedence before discourse, but rather to differentiate between the two. Stating that thinking about the body oscillates around the boundaries of discourse is not to claim an extra-discursive reality, which is then referred to through language. It is rather to assert that the intelligibility of the body relies on abstract discursive constructions. However, as Butler stresses, analysing the body as a construct demands a rethinking of construction itself and considering it as a process that creates subjects through the processes of inclusion and exclusion (Butler 1993: 11). As such, it also has to demarcate the domain of the non-subject or abject, which becomes a site of negative identifications that have been constitutively rejected from the subject domain. These processes of making one's body intelligible to oneself and to others are dynamic and subject to change and, as such, the body retains a certain corporal opacity, which is resistant to critical analyses and demarcates the borders of discourse. Nonetheless, theoretically approaching the difficulty of thinking about the body is crucial to how we conceive of others and ourselves and how that knowledge informs and shapes our bodily experience.

Regardless of the difficulties posed by theorising the materiality of the body, documentary photography leaves one little choice — the mediated bodily presence of the other is apparent and impossible to ignore. Judith Butler in *Bodies that Matter* approaches the body by referring to the classical impossibility of separating materiality and meaning, both logically and etymologically. In her writings on femininity, she underlines the etymological connection between *matter* and *mater* as well as *matrix*, linguistically indicating the indissolubility of classical Greek notions of origin, significance and materiality. In order to probe the notion of materiality further, she analyses Aristotelian ideas about the body and soul and their significance for Foucault (Butler 1993: 33). Aristotle believed that the question of whether the body and soul were one could be dismissed as meaningless, since he understood the soul as the organising foundation of the body, which invested the body with meaning, therefore making meaning inextricable from materiality (ibid.). In Foucault's work Butler notices an implicit reworking of Aristotelian ideas, whereby the soul 'is an historically specific imaginary ideal according to which the body is effectively materialized' (ibid.). In order to examine what these ideas exclude, she refers to Luce Irigaray's engagement with the Platonic distinction between form and matter, where she argues that Plato's binary oppositions are part of a 'phallogocentric economy that produces "feminine" as its constitutive outside' (ibid.). Butler's historio-philosophical account of the materiality of the body points to the impossibility of thinking about materiality and meaning as separate entities, and the role of discourse in disguising that impossibility.

The power of discourse relies on the fact that, although every human being experiences the materiality of their body, the only way in which one can make this experience intelligible to others is through language. Butler is careful to underline that this does not mean that language takes priority over the bodily experience and constructs it *a priori*. To the contrary, identity emerges through an exclusionary matrix from the nexus of bodily experience and cognition, as the latter orders and categorises that experience through language. Bodily morphology becomes intelligible through a series of categories, which, according to Butler, constitute the subject through processes of performative reiteration (Butler 1993: 10). How does this process of construction happen? What is included and what is excluded from the image of ourselves and others, and on what basis?

Butler's argument is that the exclusionary matrix, through which the subject emerges, is symptomatic of the influence of the discursive regime at its most insidious and effective. The intelligible material body emerges through language, which is to say that there can be no reference to the body, without it simultaneously being a further piece of information about that body (Butler 1993: 10). By creating the domain of the subject through a necessarily exclusionary and violent act (Butler 1993: 34), discourse also creates the domain of the abject. It designates valuable and socially acceptable identifications while, at the same time, creating those that remain ostracised and taboo in order to circumscribe the domain of the subject, and serve as its dialectical outside. The categories of subject and abject are thus mutually dependent; the abject remains indispensable as the boundary of the subject, being a constitutive *sine qua non* of the subject's existence as its 'founding repudiation' (Butler 1993: 3). This designation of abject domain that creates a field of intelligibility is the effect of power. It creates a taken-for-granted ontology, which is then referred to as material positives that can only be accessed through discourse which made them intelligible in the first place. Consequently, such discourse obscures the genealogy of power relations that constituted it.

But why does the discourse of power obscure its own genealogy, making its founding disavowal opaque? If what is rejected does not belong within the subject domain, why does it need a powerful agent to stop it from encroaching on the subject's integrity and keep it as the subject's constitutive outside? These questions expose the linguistic potential for change within any discursive construction. Hence emerges the need to guard against these changes in order to defend subject domains and protect a certain way of understanding them, as well as the power relationships that underpin them. For what the abject threatens is very serious indeed. Julia Kristeva's ideas on the abject informed Butler's view of it as a 'founding repudiation'; Kristeva argues that the process of abjection is the way in which we discriminate and reject what is other to ourselves in the course of creating the 'I'. Importantly, after disavowal, the abject remains as a menacing presence on the periphery, always threatening to violate the borders of the subject and pulverise it (Kristeva 1982: 2). Yet, the abject is also alluring through its difference, seductive and repellent at the same time. It helps to maintain the subject's boundaries and simultaneously threatens them. Despite its sickening appeal, its constant warning of the dissolution of the subject keeps it firmly on the periphery, thus providing structure to the subject's proper self (ibid.). Abjection, however, is not synonymous with negative repudiation; it is also a creative phenomenon, which produces objects of hate (Kristeva 1982: 6). Bearing in mind the appeal of the abject and the tenuous nature of the 'I', the subject domain needs constant protection in order to remain within its boundaries.

Faced with the threat of the abject, a threat all too familiar and uncanny from within, the 'I' continuously has to maintain its domain in order to reinforce the desirable identifications and spurn others. In the words of Butler, this process is achieved through a set of limits and norms that function as an aspect of power through reiterative performativity (1993: 95). These normative aspects of performativity are understood as creative constraints, since they are indispensable in compelling appropriate identifications, but do not determine them fully in advance. They help the subject emerge through a complex staging of identification processes, which can never be fully completed and which, crucially, allow for the structuring sedimentation of alterity in the construction of the 'I' (Butler 1993: 105). Power within these processes of identification is embodied through the reiterative repetition of norms, which reinstate the symbolic law. 'The priority and the authority of the symbolic is, however, constituted *through* that recursive turn, such that citation [...] effectively brings into being the very prior authority to which it then defers' (Butler 1993: 109; original emphasis).

The reiterative performativity of identification processes always carries a potential for subversion, even if it has to be constrained by the relations of power, which enable its existence. Although one does not stand at an 'instrumental distance' from material constraints or the way in which they symbolically function within processes of normative reiteration, it is still possible to figure them differently, even if the agency which enables that challenge originally stems from the discourse it seeks to oppose (Butler 1993: 123). As such, power creates what Spivak refers to as an 'enabling violation' (ibid.) and allows for certain elements of the abject to enter into the domain of the subject, challenging, changing and moving its boundaries without annihilating it completely.

How does this explanation of the power of discourse inform my analysis of photographs of the marginal body? First of all, it allows for a broader understanding of John Berger's assertion that the relationship between what we know and what we see is never settled (Berger 1972: 7). More specifically, it explains that there is no neutral visual field where images can be viewed, for there are no objective eyes — everyone is implicated in the epistemological field, as their very subjectivity is partly determined by it. Knowledge and discourse, therefore, influence seeing as a socially and culturally constitutive act, one which is visually complicit in determining the domain of the subject and the abject. Just as discourse encompasses within itself the potential for transgression, the visual field is also open to phenomena and images that may unsettle current regimes of visibility. However, similarly, this unsettling will draw its agency from the constructed field of vision which it seeks to challenge. Secondly, it helps to approach the compelling nature of images of subalternity. Through showing the domain of the abject, it shifts the subject by confronting it with its constitutive reliance on the abject, therefore creating potential for a different site of identification.

The importance of the concept of embodiment in relation to analysing Goded's photography is not limited to its subject matter, but extends to her practice as a documentary photographer. Goded is very much aware of her role and her power within the processes of representation as the one whose presence and ability to mediate representations alters the situations and behaviours she witnesses (Goded 2013). She asserts that she likes participating in the events that she photographs (Goded in Light 2010: 257), which is, ultimately, a conscious reiteration of the witness paradox. Thus, she constructs herself as part of the process of witnessing and participating, and discursively links the materiality of her own body to that of her subjects, thereby attempting identification and unsettling the boundary between subject and abject domains. In order to gain access to the bodies of her subjects, Goded interferes in their private spheres. She photographs them at home, in places of worship, at work, in happiness and in mourning, entering into an intimate relationship within which she can always wield more power than they can. The choice of her photographic subjects proves that she consciously seeks out abject bodies. Her declarations about personal motives for such choices give weight to Butler's argument about the structural indispensability of alterity in the creation of 'I'. Goded's interest in her own body impels her to represent the abjected bodies, therefore indicating the link between alterity and abject, which both serve as the constituting repudiations of the self.

The Body and Race

Following on from Judith Butler's rejection of the pre-discursive body stems a need to re-examine the concepts and identifications that circumscribe bodily existence by referring to its presupposed material characteristics, such as the concept of race. Recent race theory has re-examined the term not as a referent to an extra-discursive materiality, but as a constitutive concept that plays a crucial role in the process of 'racialization' (Butler 1993: 229). Indeed, the notion itself is what enables both racism and any resistance against it. Before laying out the main theoretical underpinnings for analysing the notion of race in photographic representation, it is worthwhile to consider one of Goded's photographs from *Tierra Negra*, where she and her subject visually probe this notion.

One of the most poignant photographs included in *Tierra Negra* is that of a little girl holding a white mask in front of her face (Figure 4.1). She stands barefoot at an entrance to a large, bare room. The concrete from which the floor is made

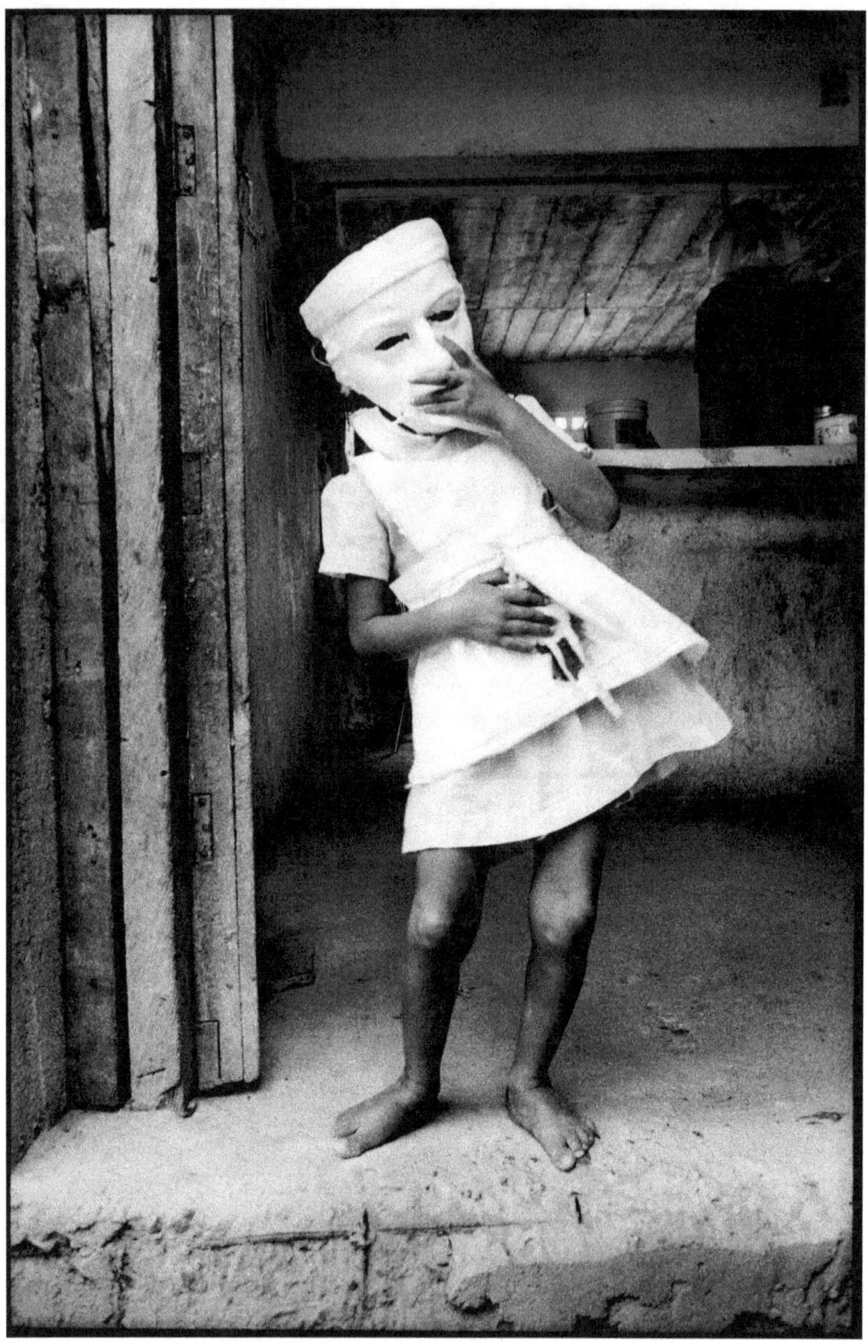

Fig. 4.1. M. Goded, *Tierra Negra* (1994).

has crumbled at her feet revealing the steel reinforcements. Her face is completely obscured by a white mask she is holding up with her left hand, making the colour of her skin and her small frame the only recognisable features. The mask she is holding has features typical of white adult men, creating an odd contrast with her childlike body clothed in a dress with a pinafore. Her hidden face is an allusion to the invisibility of black Mexicans within the social and cultural landscape of their own country. It suggests that her individuality does not matter, as her identity is already determined and marginalised because of her race, gender and economic status. Furthermore, holding the mask in a way that covers its lips not only highlights her lack of agency to reiterate her own identity on her terms, but also visually exposes the limits of discourse, which pushed her into a marginal position. Indeed, as the constitutive outside of the socially acceptable norms, she cannot say anything that would not compound her own abject status. She looks small and fragile, despite being shot at her own eye level. However, the girl is still the main subject of the photograph, albeit partly obscured and disguised. What if, behind the mask, there is a face of defiance?

As Butler claims, to be implicated and circumscribed by the discourse of power is not the same as being determined by it. After all, donning a mask is a carnival tradition, which has for centuries helped to invert and question power hierarchies. The etymology of the word carnival, from Latin *carne* for 'flesh' and *levare* for 'to remove' or 'to release', in itself hides a promise of questioning and rearticulating the meanings entrenched within the materiality of the body. Moreover, the physical positioning of the girl holding a white face is a clever comment on how subaltern identities sustain the subject domain — quite literally, she is inside the mask. Her body is tilted to the left and she is holding her stomach, as if she was in a fit of laughter. She is visually mocking the very idea of race and one can imagine her chuckle resonating against the white mask. In a carnivalesque reversal of roles (Bakhtin 1984a, 1984b), the girl is no longer an objectified victim, but an active agent capable of questioning racist power hierarchies. The grotesque image of a small dark body holding up a large white face is not just a picture of abjection. By playing with an established norm and mocking its reversal, this representation of a small child becomes a visual tool capable of interrogating hegemonic views that sanction its subalternity. In terms of a marker of difference such as race, which hinges on the visual, this carnivalesque play becomes all the more important in analysing how difference is understood and embodied.

This photograph of a girl holding a mask helps to delve immediately into recent race theory. David Goldberg and John Solomos argue in the 'Introduction' to *A Companion to Racial and Ethnic Studies* (2002) that race is a medium through which difference is represented and that is socially made and politically motivated (Goldberg 2002: 3–4). As such, race is not understood as a natural category corresponding to an extra-discursive, bodily reality, but rather a discursive construct circumscribed by socio-historical realities and vested with political, social and cultural interests (ibid.). Nonetheless, that is not to deny that it produces material effects and at the level of everyday experience remains a potent social category around and against which groups organise their identity and their politics (ibid.). Within the colonial context Frantz Fanon explained his view of the way in which race shapes one's place in the world in his seminal work, *The Wretched of the Earth* (2001). Although his reflections are rooted in the environment of colonial French Martinique, his theory of race as an effect of colonisation, which produces and sustains difference, is indispensable to understanding the process of racialisation in colonial and post-colonial settings.

His earlier work *Black Skin, White Masks* and *The Wretched of the Earth* are Fanon's attempts to formulate a political response against racist social structures and put the racially discriminated subject in a position where he can contest (or ignore) prejudiced epistemes (Fanon 1986: 100). Therein, Fanon strives to offer a way out of the 'turn white or disappear' dilemma (ibid.). He describes the process of being subjugated by the colonizers, which has a crucial racial dimension, since the site of racial difference is also a site of power (Goldberg and Solomos 2002: 5). This discursively produced difference is then, according to Fanon, internalised and reimagined as a twofold inferiority complex of the black man; he is economically dependent on the white man and that inferiority is internalised or, as Fanon would have it, 'epidermalized' (1986: 13) As such, the black man comes to experience himself as alien and other (Goldberg and Solomos 2002: 5) according to the discourse which denigrates him. Importantly, Goldberg and Solomos underline the limits of such identity politics. Fanon's ideas, however, understood as a significant development in race theory rather than a definite prescription for the correct identity politics, still forge a different way of representing and reimagining the black subject. How does this epistemologically constructed racial dimension function within the visual field where Goded's photographs appear?

The issues of racial identity in Mexico are inextricably linked to the concept of national identity, impossible as it is to fully define. The Mexican population is ethnically described as mostly comprising the descendants of Spaniards and Indians, creating a *mestizo* identity that is seen as quintessentially Mexican. Despite it being something of a contradiction in terms, *mestizaje* remains at the core of the way in which Mexicans imagine their nation, exemplifying Goldberg and Solomos's assertion that racial identities are sites of political struggles, whose valence, meaning, and referents are defined by socio-historical circumstances (2002: 3). The influential Mexican philosopher Leopoldo Zea saw the *mestizo* as 'a fruit of the union between the conqueror and the conquered' and through which the 'hateful racial discrimination disappears' (Zea in Oliver 2011: 254). Certainly, the concept of *mestizaje* is an attempt to resolve problems stemming from the colonial discourse of racial difference, which relied on the subject–abject opposition between the colonisers and the native population. By inviting the previously disavowed identity into a syncretic concept of race, an imaginary union is created, which establishes its own subject domain by renouncing other possible identifications and entrenching the *mestizo*. To this day, Mexican authorities financially support villages with indigenous inhabitants and provide them with cultural recognition through the Instituto Nacional Indigenista, which also commissions photographic projects to document their way of life, producing a layering of political, visual and discursive dimensions. Nonetheless, it is important to note that *mestizaje* as a socio-cultural and political project aims to incorporate the heterogeneity of the indigenous population into an idea of a homogeneous national identity.

The cohesiveness of that fixed identity relies on excluding any other racial groups from the mix of *mestizaje* and, therefore, ignoring Mexico's black population. Such figuring of the imaginary Mexican self forecloses any possibilities for positive identifications for those who are seen as black. As B. Christine Arce argues, the history of black people in Mexico is that of erasure, silence and invisibility, despite their consistent presence, both physical and cultural, since the conquest (Arce 2018: Location 195). The Mexican concept of national identity not only does not recognise racial identities outside the Spanish/Indian paradigm, but specifically sanctions against such recognitions. The effects of this powerful discourse are clear in the resistance to identify with black racial identity by the inhabitants of the Costa Chica. Although outsiders characterise many of its residents as black (*negro*), ethnographic evidence suggests that the villagers identify themselves as *moreno* as a way of underlining their ethnic link to the indigenous heritage of their Indian ancestors, making a bodily claim to *mexicanidad* (Lewis 2000: 898). The recent scholarly and national projects, such as the Third Root movement, which endeavour to reclaim Afromexican identity for a wider, multicultural understanding of Mexican identity, have been met with resistance. They are seen 'as an outside imposition that conflicts with [the villagers'] sense of themselves as Mexican while [reinforcing] their political and economic marginality' (ibid.).

Given this context, it is perhaps unsurprising that Maya Goded's initial suggestion of doing a project on the Mexican black population was met with lack of interest at the Instituto Nacional Indigenista in the early 1990s. Eventually, she secured the necessary funding through the Instituto and became the first photographer to document the life of Afromexicans on the Costa Chica. Aside from an introduction, which reclaims black identity as part of Mexican identity in bodily terms, the book is devoid of any commentary or explanation with regard to the photography. Goded confesses to writing about her experiences, but she also claims that to include these narratives in the album would be wrong (Goded in Light 2010: 255). Indeed, how does one verbally account for nearly four centuries of oppression, erasure and invisibility?

Despite the aforementioned idealisation of the concept of *mestizaje* and the symbolic power of the indigenous population within this paradigm, they are economically and socially disadvantaged in Mexico as well as in the rest of Latin America, with 80 per cent living below the poverty line (Piñeiro Iñíguez in Oliver 2011: 260). Nonetheless, their photographic presence is pervasive in the work of both foreign and Mexican photographers such as Manuel Álvarez Bravo or Graciela Iturbide. On the one hand, this visual presence underlines their symbolic power and, on the other hand, it also demarcates them as other, figuratively pointing to the racial paradox at the core of bodily essentialism of *mestizaje*. Historically, since the second half of the nineteenth century when photographic technology became

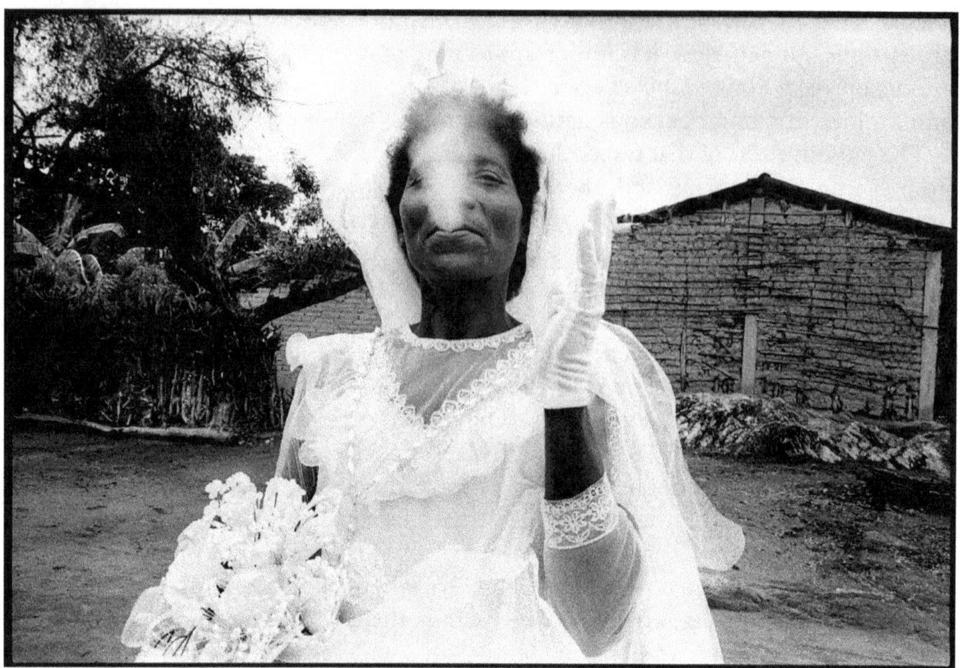

Fig. 4.2. M. Goded, *Tierra Negra* (1994).

available in Mexico, the authorities would commission projects of photographing indigenous people, conducted in order to keep records of those considered a risk to the state, including prisoners and prostitutes (Debroise 2001: 46). The racialised body was visually marked as a threat and catalogued through photographs, stigmatised and subjugated through this representation, which was vested with the power of the authorities. Moreover, photography's use in anthropology links it to academic discourses of truth and power, and reinforces the link between discourse and visual representations. Mexican photography's preoccupation with the indigenous corresponds to discursive concerns relating to otherness in the concepts of *mestizaje* and *mexicanidad*. Within Goded's body of work, however, concerns with race converge on Mexico's hitherto invisible and unacknowledged black community. That focus reflects the prevailing and often unchallenged assumption in Latin America 'that the study of blacks is one of racism and race relations, while the study of Indians is that of ethnicity and ethnic groups' (Wade in Warren and Twine 2002: 550), pointing to the discursive climate influencing Goded's photographic output. The name of the album *Tierra Negra* metaphorically links the subjects' skin colour to the land they inhabit, situating and rooting them within the geographical landscape of the country, which often denies their very existence (Warren and Twine 2002: 550–51).

One of the photographs from *Tierra Negra*, which exposes the potential for identities to be figured differently, is that of a bride smoking in her wedding dress (Figure 4.2), whom Goded described as 'the feminist of that village' (Goded in

Light 2010: 256). Getting married may seem an incongruous way to demonstrate feminist sentiments, yet the photograph is rich with potentially subversive visual content. The white wedding dress and veil signify purity and virginity in Catholic tradition, but the bride is clearly an older woman. In an environment where only young virgins can find husbands in their village (Goded in Light 2010: 257), her marriage defies convention. The contrast between her dark skin and the dress emphasises the theatricality of wedding attire in general, but also the subject's nonchalance in wearing the outfit with lop-sided jewellery, rumpled veil and awkward-length sleeves. She is enjoying a cigarette outside, which is also a defiant gesture, as women smoking in public are frowned upon. She appears relaxed and happy in her demeanour. Certainly, the photograph captures the moment when she reiterates the discursive norms by taking part in a patriarchal ceremony and reformulating them in ways which suit her. As all the props suggest, her agency and the attention she is receiving stem from the citational power of the traditional ritual in which she is participating. Nonetheless, the image subtly challenges its symbolic meaning with her confident and insolent demeanour, questioning the repudiation of older women from the socio-cultural image of brides by her very presence. Such questioning offers a mode of resistance to being defined by age and virginity, which is all the more significant because it is staged in a conservative environment of a small village. The composition of the photograph is also a departure from traditional bridal photography. First of all, the groom is nowhere to be seen and therefore conspicuous by his absence. Secondly, the low angle of the camera makes the bride appear taller and dominant within the composition. The latter characteristic may be worthwhile considered in the light of ethnographic research, which suggest that black women on the Costa Chica are seen as stronger and more dominant than white or indigenous ones, to an extent that it would impede them from having a relationship with a man who was from a different ethnic background (Lewis 2000: 905). Such ideas stem from a wider racist context where black bodies, according to Frantz Fanon, are bearers of danger and remain circumscribed as potentially violent (Fanon in Butler 2004: 208).

How does one visually challenge the racist episteme which categorises and stereotypes black bodies as agents of danger? This question is especially pertinent as perceiving racial or sexual difference is always fraught with misrecognitions and subject to pre-existing stereotypes (Mitchell 2005: 297). If pictures do indeed 'take on a life of their own [...] in the rituals of the racist encounter' (ibid.), then they can also interrogate such rituals, serving as a remainder of the unstable nature of identifications whose dynamic processes are never completed. Maya Goded's photograph of two men embracing each other (Figure 4.3) defies stereotypical portrayals of black men. The image captures two young men sharing a moment of easy intimacy. Leaning against the wall they are pictured wearing only their underwear or swimming garments. The taller person is facing the camera and holding his friend's waist. The other man is mirroring his position, with his right hand tucked behind the taller man's back above his hip. In the foreground of the image, their bare toes are touching. Their embrace is open but joined on one side,

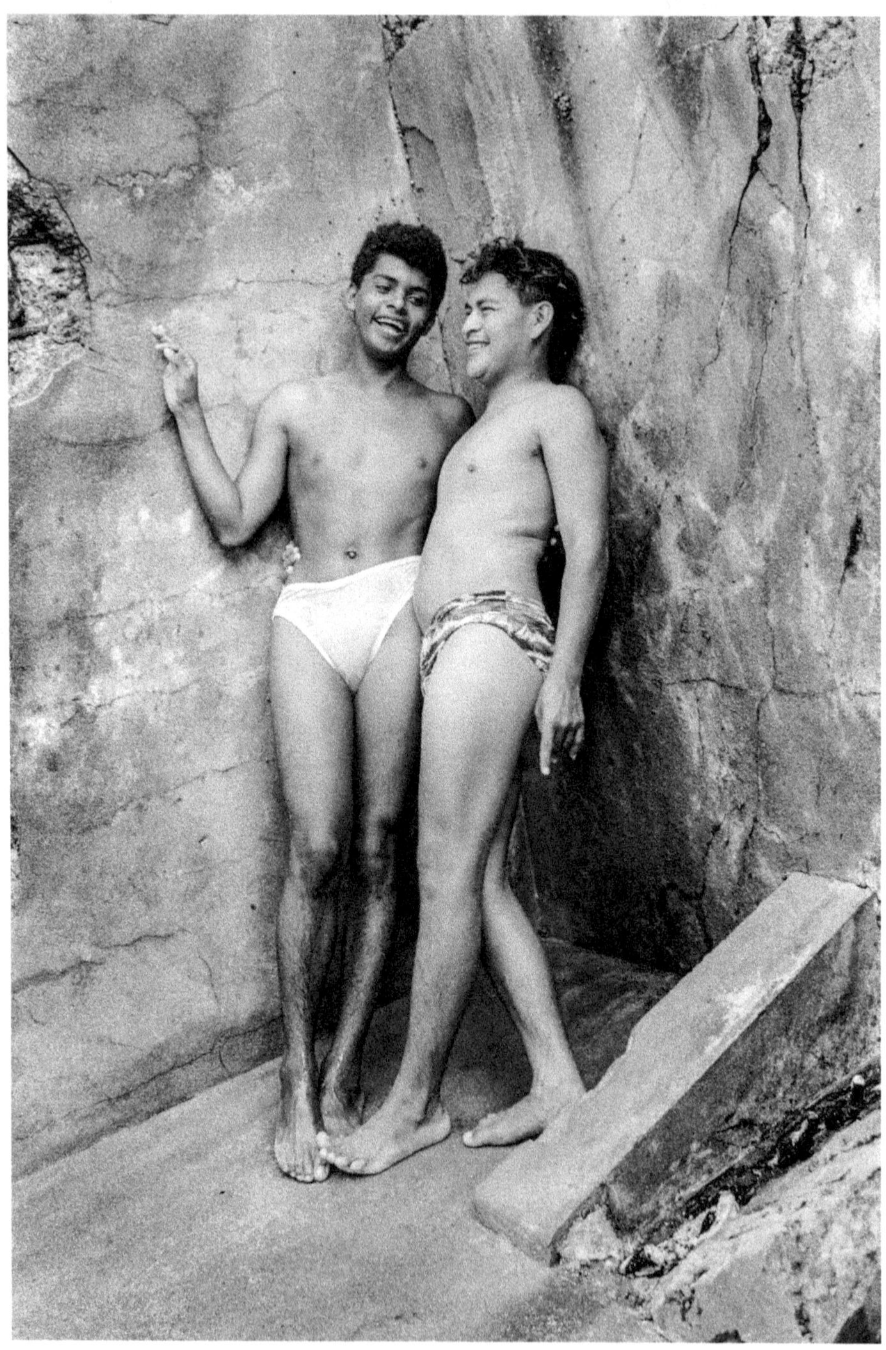

Fig. 4.3. M. Goded, *Tierra Negra* (1994).

allowing the camera to capture their relaxed, smiling expressions. The composition of the image and its subtle grayscale with low contrast emphasise the men's youth and comfortable manner instead of their skin colour or features.

The image invites the interrogation of the stereotype of a black male as aggressive and dangerous, which is an entrenched part of a wider racist episteme and a residual reminder of colonial pillage and slavery. The black body, constructed as dangerous prior to any gesture, justified violent oppression and exploitation (Fanon in Butler 1993: 229). The constitutive power of this prejudice can be appreciated through ethnographic research about the Costa Chica (Lewis 2000), which is often described as one of the most dangerous areas of the country, and studies on the local communities, which suggest links between the African origin of their inhabitants and their violent customs (Lewis 2000: 919). In this particular context, the archetypal aggressive male is the *cimarrón* — a runaway slave, whose figure and mentality is claimed to have profoundly marked Afromexican identity (Beltrán and Avila in Lewis 2000: 919). Yet research suggests that predominantly black regions have no higher incidence of violence than Indian regions (Avila in Lewis 2000: 919), giving evidence that aggressive behaviour amongst subaltern ethnic communities is used discursively as a normative paradigm to associate their race with social danger. Through Goded's lens, the two men appear touchingly vulnerable. This portrayal provokes a reflection upon the convergence of expectations, which stem from pre-existing and constitutive ideas about race.

The photographer's visual intervention has emerged within the context of the Third Root initiatives in Mexico that seek to acknowledge the cultural, social and economic contributions of the marginalised black communities (Lewis 2000: 913). Inspired by the idea of multiculturalism, it is a movement that seeks to foster Mexican cultural variety, while at the same time protecting and strengthening national unity (Lewis 2000: 913).

> If, however, common roots [...] suggest a common kinship and assumed social affinity, in embracing blackness whites are nevertheless using it to construct a national identity that is rooted in a romanticized and primitivized cultural history located in a pre-European past of which only showy vestiges remain (Stutzman 1981: 64–65; Wade 1997: ch. 3). It thus excludes contemporary *morenos* much as contemporary Indians have always been excluded from the nation even as their past is extolled and preserved for elite consumption. In the end, not only are blacks and Indians both exploited, both are folklorized as well. (Lewis 2000: 913)

The folklorisation of local customs, which are seen as exotic remainders of African roots, shifts the focus away from the needs of contemporary communities. Some traditions, such as *sones de artesa* music and dances are these days only performed for the benefit of outsiders, while the locals favour the popular Latin American *cumbia* instead (ibid.). Such artificial preservation of arbitrary cultural behaviour stems from ideas and stereotypes about a subaltern group, which, having been shunned for centuries, is now being celebrated in a prescribed manner by the same discourse of power which once placed it firmly in the domain of the abject. In fact, the Costa Chica inhabitants resist being described in terms of how others see their bodies and their perceived racial heritage (Lewis 2000: 917). They understand that their blackness has been discursively constituted as the structural outside of Mexican national identity, therefore effectively denying them any power, be it material or symbolic. This understanding of one's own abjection provides an opening in the dynamic processes of identifications, which allows for a challenge to be articulated and therefore become visible.

One of the most poignant measures of the abjection of the black community on the Costa Chica is the fact that their way of life is not understood very well. A good example of this limited understanding are the myths surrounding their customs, such as that of the *rapto*, which is the traditional kidnapping of a young unmarried woman, who is then either wedded to her kidnapper or forced to leave the village, depending on whether or not she is a virgin. Some ethnographers (Lewis 2000: 913) argue that such traditions have long disappeared and are perpetuated for their sensationalist appeal, while others (Goded in Light 2010: 258) claim that they are still practised. The powerful myths of identity and racial stereotypes do little to further the understanding of the community, which has been denied the right to self-determination and representation. Goded's photographs, quite apart from their documentary value, do exoticise and folklorise the villagers' everyday life by using techniques similar to those employed by Graciela Iturbide in her photographs of indigenous Mexican women in albums such as *Juchitán de las mujeres* (1989).

The resistance of the villagers against being defined by the Third Root movement is evidence of their agency in the processes of identification. The discourse that wants to incorporate its preconceived idea of black identity into the concept of national identity fails to account for that agency, by posing these concepts from a pre-established position of national unity. Yet, as Butler explains, identity does not belong to the world of events and can never be understood to have taken place (Butler 1993: 105). It is a dynamic process, which belongs to the imaginary realm where it is figured as a desired effect or accomplishment, which can never be completed. Subject to the volatile logic of iterability and performativity, identities escape definitions and are constantly reconfigured anew (ibid.), although they do draw on the discursive agency, whose subject domain constrains them without determining them fully in advance. As much as Goded has provided a series of photographs of a community previously absent from the socio-cultural landscape before, their sudden mediated presence does not fit neatly into the preconceived ideas about their place within the racial and cultural landscape. This swift cultural rediscovery of the long-abjected black community and the challenges in reincorporating it back into the subject domain exemplify the constant movement taking place between these two domains, mutually dependent but also continuously threatened by one another.

Tierra Negra as a cultural text reveals the power of photographic representation to make new meanings within existing hierarchies of knowledge and power. The album itself gives an impression of portraying an Afro-Mexican community, both in its introduction and in its visual content, yet the community pictured does not self-identify with *afro-mestizaje* (Lewis 2004). Scholarly criticism of the album focuses on the kind of representation Goded provides for the local communities; Mariana Ortega problematises Goded's work by claiming that Goded's representations are exoticised, and incongruous with the villagers' lifestyle (Ortega 2013: 171). Laura Lewis documents some reactions of the villagers to their own representations in *Tierra Negra*, such as misrecognition where the photographic images are seen as blacker or uglier than they are, or as photographs of people from elsewhere (Lewis 2004: 481–83). Ortega's criticism of the indexical nature of Goded's photography of blackness in Mexico, coupled with her claims that Goded's representations primitivise and exoticise her subjects, is a contradiction in terms, which points to the implicit expectations of representing shunned ethic communities. If the album appears to be probing a racist framework, then it is because the concept of race enables both racism and any resistance against it and it is a *sine qua non* of thinking about embodiment. Seeing Lewis's ethnographic research in this light also allows the framing of representations in *Tierra Negra* not as 'optical violence' (Lewis 2004: 491) but as an opportunity for Goded's subjects to contest their representation in racial terms. Their resistance to being labelled, seen or represented as black can be framed as an act of defiance against a racist framework, enabled by the photographs. This is a powerful opportunity, particularly in a country where racism is rarely acknowledged as a phenomenon (Moreno Figueroa 2010: 388). Nonetheless, it is important to note that the very need to contest one's own representational blackness stems from having to negotiate racist hegemonic symbolic structures from a subaltern position.

Photography intervenes here with a visual semiotic system, which has the power to represent the abjected and expand the horizon of vision to include the hitherto invisible. Nonetheless, its power is implicated within discourse and within its own semiotic system, since it is a tool which helps to represent difference, in the case of *Tierra Negra* based on race, which produces otherness (Goldberg and Solomos 2002: 3). The semiotic scope of the concept of race reaches beyond its apparent, designated bodily signifiers, and extends to a plethora of socio-historical and cultural consequences, which, in turn, link race to notions of class and power, helping to build an exclusive hierarchy that relies on the subjugation of the other. Nonetheless, despite photography's implication in making these divisions apparent, it also has the power to transcend them visually, for it is not fully determined by the discourses which govern and sustain it. Therefore it has the ability to mediate visually between the domain of the subject and the abject, repeatedly reframing questions of alterity and probing distinctions between the ways in which different bodies are valued according to their position within the hierarchies of power. Here the concept and representation of race are manifestations of alterity, which sanction the marginalisation of the ethnic minority on the Costa Chica, whose difference is figured as a visual, social and cultural signifier justifying their abjection.

The Commoditised Body

The medium of race is only one of the ways in which difference is discursively and visually produced, resulting in constructed hierarchies that value people differently according to their position within them. Another way of mediating differences, which produces valorising material effects, is through the focus on people's roles within communities, especially in terms of their employment. The economic and social pressure to participate in the labour market, be it formal or informal, and the role assumed within it determine one's position and agency within one's community. Karl Marx in *The Economic and Philosophic Manuscripts* (1964) explains how labour produces alienation for the labourer, understood as alienation from the self, from other workers, and from the product of their labour (Marx 1964: 17). These multiple alienations, in turn, commoditise both the fruit of the worker's labour and the workers themselves (Marx 1964: 106), where their only value is linked to their work. This commoditisation of workers is relevant because of the impossibility of separating their bodies from their employment, which becomes especially salient in the context of prostitution. Although Marx argues that prostitution is just a specific expression of the more general alienation of the labourer (Marx in Pateman 1988: 201), the inherent disposability of the body of the prostitute stemming from its commoditisation is compounded by the accompanying stigma and marginalisation.

This systemic and endemic disregard for the body of the prostitute demands analysis in relation to Maya Goded's photographs of prostitutes in Mexico City published in the album entitled *Plaza de la soledad.* As much as the word *prostitute* is often replaced with *sex worker* in current research in order to circumvent the stigma associated with the former, here it is used in order to underline the discursive stigma of sex work as an important reason behind the inherent disposability of prostitutes, regardless of their linguistic signifier. Debates surrounding nomenclature range from framing the use of *sex work* instead of *prostitution* as an empowering eschewing of stigma associated with prostitution, to deeming it a neoliberal gesture that misrepresents its precarious realities. Here, the two terms are used interchangeably in order to draw attention simultaneously to the stigma of selling sex and to its repetitive and utilitarian aspects not dissimilar from other forms of employment.

Maya Goded's starting point for the album was the experience of her own pregnancy that led to a desire to understand the female body, and the way in which it circumscribes one's life and destiny (Goded 2006: 11), especially in an environment, such as Mexico, where the imaginary ideal is the unattainable virgin mother. Photographing the bodies of prostitutes was for Goded a catalyser, which allowed her to learn about herself (ibid.), once again underlining the importance of others for one's self-image and sense of identity. The focus on her visceral desire to learn about bodies and the way in which they physically and culturally determine the life of women she encounters is paramount. It echoes Judith Butler's assertion that separation between materiality and meaning is impossible, and that all subjects emerge from the nexus of bodily experience and reiterative identifications, which enable human existence within the symbolic order. The way Goded frames the bodily experiences of her subjects shows as much about her attitude and motivation for her work, as it does about the circumstances of the women photographed.

Goded's documentary representations of prostitution are a visual engagement with a crucial cultural trope within Mexican culture, namely that of a fallen woman. Debra Castillo (1998: 4) argues that the figure of a loose woman is an object of national obsession in Mexico. Referencing Octavio Paz's *Malinche*, Cortés's lover and interpreter and the archetypical '*madre chingada*' [violated mother] (Paz 2008: 25), Castillo examines the tension between female personhood and sexuality in Mexico, arguing that the term 'woman' is defined not just in opposition to 'man', but 'also in contradistinction to this other-gendered being, the sexually transgressive female' (Castillo 1998: 7). Castillo's analysis of Gamboa's novel, *Santa* (1903), provides a crucial link between how this narrative trope came to have a visual presence (Castillo 1998: 37). Based on the book, *Santa* (1931) the film was the first Mexican feature with direct sound. It was also the first brothel melodrama, an important national form, which later spurred the *cabaretera* (cabaret/brothel melodrama) (Tierney 2007: 22) and *fichera* (Mora 2006: Location 281) subgenres, all of them concerned with portraying fallen women or their places of work. In *Cinemachismo: Masculinities and Sexuality in Mexican Film* (2006), Sergio de la Mora devotes several chapters to charting representations of prostitution in literature and cinema throughout the twentieth century, examining them as repositories of the nation's anxieties about its myth of origin and changing gender roles over the decades. The marginalisation of the country's prostitutes past and present underpins this lasting fascination, which is critical for understanding Mexican cultural production. Goded's documentary engagement with the topic shines a spotlight on an environment steeped in patriarchal mythology, moralistic Catholic teachings, and woefully under-researched (Castillo 1998: 8), although recent studies, such as Patty Kelly's *Lydia's Open Door: Inside Mexico's Most Modern Brothel* (2008) and Marta Lamas's *El fulgor de la noche: El comercio sexual en las calles de la Ciudad de México* (2017) have begun addressing that scarcity.

In addition to the country's obsession with fallen women, the popular reverence of *Virgen de Guadalupe* as a symbol of national unity also influences attitudes to women. Octavio Paz points out that her unifying potential is twofold — firstly, she is an Indian virgin, secondly, she appears at the site of a destroyed temple dedicated to the Tonantzin, the Aztec goddess of fertility (Paz 2008: 24), the racialised image of her body a visual reminder of the colonial fusion. Seen as the refuge for the unfortunate and dispossessed, she is the imaginary maternal womb (ibid.) in a symbolic embodiment of feminine perfection. Therefore, her image becomes a source of feminine empowerment and superiority, albeit within clearly demarcated areas, and an archetype of an idealised female body. The issue of positive bodily identification with the virginal mother is problematic in itself, since it creates an imaginary ideal that remains entirely inaccessible through the lived, bodily experience, therefore constituting a constant lack and inadequacy within the subject domain. Nonetheless, Jeanette Rodríguez (1994: Location 676) argues that Guadalupe provides a crucial identity template, particularly for women who are marginalised and poor. As for the borders of this imaginary ideal, the figure of the violated mother, *la Chingada* or *Doña Malinche*, Cortés's interpreter and betrayed lover, is its model antithesis (Paz 2008: 25), disavowed for her sexual vulnerability and yet threatening to unravel the discursive fabric of the subject. According to Paz,

> Her taint is constitutional and resides [...] in her sex. This passivity, open to the outside world, causes her to lose her identity: [...] she disappears into nothingness, she is Nothingness. And yet she is the cruel incarnation of the feminine condition. (Paz 2008: 25)

La Chingada is the Mexican maternal guise of the pervasive Madonna–whore duality, where the domains of being and of non-being are demarcated through symbolic embodiments that hinge on the question of sexual vulnerability. In that context, a prostitute who allows her photograph to be taken is explicitly expressing a desire to be seen, a desire to visually represent her own embodied experience within a framework that explicitly denies it. Goded's work, therefore, challenges the constitutive dichotomies outlined above, that of masculinity and femininity, Madonna and whore, *Virgen de Guadalupe* and *La Malinche.* Goded's *Plaza de la soledad* visually probes anxieties surrounding the female body and its legitimate presence within the subject domain, representing the bodies of the prostitutes and thus visually exposing the consequences of their socio-historical, economic, cultural and discursive marginalisation.

Mexico has a long tradition of artistically reinterpreting female embodiment, both in relation to national identity and to wider frameworks of artistic conventions. One such example is the fact that *Virgen de Guadalupe* representing a gendered national sentiment encounters its nemesis in Frida Kahlo's self-portraits, which 'defamiliarize and distort the meaning of the maternal body, the European nude, the Catholic icon, the viewer's gaze' (Franco 1989; Chedzgoy in Redclift 2003: 496). Nonetheless, here the female body also appears as a space for expressing the national and the suffering within the national. In such a context, the prostitute becomes a symbolic repository for the country's anxieties and an embodied presence through which national and personal dramas are played out. This interest in romanticised visual notions of sex work is more indicative of patriarchal symbolic structures and their bearing on possible female identifications defined by the binary Madonna–whore duality, than of the material, embodied realities of prostitution on the streets of Mexico. Goded's documentary photography can, therefore, be framed as an attempt to de-romanticise and destabilise the image of a sex worker in Mexico by contrasting viewers' expectations with a different point of view. That is not necessarily to deny Goded's photographs the power to idealise their subject, but rather to underline that they visually contest expected romanticised visions of sex work, prevalent in Mexican cinema and popular culture.

Long before the development of the cinematic interest in prostitutes, or even of cinema itself, towards the end of the nineteenth century the Porfirian state apparatus forged a close relationship with prostitution through photography. It was then that the state's avant-garde project of photographing criminals for identification purposes was extended to prostitutes in the name of protecting public health and decency (Debroise 2001: 46). John Tagg in *The Burden of Representation* argues against the perceived neutral nature of the camera, claiming it to be always vested with particular authority (Tagg 1988: 63). Its power of surveillance in particular turns its ability to represent others from a mark of celebration to a burden of subjection (ibid.). The photographs of the nineteenth-century Mexican prostitutes and descriptions accompanying them were the precursors of systematised public health records established during the Porfiriato and the many *Reglamentos para el ejercicio de la prostitución* [Regulations Concerning Prostitution] that survived, in more or less unchanged form, to this day. Here, visual representation is a means of control. However, the photographs also inadvertently encouraged and showcased an erotic performance (Debroise 2001: 46), which, in turn, displays the potential for visual representation to be manipulated and misconstrued, even when personal agency is limited and one is ultimately at the mercy of the state authority. Although the images were conceived as a way of controlling prostitutes, they were able to use their representation as a way of advertising their services, which underlines the potential for ambiguity within the medium.

The state's efforts to control prostitution extended beyond the creation of photographic records. The authorities have also sanctioned physical containment of prostitutes in designated areas known as *zonas de tolerancia* where prostitution was approved and where the women were allowed to live and work (Uribe-Zúñiga et al. 1995: 594). By designating these areas specifically for sex commerce, the state has effectively helped to market and commoditise the women's bodies. Despite Carlos Monsiváis's critique of the creation of such areas and his comparison between them and concentration camps (Monsiváis in Mora 2006: 35), the reasoning behind creating such spaces has not changed much over the last hundred years and focuses on the need to control prostitution and protect public health from sexually transmitted diseases (Uribe-Zúñiga et al. 1995: 594). Consequently, apart from the moral and social stigma of being a prostitute, the state adds a spatial dimension to the women's marginalisation by effectively imprisoning them in ghettos. Their stigma is mapped out onto the city and they are the only ones who suffer from it — neither their procurers nor their clients are bound by this constriction of movement. Yet, just as Baudrillard (1994: 12) once wrote that prisons exist precisely to hide the carceral nature of society, *zonas de tolerancia* are a similar exercise in distancing individuals from themselves, creating and perpetuating divisions and concealing the fact that everybody is part of this unfair economy of exchange. The prostitutes, however, bear the brunt of their spatial relegation, as their confinement underlines their status as commodities. The state helps to market their bodies by providing legislation, which detains the women for the convenience of their procurers and clients. Moreover, it is important to acknowledge the futility of trying to protect prostitutes from spreading sexually transmitted diseases through containing their movement within the city if their clients face no such restrictions. Consequently, the explanation for the *zonas de tolerancia* provided by the authorities cannot be accepted at face value and should rather be seen as an attempt to justify controlling and sanctioning socially undesirable behaviours through spatial relegation and marginalisation.

Expelled from the subject domain, prostitutes constitute the saint–whore duality. Their abjection enables the commoditisation of their bodies, and, in turn, the fact that their bodies are on sale compounds their confinement to the domain of non-being, making any claims of bodily integrity impossible to sustain. The work they perform produces a particularly acute case of Marxist alienation (Marx 1982: 17) because of the social stigma attached to it and the impossibility of separating their bodies from the services they perform. Their spatial relegation forces them to live in ghettos and surrender to the control of procurers and the state, thus turning their bodies into commodities which are available for others to look at and buy. The reason why prostitutes are so feared, despite the fact that they appear to have very little social agency and are easily imprisoned and inspected by the authorities, is precisely because of what their bodies signify within traditional gender paradigms. Their abject existence, however marginal, is always a threat not just to women who live according to the more socially rewarded moral codes, but also to men, since femininity is the founding repudiation of the concept of masculinity. This powerful disavowal produced by gender binaries has a creative aspect, as rejection spurs the creation of the object of hate, reinforcing the constitutive borders of the subject domain through fear and remaining a menacing presence on the periphery. In that sense, Goded's photographs are an engagement with social fear and repudiation, since prostitution can be both alluring and terrifying.

Despite the fact that representations of prostitutes abound in Mexican visual culture, they usually function as a border to the model of family life and a constitutive outside of desirable identifications. Prostitution, therefore, shores up Catholic family values and perpetuates the patriarchal value system by framing it as a safety-valve phenomenon, a necessary outlet for masculine desire. Seemingly on the outside of the sanctity of a Mexican Catholic family, prostitution becomes its indispensable border, creating a paradox whereby the rejected phenomenon is necessary for the functioning of the subject domain of traditional family values. Goded's photographic intervention is significant here, since she represents the lived, embodied experience of women, who are normally either vilified or romanticised as victims, showing how their daily lives and struggles defy stereotypes. Furthermore, she also pictures their marginality and its material effects on their lives and bodies. It is precisely the photographic close-up of a shunned community of women that has the power to visually destabilise and challenge perceptions of prostitution, but also of the patriarchal values underpinning traditional family life. The following analysis of Goded's album *Plaza de la soledad* will show how these effects are achieved through a close examination of a selection of photographs, which probe, frame after frame, the mutually exclusive dualities of *La Malinche* and *Virgen de Guadalupe* in their representations of marginal embodiment.

In *Plaza de la soledad*, Maya Goded photographs men, women and children entangled in a web created by prostitution, which is often perceived as a 'victimless crime' (Reanda 1991: 203). Her photographs clearly show its victims, thus opening up an abject domain and challenging perceptions and assumptions about a socio-cultural taboo, which affects millions of lives across the globe every year. In that sense, her work carries an urgent humanitarian message, because it exposes a particular local example of international human trafficking. Laura Reanda (1991: 204) argues that in the contexts where extreme poverty, domestic violence, sexual abuse and trafficking are rife, the boundaries between enforced and voluntary prostitution become very difficult to sustain.

The past few years have brought a new awareness of the problems of child abuse and domestic violence as possible root causes of prostitution. An international expert meeting organized by the United Nations Educational, Scientific, and Cultural Organization (UNESCO) found that the majority of female prostitutes had been victims of incest, violence, or rape, which resulted 'in the destruction of a woman's identity, an essential step in subsequently transforming the human body into a sexual item of merchandise for commercial purposes.' Consequently, the arguments of those who consider any prostitution a slavery-like practice have become more compelling and the focus of greater international attention. (ibid.)

The body in postmodern Mexican art is often configured as a space where cultural, social and economic discourses can be played out. An excellent example of this is Teresa Margolles's work entitled *Lengua* (2000) consisting of a preserved human pierced tongue, which the artist bought from the family of a deceased youth killed in a drug-related street-fight. The artist was able to buy a part of a human body because of the economic situation of the people from whom she acquired it. The body part on its own was displayed as a visual commentary on the issue of drug wars, thus becoming separated not just physically but also semantically from its original owner and function. *Lengua* helps to shed light on the bodies of Goded's subjects, since their work consists of giving up autonomy over their bodies in return for money. Their flesh is no longer just their own, they belong, at least temporarily, to their procurers and clients and become fragmented through commoditisation. Their skin has been cut and burnt, underlining their fragility and vulnerability. Moreover, they are also subject to photographic fragmentation, whereby their bodies are cut and sectioned by Goded's framing in order to fit within a visual narrative. The abject, marginal body lacks agency over itself and is marked and portioned by others. Is this 'an enabling violation' within the visual field or a further marginalisation?

The question of exploitation in *Plaza de la soledad* deserves consideration in order to avoid denying photography the power to destabilise viewers' assumptions. Crucially, when photographing prostitutes, Goded takes the place of the client when she pays the women for their time, asks them to strip and takes photographs of their naked bodies. Just as many cultural critics underline the similarities between the vocabulary used for photography and warfare (Berger 2003, Sontag 2005), there are also similarities between the colloquial lexis of sex and that of photography, especially when one considers the double meaning of words such as 'to shoot' and 'to take'. The scopophilic, sometimes even parasitic, gaze mediated by the camera is not unlike that of a client searching for satisfaction in a *zona de tolerancia*. Goded's subjects through their bodies become a vessel for a story which is not their own. Despite the intimacy of the photographs and the interviews included with the album, it is the photographer and editors who are in charge of the visual narration and who control the content of her album. Consequently, there is an element of exploitation in Goded's photography, which feeds viewers' desire to see the reality of prostitution and makes a voyeuristic spectacle of their misery, compounding and visually sanctioning their abjection.

How can these two contrasting and conflicting arguments be reconciled? More importantly, how can they coexist on a two-dimensional piece of photographic paper? Here photography allows for a reflection on the plasticity of human understanding and ways of conceptualising one's own identity and those of others. Even though the categories of subject and abject are indispensable for human understanding of the world and are a *sine qua non* of thinking (Butler 1993: xi), their boundaries are not fixed and impenetrable. On the contrary, there is constant epistemological movement between the two, which threatens annihilation, but also enables transformations. Here a still photograph is not just a space where two conflicting questions can be played out and analysed, it is also a space where viewers are compelled to reflect not just upon what they see but also upon their reaction to it. Thus questions surrounding the representation of abject bodies lead to questions about the subject domain and its discursive as well as visual limits. A photograph, despite its apparent stillness in representation, is in fact a place of interrogation because looking has to be an active choice. Therefore an image 'oscillates between the statement and the question, the two never dissociated but always dependent upon one another' (Nair 2011: 228). The close analysis that follows considers this movement within Goded's still photography.

Plaza de la soledad is a visual black-and-white narrative accompanied by interviews conducted by Goded with some of the subjects. They provide a verbal anchoring for the photographic narrative of the photographs and imbue the images with additional meanings, although the focus of this chapter's critical engagement remains with the photographs. However, their role is important because their very presence in a photographic album points to the need for contextualising and anchoring of images. The interviews themselves will be referred to for the study of certain photographs, since they provide a written perspective that, through mediation, includes voices of Goded's silent subjects. This inclusion of the women's perspectives on their own lives, their profession, their relationships and their choices in life indicates that within the album the women are represented not just in terms of their image, but also framed within their own narratives. For subaltern subjects such as sex workers, whose voice is all too often silenced by stigma, having an opportunity to narrate their own experience means already overcoming the silence pertinent to their subalternity.

The visual story starts and ends with images of the street, alluding both to the street life of prostitutes and to the fact that prostitution is inscribed into the urban landscape of Mexico City. The vast majority of the photographs are taken in confined spaces, either in small, poorly furnished rooms or against walls. They serve as a metaphor of the subjects' restricted position in the society and their accessibility, which illustrates the commoditisation of their bodies. The album

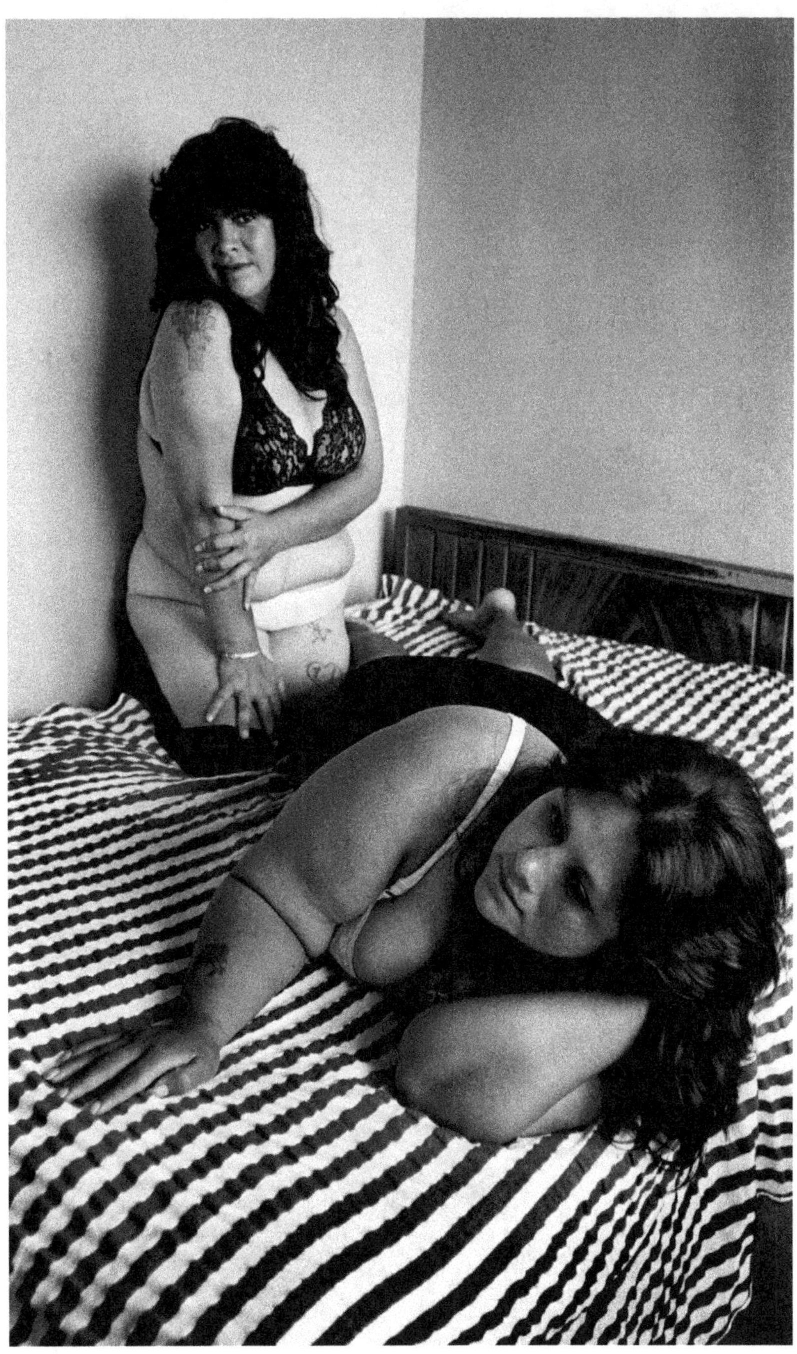

Fig. 4.4a. M. Goded, *Good Girls* (2006).

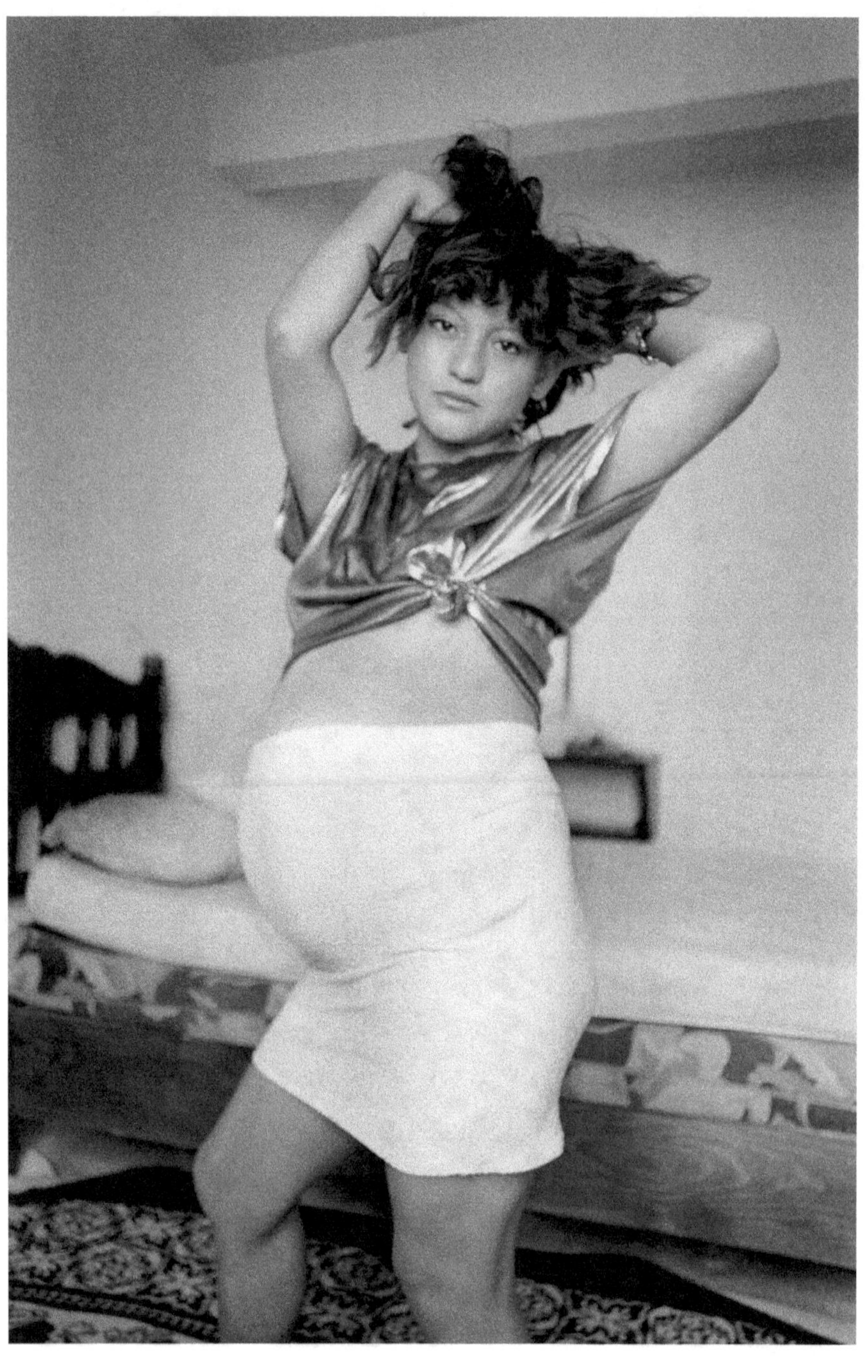

Fig. 4.4b. M. Goded, *Good Girls* (2006).

also defies expectations by showing sex workers' attempts to fit into mainstream socio-cultural life by including photographs of marriages, first communions and other events, which in Catholic contexts normally define the sanctity of family life. Participation in these liminal rituals deeply rooted in Catholicism and its morality are for sex workers a way of overcoming the stigma society associates with prostitution and a creative reworking of norms, which relegate them to the margins of public life. Goded's use of family album conventions to represent prostitutes, normally considered as the antithesis of mainstream family life, indicates her desire to draw viewers' attention to their paradoxical exclusion from and indispensability to such strict norms.

The matter of selling sex and the erotic displays required to entice likely customers is showcased by Goded in ways that actually reduce its erotic potential. The photograph on page 17 shows just a pair of legs clad in stilettos and a very short, tight skirt photographed against a wall. Immediately afterwards, on pages 18 (Figure 4.4) and 19 there are four photographs of different women in various stages of undress photographed in small and poorly furnished hotel rooms. The photographs on pages 20 and 22 take viewers back to the street, framing one corner from two different perspectives and showing women in tight blouses and short skirts waiting for their next client. Another turn of a page reveals a composition, which mirrors the one from pages 18 and 19, again framing prostitutes in hotel rooms (Figure 4.5). The juxtaposition of photographs of the streets and those taken inside are a visual metaphor of a routine experienced by Goded's subjects and its spatial confinement. The photographs force viewers to undertake the same repetitive journeys from the street to the hotels, which the women regularly take. The symmetry of the composition underlines not just the restricted character of Mexican prostitution but also its quotidian nature, therefore stripping it of its mysterious allure. Despite the fact that Goded shoots different women for every photo between page 17 and page 24, the composition she chooses does not focus on individuals' characteristics but on the unremarkable regularity of their employment instead. With some women in the photographs seeing over sixty clients a day (Goded 2006: 109), the images focus on the similarities between the prostitutes and their environments. The women photographed inside the hotel rooms on pages 18 and 19 as well as pages 22 and 23 are framed from above and most of them look into the camera while striking a seductive pose. The framing does not emphasise their attractiveness, even when they are young and conventionally beautiful, underlining their vulnerability and commodification instead by making their bodies appear small and defenceless. They are looked down upon by the photographer and by viewers of her photographs, just as they are looked down upon by the society. This composition echoes that described by John Tagg in relation to photographing the Other:

> There are bodies and spaces. The bodies: workers, vagrants, criminals, patients, the insane, the poor, the colonised races — are taken one by one, isolated in a shallow, contained space; turned full face to an unreturnable gaze; illuminated, focused, measured, numbered and named; forced to yield to the minutest scrutiny of gestures and features. (Tagg 1988: 64)

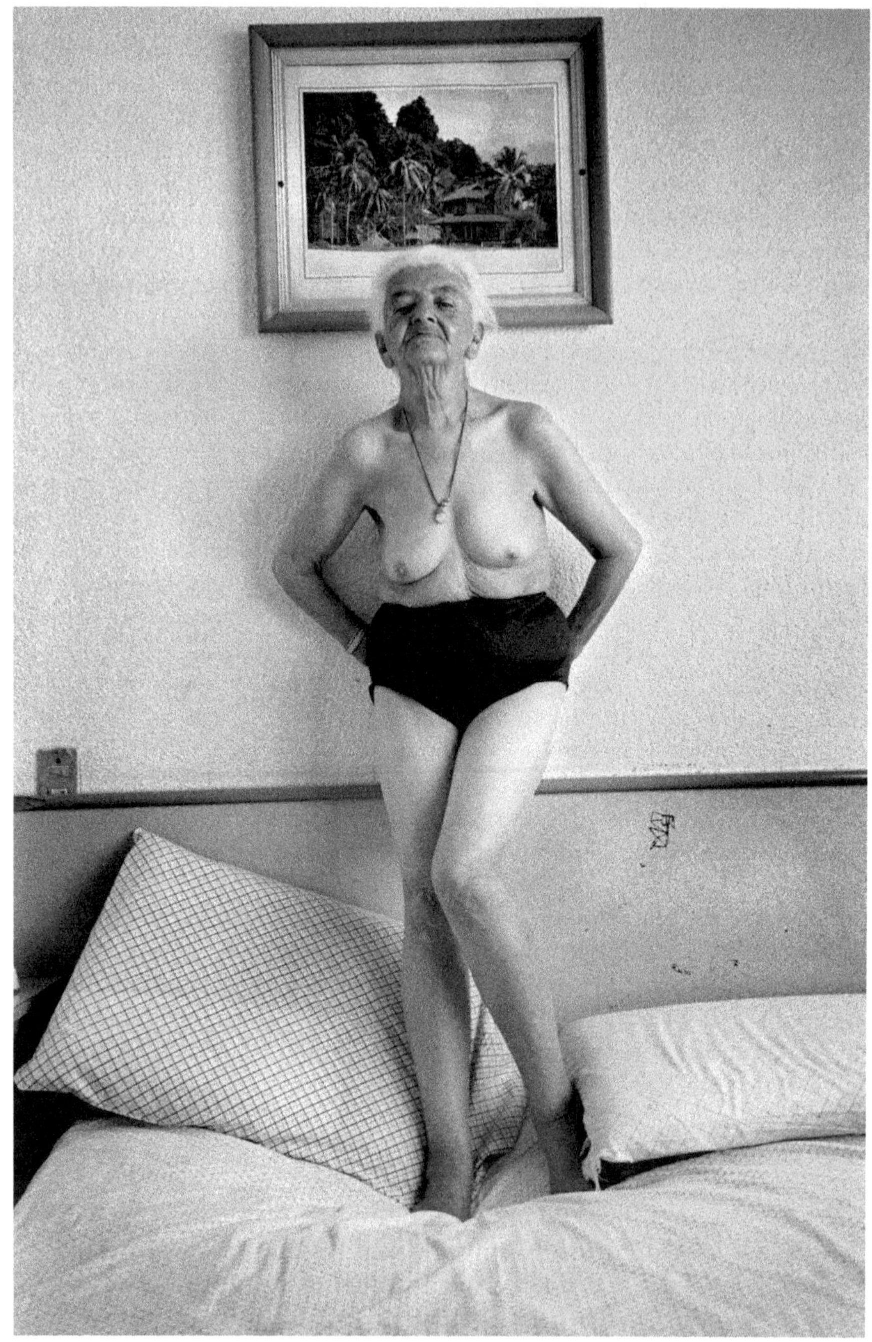

Fig. 4.5a. M. Goded, *Good Girls* (2006).

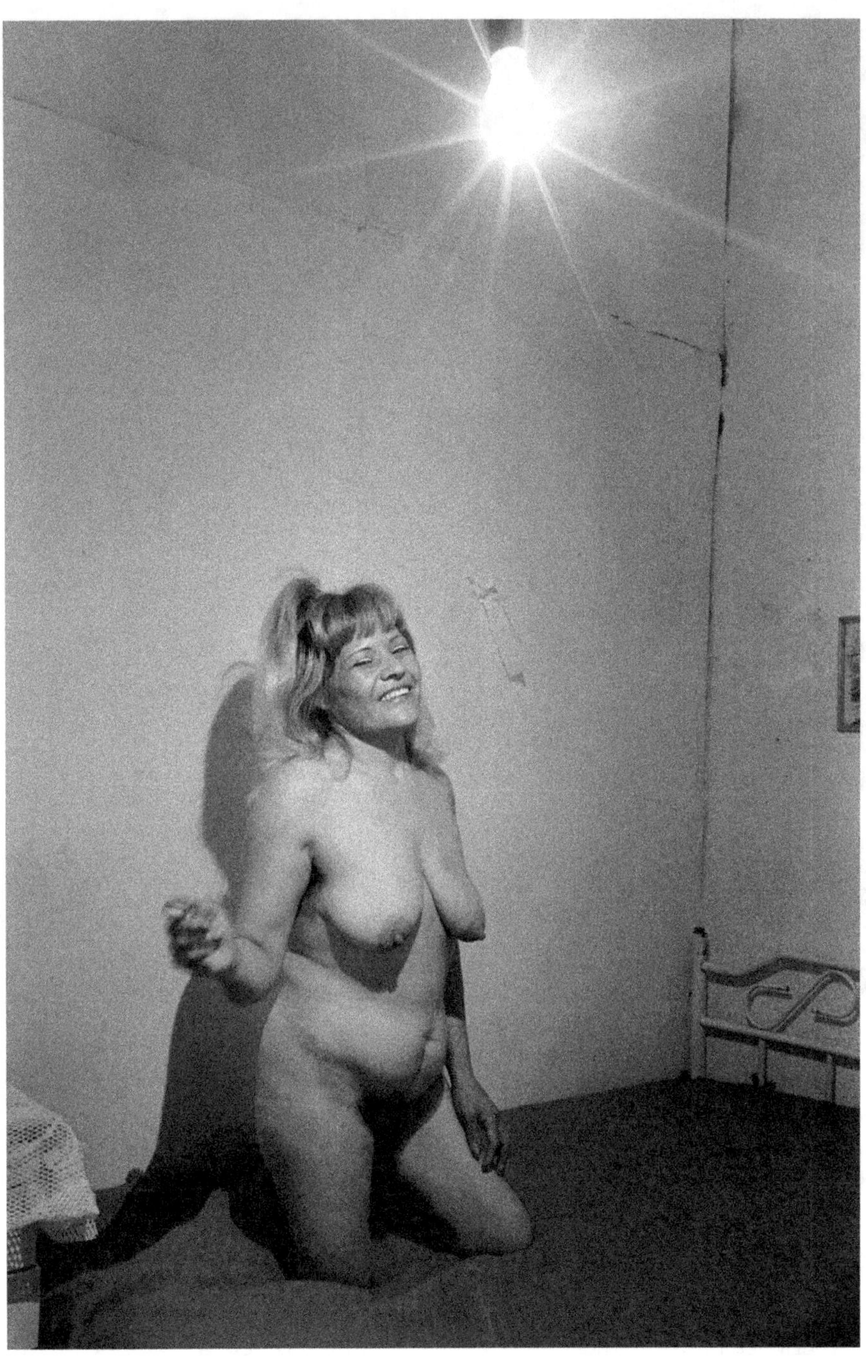

Fig. 4.5b. M. Goded, *Good Girls* (2006).

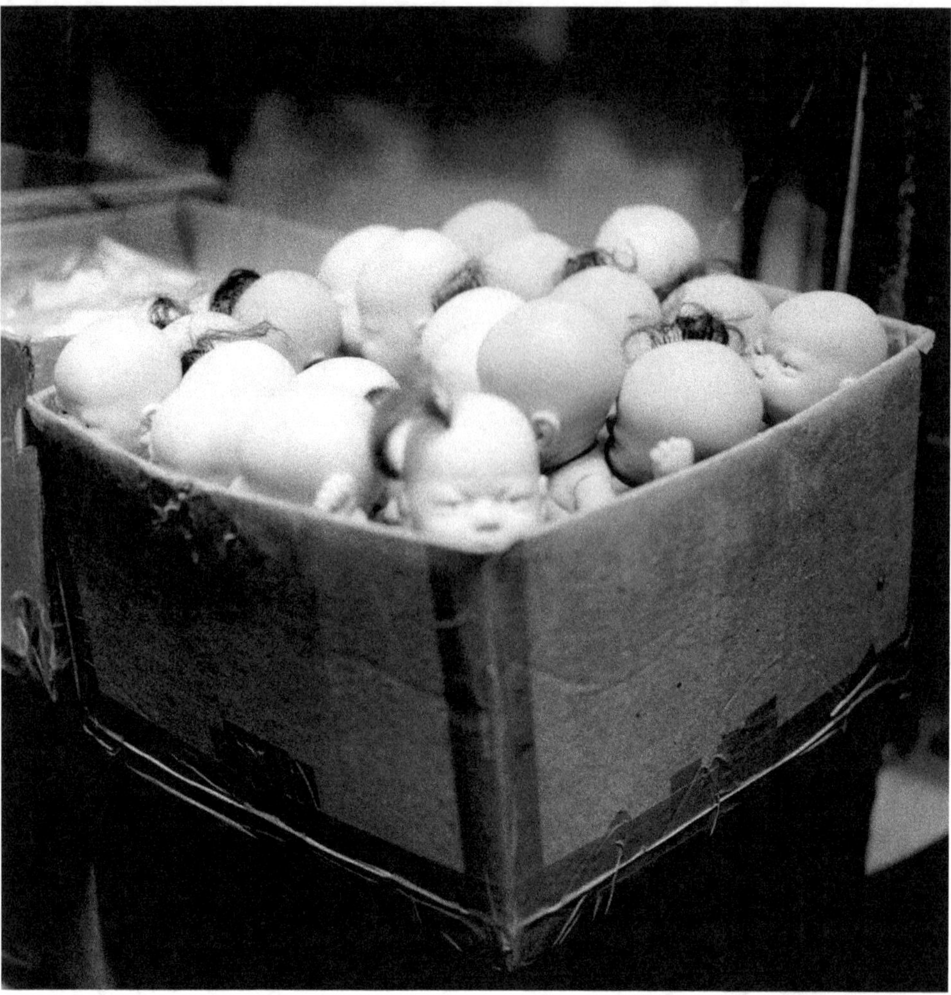

Fig. 4.6. M. Goded, *Good Girls* (2006).

The camera is an aggressor in this encounter, taking the place of a client who would normally purchase the flesh offered by the women before Goded's lens, yet this only draws further attention to the subjects' commoditisation. Hence looking at those photographs becomes an uncomfortable experience, since one consumes the sexual display on offer in a manner that does not differ widely from that of a client purchasing sexual services. This discomfort is, according to Žižek (2000: 525), the result of the experience of our own gaze coinciding with the gaze of a pervert. In *Looking Awry* he states that '[t]here is something extremely unpleasant and obscene in this experience of our gaze as already the gaze of the other' and in viewing images that bare all (ibid.), since erotic pleasure relies on the mystery and uncertainty of the other or its representation. The awareness that everything is on display and can be had precludes potential gratification. The women's commoditisation is compounded by their economic poverty, which is evident from their surroundings and their dress. For it is both their job and their economic situation which makes their bodies somewhat disposable, therefore forfeiting any erotic pleasure which could be had from gazing at them. Here the aggressive position of the camera, which usurps the place of a client, actually results in images that underline the abhorrent throwaway attitude inherent in the practice of prostitution.

Goded visually alludes to this disturbing disposability of the body through a photograph on page 35 (Figure 4.6). It is an image of an old cardboard box, stuck together with pieces of tape and filled to the brim with little dolls. The dolls are packed very tightly and appear to be very similar to one another, some with a random lock of hair stuck to their heads, others with their little fists rising above the sea of identical baby faces. Placing a photograph of discarded dolls in an album where photographs of prostitutes are published creates a visual critique of sexual exploitation, which leads to the commoditisation of the body. Entering one's body and its ability to perform sexual functions into an economic exchange is a selective and reductive way of treating oneself. One that, according to Carmen interviewed at the end of the album, requires an ability to disassociate body and mind. 'Look, when we work, our mind goes blank, and we never really see the person. Logically we feel nothing' (Goded 2006: 101). Thus, the body becomes nothing more than a plaything and a tool, much like the dolls in the photograph. This desire to 'feel nothing' (ibid.) is testament to the unpleasant and draining nature of the job itself, as well as the necessity to fake emotions and conceal real ones. Catharine MacKinnon in *Are Women Human?* (2006) describes this desire for disassociation from one's own body as a common response of those suffering torture and trauma, one which, while promoting survival, can also be hard to reverse and invariably produces devastating psychological effects (MacKinnon 2006: 19). Moreover, just as it is impossible to disassociate meaning from materiality, striving for the separation of body and mind is a similarly futile activity. As much as the desire to feel nothing may serve as a protecting mechanism from the trauma of having to sell one's body, prostitution undoubtedly requires mental as well as physical engagement in order to provide sexual services. As Maggie O'Neill argues in *Prostitution and Feminism: Towards a Politics of Feeling* (2001) emotional involvement is a necessary part of prostitution because sex workers use emotional energy to make clients feel good (O'Neill 2001: Location 3230). A disassociation between body and mind is not only hard to fathom but would also render the sex worker unable to perform her job. Moreover, prostitution places the body at risk of unwanted pregnancies, of which the baby dolls could be read as a metaphor, alluding not just to the disposability of the women's bodies but also to the redundant nature of their offspring. Once again, materiality, as an effect of power, and meaning are intertwined to enable the transfer of social stigma through the mother's womb.

Another aspect represented by Goded in *Plaza de la soledad* concerns the effects of marketing one's body as a commodity, which are visually traced on the bodies of her subjects. A number of the photographs show tattoos clearly visible on the skin of the prostitutes, which are a visual allusion to the social stigma of their profession as well as, more generally, to the need for adornments in commoditising human

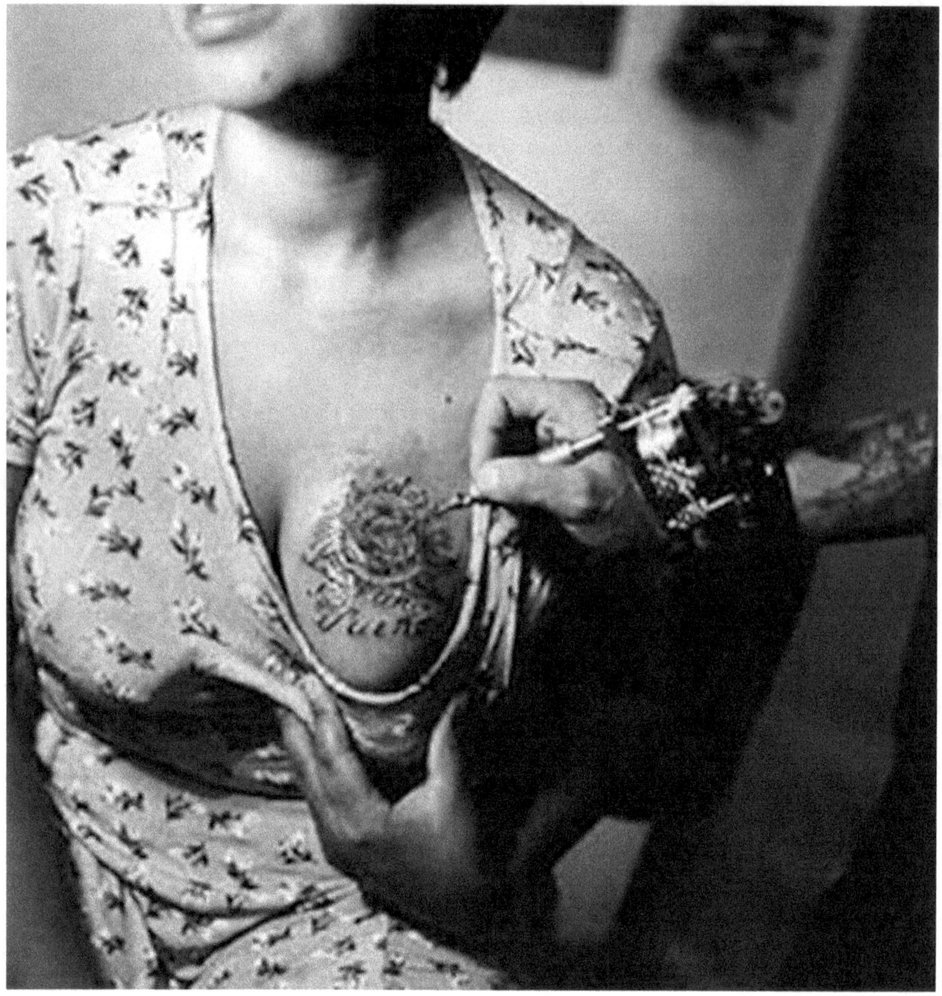

Fig. 4.7. M. Goded, *Good Girls* (2006).

beings. One of the images in the album is a photograph of the torso of a young woman, whose breast is being tattooed (Figure 4.7). The mark on her skin is being made with a special tattoo gun, which penetrates her skin repeatedly with a needle and leaves a mark with every incision. In the context of the woman's job, the phallic tattoo gun is an allusion to the physical act of penetration, which also marks prostitutes not just physically but also socially and culturally. The composition of the photograph, showing just the woman's torso and her full breasts, clearly emphasises the importance of the fetishised body in prostitution. The hands of the tattooist, however, come from the outside of the frame, making them invisible despite the power they exert over the woman's body in this photograph. There are many other women with tattoos among the women photographed by Goded, and her interest in the skin of her subjects is indicative of an attempt to capture their experience in physical terms. Skin becomes a boundary, an external, finite and concrete limit

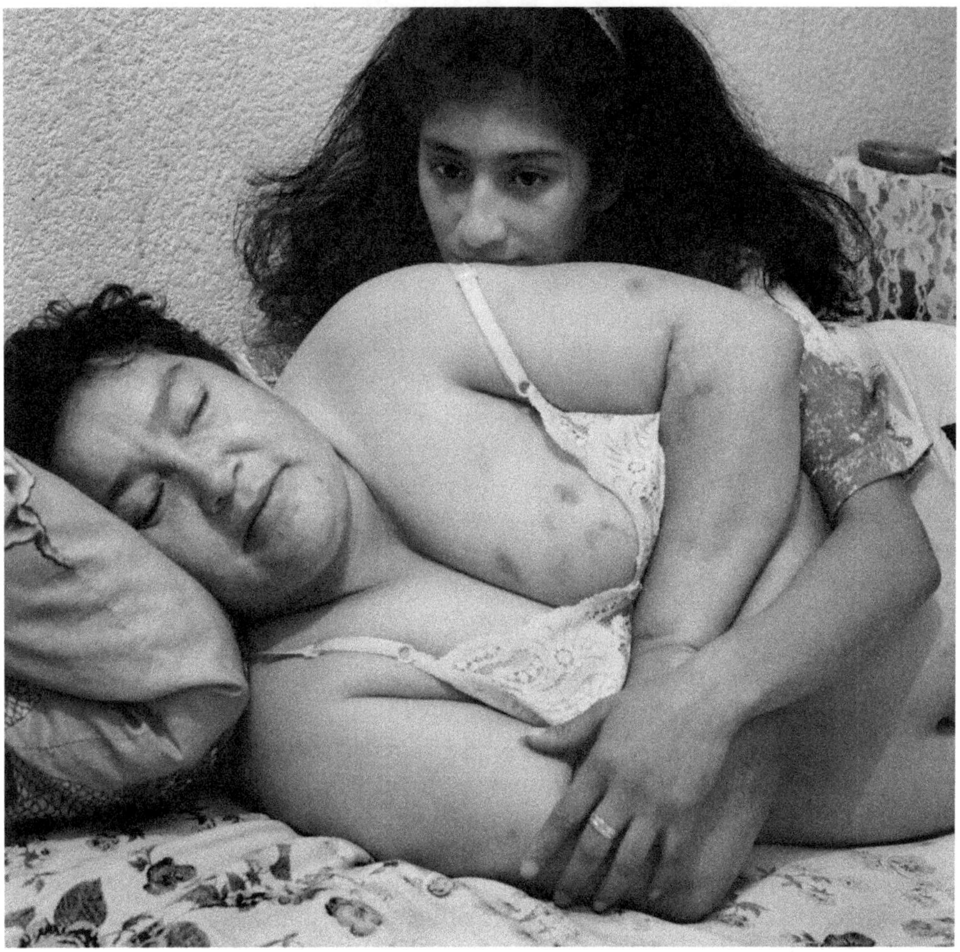

Fig. 4.8. M. Goded, *Good* Girls (2006).

of one's body, which is also permeable and open to interactions with the outside world. For all the protection it offers, it can also be quite vulnerable, especially for those occupying the precarious position on the borders of the subject domain.

Apart from tattoos, Goded explores the vulnerability of her subjects' skin by photographically tracing marks and scars. They become important visual traces of the humanity and vulnerability of her subjects, turning her photographs into spaces for envisioning the prostitute otherwise, and mediating the personal suffering entailed in being treated as a commodity. The image on page 84 (Figure 4.8) captures two women lying on a bed. It is cropped in a way which invokes closeness and intimacy, since the women's heads and torsos take up 80 per cent of the image. The older woman in the foreground appears to be asleep in just her bra and her breasts are covered in bruises, which were left by fingers groping her violently. Her arms bear knife scars and her face is weathered and appears to be swollen. The younger woman in the background is hugging her belly and looking down outside the frame. Her eyes are dark and sunken and her face bears small bruises and scars. Both women seem very tired and downtrodden, and the focus on their bare and scarred skin emphasises their vulnerability, which is the direct effect of the commoditisation of their bodies. Indeed, they both adopt a defensive pose, the older woman crossing her arms in front of her belly and the younger one hiding behind her. The violence they must have suffered is implicit in the atmosphere of the photograph and yet understated and somewhat muted. The fragility of their bodies and their susceptibility to being marked by tattoos and scars is very much in keeping with the rest of the photographs in the album, where the extreme close-ups allow viewers to see details they normally would not be able to notice. The revealing points to the women's availability, which extends not just to sexual services but also to their image. Their scarred, wrinkled and burnt skin draws attention to the fragility of their bodies and their fragmentation, which symbolically embodies the domain of the abject as one that cannot protect its own boundaries due to serving as a border for the powerful other. The image is captured at the moment of intimate stillness which occurs after trauma and the subjects do not engage with the camera — their defensiveness is palpable in their poses and in the closed eyes of the older woman, whose strategy of avoiding being seen resembles that often used by children who do not want their photograph taken. Nonetheless, viewers have the power to look through Goded's lens and watch the stillness of the women's suffering. It is photographs such as this one which evoke in viewers the unfamiliar inadequacy of being confronted with a silent torment. Once seen, it cannot be unseen and the discomfort experienced by a witness stems from a combination of understanding trauma and despair and from the awareness that it is very isolating and lonely — a combination of empathy and helplessness. Again, a photograph of the other leads viewers to the self, probing relentlessly the subject–abject distinction.

Goded's photographic witnessing of the trauma, which leaves visible material marks on the bodies of her subjects, visually exposes the consequences of bodily commoditisation. Regardless of the nuanced theoretical debates on the issues surrounding sex work, most scholars agree that what differentiates it from other types of work most significantly is the precariousness and vulnerability of the women's position (Sanders et al. 2009: 11). Sex workers are much more likely to be violated, battered or killed in the course of their work than any other group and many die very young. The open discrimination, stigmatisation and marginalisation of prostitutes — in other words, their abjection — impedes any attempt to defend themselves against bodily injury, partly because of the vulnerability inherent in sex work and partly because of violence against prostitutes condoned by the popular molar doctrine, which not only tolerates but promotes hostility towards 'dirty whores' (O'Connell Davidson in Sanders et al. 2009: 11). Here, photographic representation exhibits the power to show bodily injury of those who are denied their right to protect their own bodies. It visually probes the abjection of prostitutes, validating their accounts of suffering and therefore visually and epistemologically transforming their pain from an acceptable occupational hazard into an abuse of human rights (MacKinnon 2006: 42).

The shocking and compelling nature of the photographs included in *Plaza de la soledad* cannot be explained just by referring to the irresistible appeal of the abject. By photographing the prostitutes' bodies Goded showcases the material effects of power, which condemn certain lives to an existence full of pain and suffering by denying them the status of the subject. Moreover, the limited reach of such denial can be appreciated through photographs where the women chose to participate in rituals, which belong to the subject domain, therefore defying their marginal position and claiming agency. Despite the fact that their bodies are to some extent dehumanised because of the monetary value put on them by their procurers and clients, they also always escape commoditisation, as their identity cannot be fixed and remains a dynamic process. Goded's visual narrative is not confined to notions of victimhood, but it does underline the human fragility of her subjects, whose vulnerability is intertwined with their subalternity. Despite that image of defiance and self-determination within creative constraints, one cannot also fail to appreciate their marginalisation and confinement, underpinned by misogyny. Many of the photographs in *Plaza de la soledad* engage directly with themes of death, visually underlining the fragility of Goded's subjects, which is a direct result of the commoditisation of their bodies. This bodily vulnerability and precariousness is a feature which prostitutes share with most other subaltern groups, whose lack of agency and visibility renders their already disadvantaged position ever more perilous. Therefore, a discussion of the presence of marginal bodies in representation must acknowledge their risky proximity to absence.

The Body in Absence

One of the most shocking images illustrating the effects of prostitution on the skin and the body is the photograph of a dead woman on page 96 (Figure 4.9). Goded toys with the subject of death throughout *Plaza de la soledad*, which is undoubtedly a nod towards Mexican popular culture with its extravagant *Día de los muertos* celebrations and Western fascination with it.[1] On page 93, a figurine of death holding a skull surrounded by candles is photographed next to a woman's feet dressed in black tights, metaphorically showing the precariousness of working on the streets of Mexico City. Nonetheless, the photograph on page 96 is far more direct and shocking. It depicts a naked body of a young woman lying on a steel slab inside a morgue. Underneath her neck there is a card with her details on it — they are not clear enough for a viewer to be able to read, but they are a proof of institutional intervention. Just as prostitutes are relegated to *zonas de tolerancia* when they are alive, they are also subject to being measured and catalogued even in death. Her skin looks smooth and young, but there is a huge scar running all through her body from the post-mortem performed on her. It cuts her chest in half and disappears behind her ear into her abundant hair. Just as the skin of the women on the other photographs was tattooed and scarred, hers also bears the signs of being violated even after death. Her body was a commodity when she was alive and it remains so, this time in the form of a gruesome photograph. The atmosphere of this photograph is still but also rather horrific.

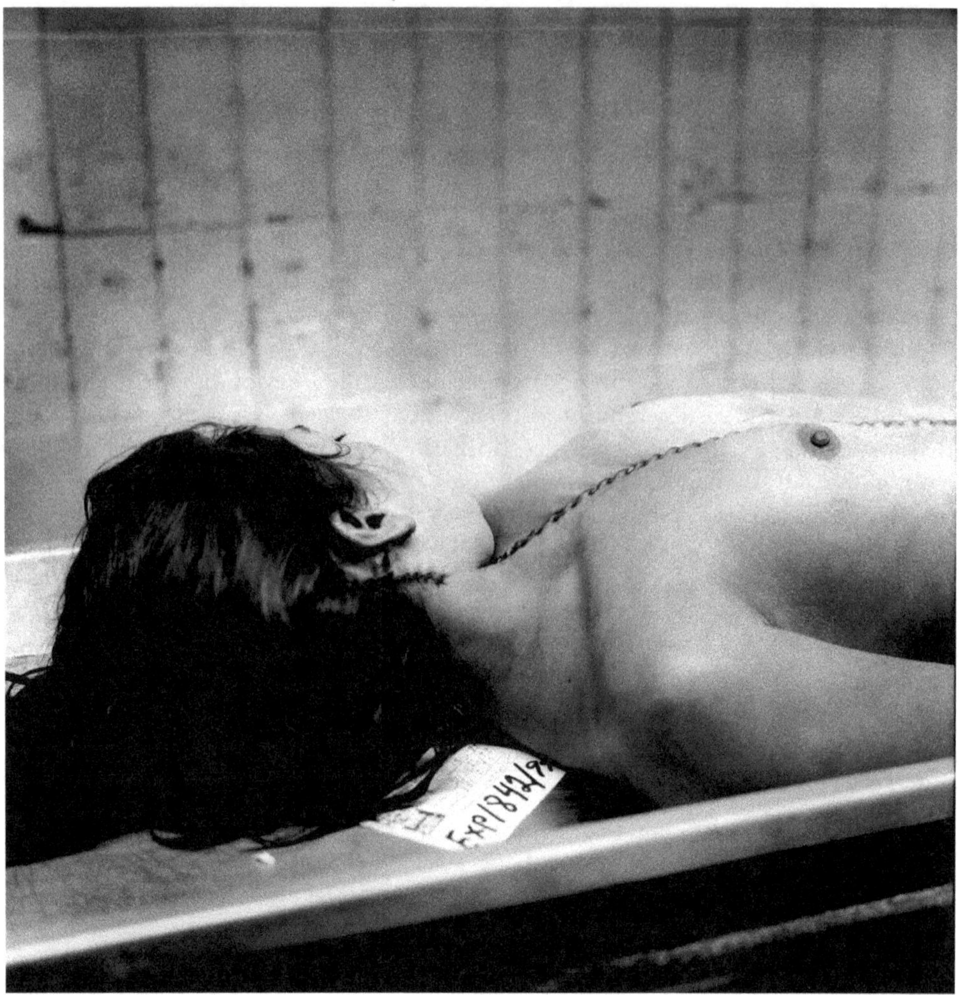

Fig. 4.9. M. Goded, *Good Girls* (2006).

The clinical, tidy environment of the city morgue captured in the photograph is an attempt to contain and sanitise the ultimate object of abjection, namely the corpse. Julia Kristeva argues that the corpse, despite being rejected, is at the same time 'something from which one does not part, from which one does not protect oneself as from an object' (Kristeva in McAfee 2004: 47). One of the ways in which the anxiety surrounding dead bodies is often expressed within the subject domain is through elaborate burial rituals. On the one hand, they help the living to mourn the dead, and, on the other hand, they also ensure that the corpse is buried, burnt or otherwise disposed of in accordance with relevant customs. In most contexts, the families of the deceased have the right to their body and normally remain protective of the remains of their close ones. This is why Goded's access to the body of the young girl, evidenced by her photograph, is a reminder that bodies, which do not enjoy the status of subject, are treated in a pejorative way whether they are dead or alive. The photograph may illustrate the dangers of prostitution, but on an individual level it also reduces a corpse of a young woman to a symbol of subjugation and institutional gendered violence.

The photograph taken in the morgue becomes especially poignant when contrasted with an image of a dead baby, which is included in *Tierra Negra*. It is impossible to determine the gender of the baby, but judging from its elaborate, lacy dress one can reasonably assume that it is a girl. She is photographed from above, lying on a carpet, her remains comfortably rested on a folded towel. Her little body takes up most of the frame and her dress, which covers all of her body, is probably a christening outfit. She is additionally adorned with tulle. The care her family has taken in dressing her for the funeral is a symbolic expression of how much her young life was valued, especially when contrasted with other images of live children in *Tierra Negra*, which often show them half-naked, barefoot and sleeping with domestic animals. The funeral dress can also be read as a figurative representation of the tragedy of losing a child — the only act of love that the family can perform for her is to dress her dead body and make her comfortable, which is why it is done with utmost care and best clothes. It is a culturally and socially important way of saying goodbye and beginning the process of mourning. Moreover, the presence of Goded taking a photograph of the corpse also takes on a different meaning in this context. It is a way of acknowledging the short life of the baby and recognising her family's efforts in caring for her body.

The most tangible limit of body intelligibility is its mortality. Death pertains to the domain of the abject; it has to be relegated to the limits of the subject's consciousness in order to make life, understood here as a logical category, possible at all. Julia Kristeva writes of the corpse as the ultimate abject, as 'death infecting life' (Kristeva 1982: 13). Despite the imperative repudiation of death, its threat does not leave and continues to haunt the living. This haunting is precisely the constitutive outside of the category of life, whose discursive borders are threatened by frissons and fissures that have the potential of annihilating it. The corpse has its materiality and death produces effects, material as well as discursive, not just in relation to the corpse but also in relation to the discursive regimes of power that sanction it. The material abject corpse turns into an absence over time, but does not disappear from the constitutive outside of the subject domain and continues to haunt it. The issue of this haunting will be examined below in relation to Maya Goded's work on the missing women of Ciudad Juárez.

In terms of the representation of loss, the role of photography, especially family photography, as an affective prosthesis has to be acknowledged. As Jay Prosser outlines in the 'Introduction' to the *Light in the Dark Room: Photography and Loss*, photographs are not evidence of presence, but instead proof of the present absence of their subjects (Prosser 2005: 1). Photographic presence always signifies loss within the inevitably temporal viewpoint of the viewer and exposes the irreversible passing of time (ibid.), foretelling our own future death (Prosser 2005: 7) by capturing and representing the temporal changes of the human body. As such, the preoccupation with death is at the very core of photographic representation, as part of the chronological constraint of lived human experience and of the medium itself.

If photography is 'the medium in which we unconsciously encounter the dead' (Prosser 2005: 1), then photographs of corpses bring that encounter to the forefront of visual engagement, often making for jarring and shocking images because of the abject nature of the corpse, as outlined above. They confront viewers with a visual statement of the fragility of life and expose the uncanny nature of the photographed corpse, which, although very similar to living human beings, is also fundamentally different since it is no longer alive. Goded's photographs of the dead seem to imply that bodies are bound by certain conventions and discourses of power in life as well as in death, as shown in the visual analysis of photographs of corpses above. Significantly, these two images of corpses form part of photographic projects that do not explicitly concentrate on death. In her photography of the missing women of Ciudad Juárez, where violent deaths are a specifically articulated focus, the images of corpses are conspicuously absent. The following section will focus on the ways in which Goded's photographs deal with the absences left by the dead women and ways of visually signalling them.

Ciudad Juárez is a border city between Mexico and the United States which is separated by the Río Bravo del Norte from its US counterpart El Paso. The Inter-American Commission on Human Rights in its report entitled 'The Situation of the Rights of Women in Ciudad Juárez, Mexico: The Right to Be Free from Violence and Discrimination' describes the wider context of the murders by defining the main challenges which plague the city. First and foremost, Ciudad Juárez's marginal location has its advantages and disadvantages. On the one hand, the city is severely affected by the drug trade between Latin American countries producing substances for consumption by the Western markets, which finds one of its trade routes through the state of Chihuahua, largely causing the high crime levels within the city for all of its inhabitants regardless of age or gender. On the other hand, it is also seen as a place of opportunity due to the flourishing *maquila*[2] industry dominating the border region. The people who migrate into the city in search of better economic prospects contribute to the rapid population growth, which then affects public cohesion due to significant social, economic and cultural differences within the population. On a more practical level, the city suffers from the shortage of infrastructure and resources necessary to accommodate the needs of its growing demographic, effectively condemning the economically disadvantaged sectors of the population to inadequate living conditions, which lack proper sanitation or health services. The power of this border economy reliant on the *maquila* industry has shifted the traditional patterns of work outside the home, since reports suggest that over half of the *maquila* workforce is comprised of women, which affords them greater economic, and therefore social, independence. In a landscape marked by inequalities between men and women such shifts cause tensions, especially since there are few resources employed in changing gendered prejudices and expectations. The report implicitly suggests, therefore, that one of the motivations behind the endemic violence directed at women is to curtail their independence and preserve traditional gendered roles.

It is also important to frame this epidemic of gendered violence within the wider context of violence that plagues Ciudad Juárez. Its proximity to the United States is not just fertile ground for the proliferation of *maquilas*, but also a place where conflicts over lucrative drug trafficking intensify. As such, the city is a backdrop of a vicious conflict between the Sinaloa cartel and La Línea, which is the armed wing of the Juárez cartel and includes Chihuahua police officers, in a fight to control the cocaine market. Moreover, it is not only women and men involved in drug trafficking who are at risk of violent assault. In *Crímenes de odio por homophobia. Los otros asesinatos de Ciudad Juárez* [Homophobic Hate Crimes: The Other Murders in Ciudad Juárez] (2010) Efraín Rodríguez Ortiz reveals that the city's endemic violence extends to murders of people displaying non-heteronormative sexual preferences or behaviours, who are victims of homophobic persecution. Through interviews with Rodolfo Milán Dena, the judicial coordinator of the Comisión Ciudadana Contra Crímenes de Odio por Homofobia [Citizens' Commission Against Homophobic Hate Crimes] in Ciudad Juárez, Rodríguez argues that violence against homosexuals is only one symptom of widespread homophobia, which manifests itself in a variety of ways, from inadequate police investigations to families not claiming bodies of their loved ones due to a sense of stigma (Rodríguez 2010: Location 2087). Seen in this context, Goded's photography only accounts for a small selection of subaltern stories of loss in Ciudad Juárez, but it does, nonetheless, provide an opportunity to analyse how the pervasive violence and persistent impunity affect the lives of those left behind.

Although for decades the response of local and national authorities to the crisis of violence in Ciudad Juárez has been inadequate, the presidency of Felipe Calderón heralded a shift in policy towards drug trafficking by deploying the Mexican Army to deal with cartels, most notably in Tijuana and Ciudad Juárez. In a commentary written for the *Latin American Policy Journal* he outlines the principles of his project Todos Somos Juárez, which aims to combine army intervention with state support for local authorities and rebuilding 'the social fabric' in the city (Calderón 2013). In a seamless narrative of diminishing violence following the introduction of his policy, Calderón claims a significant reduction in murders between 2010 and 2012 (ibid.). Although the very existence of the programme is a change in the socio-political landscape of Juárez, Calderón's claims of its success are widely contested. For example, Victor offers a scathing critique of the programme.

> El [...] programa [...] ha sido muy cuestionado por las organizaciones sociales de Ciudad Juárez. Organizaciones de trabajo con niños, con adolescentes y con mujeres han señalado, por ejemplo, que se gastó demasiado en cemento y muy poco en reconstruir el tejido social y fortalecer a las organizaciones comunitarias. [...] Llegó a muy poca gente, se beneficiaron grandes contratistas, y no hubo una atención y respuesta consistente a las víctimas. Diez mil muertos después, Calderón, el gobierno de Peña Nieto y el propio de César Duarte celebran el abatimiento de la violencia en Juárez. [...] Lo que no se dice es que buena parte de esa reducción se debe a que uno de los cárteles prevaleció en la disputa por el territorio, a que salió de Juárez la Policía Federal, nido también de delincuentes, y que la policía municipal dejó de perseguir sicarios para perseguir jóvenes y pobres. (Quintana 2013)

> [The [...] programme [...] has been widely questioned by the social organisations of Ciudad Juárez. Organisations that work with children, adolescents and women signalled that too much money has been spent on cement, but very little went to strengthen the social fabric and community organisations. [...] It reached very few people, but benefited big contractors and never provided attention and consistent responses to the victims. Ten thousand deaths later, Calderón, Peña Nieto's government and César Duarte's initiative celebrate the reduction in violence in Juárez. [...] What they do not mention is that a good part of this reduction was due to one of the cartels winning a fight over territory, as well as the Federal Police, another nest of criminals, leaving Juárez, and the city police ceasing to pursue hired assassins in favour of harassing youths and poor people.]

Similarly, Marcela Turati in '...Y Todos Somos Juárez, gran negocio' (Turati 2012) underlines that most of the investment that was meant to contribute to social cohesion went to benefit big businesses.

Todos Somos Juárez notwithstanding, the murders of young women in Ciudad Juárez, which have received plenty of national and international attention, continue and remain unsolved to this day. What can photography say about the dead? What is there to understand of the bodies that have perished? Although all human beings die, there is certainly no equality in how we die — just as there are better and worse ways of living, so there are better and worse ways of dying. Particularly in the case of the Juárez murders, the hierarchies of power within which they occur are complicit in the killings. The investigative journalist Sergio González Rodríguez, who wrote a book about the murders entitled *Huesos en el desierto* (2010), declares that not only is the scale of the crimes impossible to imagine without a significant involvement of those in power, but the constant denial, minimisation and impunity sustained by the authorities are evidence enough of their complicity. The endemic failure of the authorities to address the problem is illustrated on the Inter-American Commission on Human Rights website by the following story:

> Lilia Alejandra was 17 when she disappeared on February 14, 2001. She worked in a *maquila*. Lilia Alejandra's mother began passing out flyers as part of the search. Days later, the window of the mother's car appeared broken, and a roll of those flyers was found inside. When the police did not arrive in response to her call, she took the car to the station herself, but no clues were uncovered. Lilia Alejandra's body, naked and strangled, was found in a vacant lot just over a week after her disappearance. She left two children, the younger five months old. When Lilia Alejandra's mother went to the authorities to ask about the investigation, she was told she was 'drowning in a glass of water' and that women like that die all over the world. (Inter-American Commission on Human Rights 2012: unnumbered pages)

Why does the discourse of power designate young girls' and women's lives as not worth protecting, not worth saving and not worth mourning?

This state-led minimisation of the crimes has galvanised grassroots support. The resistance to ignoring the crimes is significant, and has produced an eminent counter-narrative. Goded's project on the murdered women and their families forms part of an immense body of work comprising documentaries, photographs, public art projects, installations, articles, books and websites. She witnesses their grieving process in an attempt to honour the memory of the victims and validate the claims of those seeking justice on their behalf. Strikingly, despite the gory nature of the crimes that leave decomposing bodies of young women, who have been mutilated, sexually assaulted and tortured, in ditches for all to see and for the media to make a spectacle of, Goded's photographs focus more on the everyday absences they left behind. In this manner, she underlines that they were valued, and that their lives are worth remembering and mourning. Through visualising the pain of the families left behind, Goded brings the victims' haunting absence back into the domain of the subject.

Maya Goded's photographs taken in Ciudad Juárez address the wound created by the crimes committed with impunity and the many absences which they produce — from physical through social to judicial ones. She engages with these absences by photographing the urban space of the city and producing haunting images of empty, run-down streets. One particularly jarring image (Figure 4.10) depicts a mural on the side of a road. It is a long shot of a dirty street, which frames the mural as the central focus of the composition, with the road surface occupying the foreground and white buildings in the background. The main contrast within the photograph is that between the dirty street smeared with oil and strewn with rubbish and the pristine whiteness of the wall on which the mural of a solitary man had been painted. There are no people and no cars on the street, apart from a few distant, small, hardly discernible figures blended into the background. This haunting absence is amplified by the lighting — the scene is flooded with natural sunlight, but the sky within the frame of this photograph is very overcast with dark, low clouds. The wall in the middle of the photograph seems almost out of place — it extends from the left-hand side in a white rectangle, surreal and overpowering through its symmetry within the composition.

The mural in the middle of the photograph is painted with brown paint on the white background and depicts Emiliano Zapata in instantly recognisable Mexican paraphernalia, wearing both a sombrero and a moustache. The painting does not have lifelike proportions; the man's figure is enlarged to occupy the entire height of a tall wall, and appears altered because of the fact that his torso and his arms appear too short for his head and his thighs. Unsettlingly, his fixed painted gaze is directed straight at the camera and he is pictured with two rows of ammunition for an automatic gun worn across his chest, and a strap with a gun-holder, hidden underneath his jacket on the left-hand side. He appears suspended in mid-air, looming over the street. He is an image of Mexican masculinity in Ciudad Juárez, signified here by the obligatory sombrero painted side by side with heavy ammunition. The portrait immediately links masculinity and violence, due to the man's intimidating and magnified presence on a deserted street.

Moreover, it suggests the normalisation of gang warfare and casual familiarity with guns, whose threat permeates everyday life in the city. The conspicuous absence of any other human presence or representation make this visual threat all the more alarming and reminds one of photographs taken in war zones, where people hide inside their houses in order to avoid becoming targets. Indeed, the authorities in

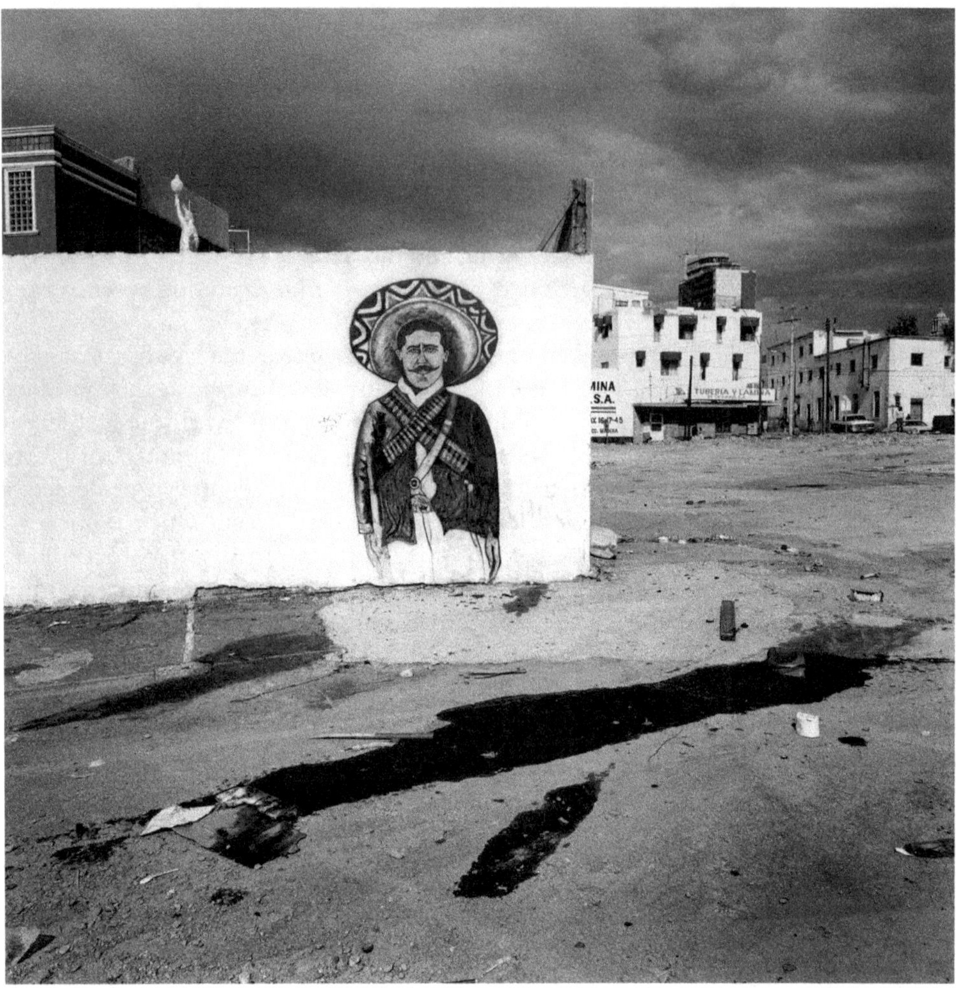

Fig. 4.10. M. Goded, Work for Justicia para nuestras hijas (2007).

Ciudad Juárez have been known to claim that the murdered women should have avoided going out in order to stay alive. Thus the subject of the photograph — the painted armed man — claims the street with his domineering presence. The haunting absence around him is testament to his strength. As for the urban landscape that surrounds him, the lack of infrastructure mentioned in the Inter-American Human Commission on Human Rights is very apparent. The street, made out of concrete and dirt, is stained with oil and full of rubbish. The road markings are hardly discernible, there are no pavements or obvious pedestrianised areas, and the only evidence of cars having used the road are cardboard boxes and plastic bottles flattened by traffic. The houses in the background appear deserted. The environment seems to be in collusion with the man in the mural, uninviting and full of hazards for cars as well as people. The empty, haunted absence around him is a visual reference to the invisible marginalised victims and those who mourn them.

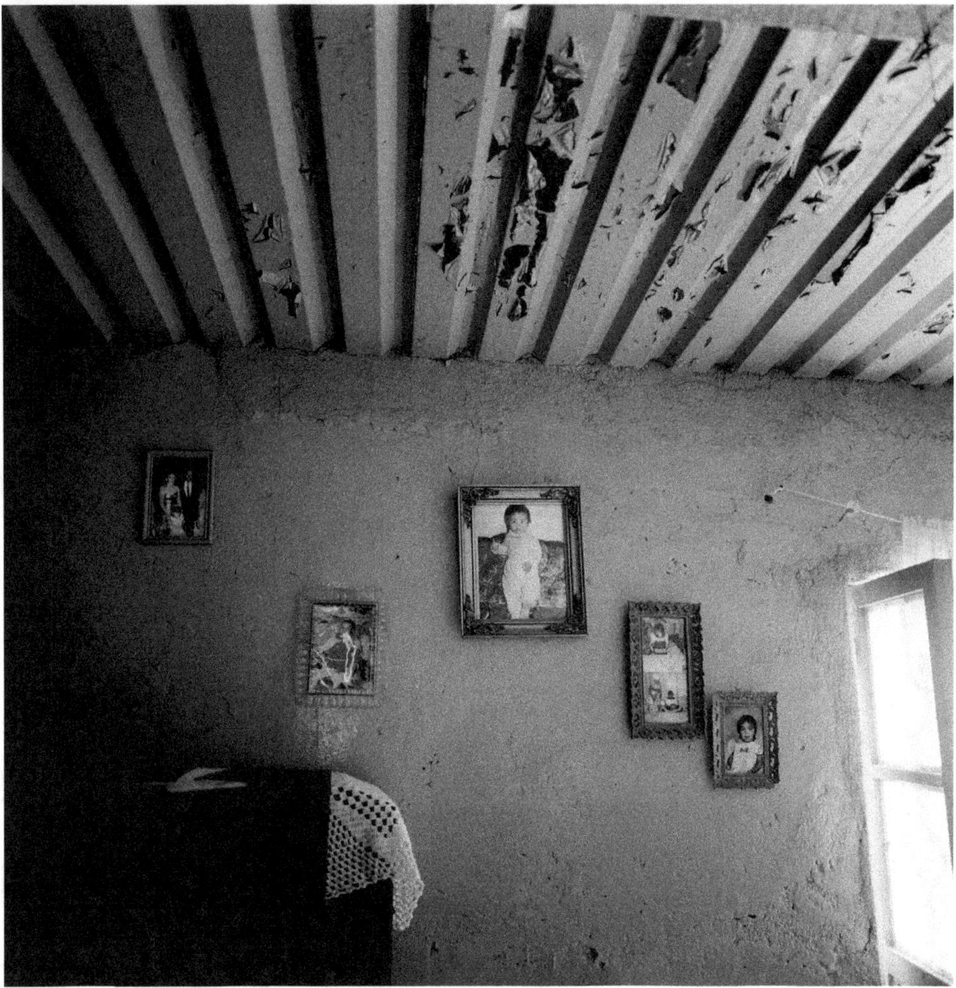

Fig. 4.11. M. Goded, Work for Justicia para nuestras hijas (2007).

The marginalisation of the victims and their families does not stem from the violent way in which they were killed. Most of the women murdered with impunity come from underprivileged backgrounds and very often migrate to Juárez in search of a better life. The socio-economic status of their families is evident from the photographs which portray their modest houses. One of the images (Figure 4.11) pictures a detail of a room in one of the victim's houses. The pockmarked, concrete wall painted blue meets a ceiling made of corrugated iron. The paint is flaking, exposing grey metal underneath. In the right-hand corner, a part of an open door can be seen, as if someone has just gone out. The room seems deserted and the only human presence is that of the young children and a family pictured on the five photographs hung on the wall. The composition of the photograph is unsettling because the line of the ceiling is out of alignment with the frame of the image, which is a visual metaphor for the way in which grief unsettles and changes

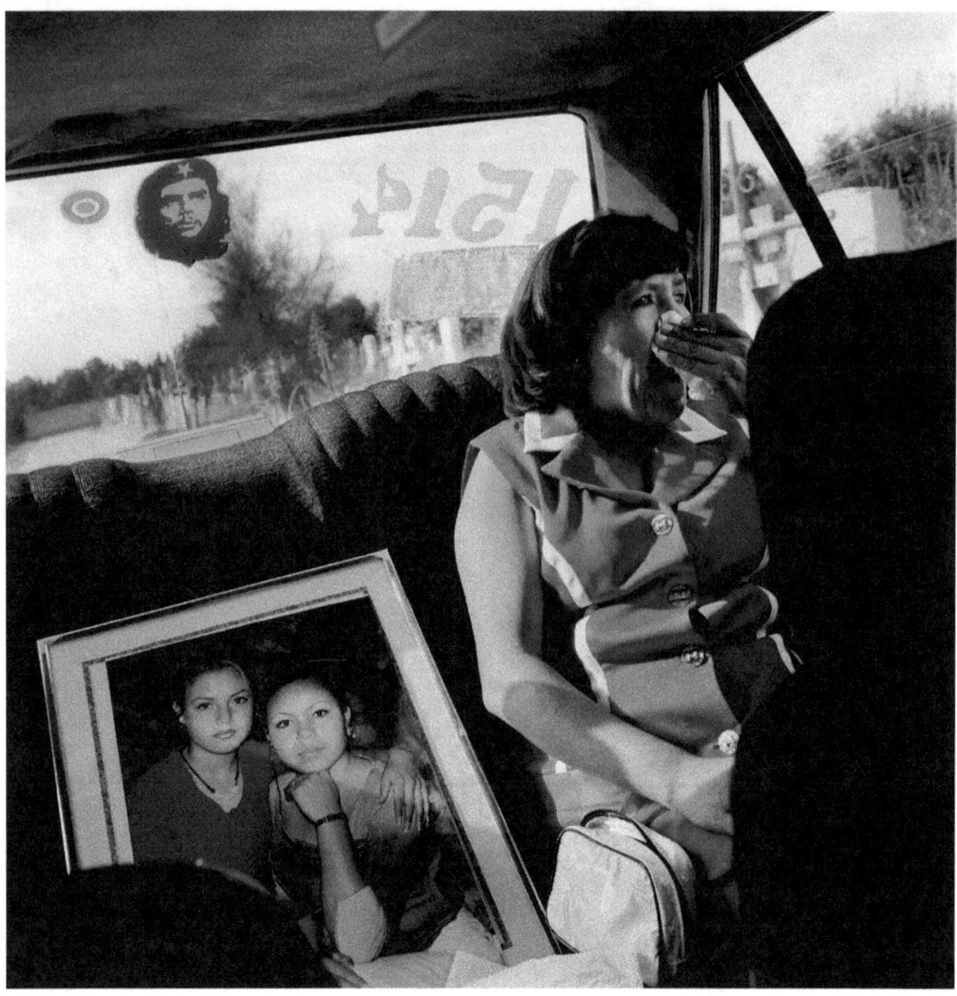

Fig. 4.12. M. Goded, Work for Justicia para nuestras hijas (2007).

everyday reality. The child whose childhood someone lovingly recorded with a camera will never have another picture taken. In fact, the only traces of her bodily presence are now to be found in the precious family mementos, contrasted with the haunting emptiness of the room. Grief invests ordinary family photographs with a different significance, since they are now traces of a life which is gone and which will never be captured again, therefore becoming all the more cherished. This is evident in another photograph in the series, where one is confronted with a surreal composition portraying a woman sitting at the back of a taxi with a large portrait of her missing daughters (Figure 4.12). It is a visual metaphor of bereavement which, compounded by the injustice and impunity, never leaves, and makes everyday actions a struggle precisely for their quotidian continuity despite the tragedy. Including photographs of missing women in her own compositions, Goded documents their unsettling, conspicuous absence, thus refusing to forget about the victims despite the claims that publicising the murders damages the reputation of the city (Reyes Baeza quoted by Amnesty International 2005).

The inclusion of ordinary family photographs in Goded's compositions has several aspects. On the one hand, it underlines the connection between photography and death, as every photograph, especially that of people, is a reminder of the passage of time and therefore of death. Every image is a presence, which refers to an absence, since to make an image 'is to mortify and resurrect in the same gesture' (Mitchell 2005: 53). When Roland Barthes contemplated the horror of death and photography in *Camera Lucida*, he stated:

> The horror is this: nothing to say about the death of one whom I love most, nothing to say about her photograph, which I contemplate without ever being able to get to the heart of it, to transform it. [...] I have no other resource than this *irony*: to speak of the 'nothing to say.' (Barthes 2000: 92–93)

In other words, the absence of someone's presence is so overwhelming that nothing can abate it. However, in the same book, Barthes writes touchingly of finding his dead mother in an old photograph and being able to rediscover her longed-for presence in an image of her as a child. Similarly, the photographs of the Juárez victims captured within Goded's compositions are bound to have a unique appeal for the families. To everyone else they may seem perfectly ordinary, but to those who lost their daughters they become the only mechanical or digital traces of the lives, which are missing and missed. As Marianne Hirsch argues,

> [T]he familial gaze situates human subjects in the ideology, the mythology, of the family as an institution and projects a screen of familial myths between camera and subject. Through this screen the subject both recognizes and can attempt to contest her or his embeddedness in familiality. The looks family members exchange, on the other hand, are located in specific points; they are local and contingent; they are mutual and reversible; they are traversed by desire and defined by lack. (Hirsch 1997: 11)

In situations concerning missing family members, the attraction of photography is compounded for those left behind by the fact that, as Barthes argues, a photograph does not necessarily show what is no longer, but instead it captures for certain what has been, meaning that one's consciousness does not necessarily follow the linear timeline of events (Barthes 2000: 85). Prosser claims that our experience of photographs as frozen, disjointed moments is close to the way we experience life and our own memory (Prosser 2005: 9). Finally, bearing in mind that women in Juárez have been disappearing for almost two decades now, ordinary family photographs of them help their dear ones remember them despite the passage of time. They are a desperate attempt to resist what Prosser calls 'the inevitable fading of lives in our lives' (Prosser 2005: 9). When justice has been denied, forgetting the victim may be construed as an act of betrayal by those left behind. Moreover, quite apart from being aids to familiar memories, the images of the missing constitute a physical, irreducible evidence of the women's existence that, by its very presence, helps to address the impunity of the murders. They provide material for artists such as Tamsyn Challenger (2010) and Ilán Lieberman (2009) to create works of

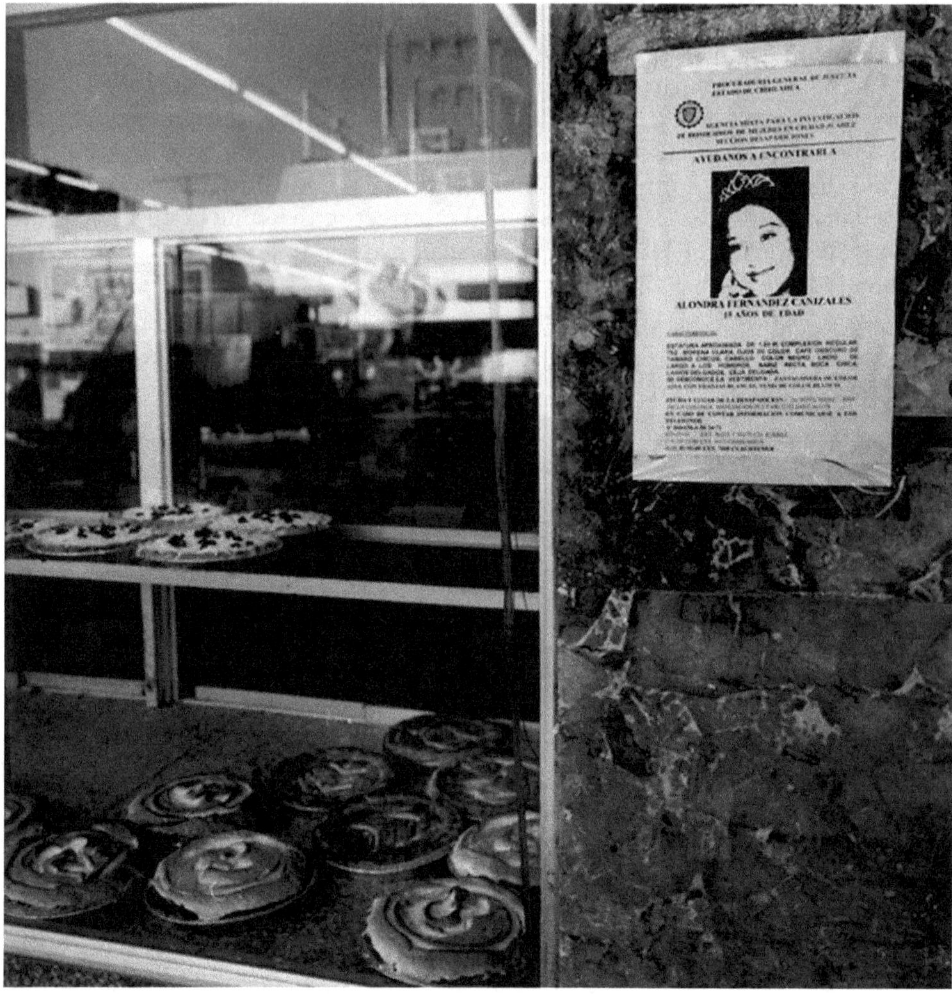

FIG. 4.13. M. Goded, Work for Justicia para nuestras hijas (2007).

art, which through contemplative consideration and reworking of the photographs of the missing create new artistic and social spaces for challenging the impunity of the murders and preserving the memory of the victims. Such artwork artistically transforms and expands what W. J. T. Mitchell calls 'the life of an image' (Mitchell 2005: 2). By creatively reworking the photographs of the missing, the new images metaphorically challenge the boundaries of death through the assertion of their absent presence.

Family photographs of the missing are also indispensable as a visual clue for the authorities, who are looking for them. As such, intimate family images become public property in the search for the missing person. An unsettling everyday image from Ciudad Juárez captured by Goded is a photograph of an official missing person poster stuck onto a wall (Figure 4.13). The notice asks for help in finding the fifteen-year-old Alejandra, but the picture that is meant to help people recognise the girl is badly photocopied. The high contrast of the image makes her face drained of all colour against a black background, which does not even allow the viewer to distinguish between the girl's hair and the backdrop. It is almost as if her reproduced photographic representation was slowly disappearing as well, following in her footsteps. The tiara carefully placed in her hair, most likely from her recent *quinceañera* party, is a reminder of social expectations of her conduct as a girl who has just become a woman through a ritualised cultural celebration. Receiving the tiara during the celebration is a token gesture of respect towards the teenager, which, on the missing poster above her young face, makes for a particularly poignant *mise en scène*. Just as Octavio Paz (2008: 73–74) once noted that the proliferation of different Mexican fiestas was a measure of Mexican poverty, so in this case the exaggerated birthday celebration reserved only for girls, often requiring weeks of preparations and considerable expense, is a measure of women's oppression. Meanwhile, despite Reyes Baeza's concerns, the photograph proves that life in Juárez carries on as normal. The patisserie presents its cakes in a glass display window next to the poster, despite the fact that the missing girl captured next to them probably met a rather gruesome end. Jarring as this contrast seems, it is also quite obvious that the city must be littered with similar posters, as such kidnappings and the accompanying futile appeals come to form part of the fabric of the city.

The commonplace nature of violent deaths of young women in Ciudad Juárez has the potential of desensitising public opinion to news of yet another disappearance, inasmuch as hundreds have disappeared before. The posters, flyers and newspaper appeals start to form a part of the cultural landscape, alongside local news, sport and weather reports, and advertising leaflets. This normalisation of violence, however, does not make mourning any easier for the people left behind but may actually aggravate the grieving process for several reasons. First of all, the loss is not acknowledged as important or even particularly newsworthy, despite the fact that losing a young member of the family is devastating. Secondly, mourning for the missing is particularly difficult, as closure remains elusive and the only immediately accessible phenomenon is absence. There is no body and no grave, yet somebody has gone leaving behind a space without a voice, and there are limited ways in which this loss can be acknowledged without giving up hope of finding them. Their abject absence haunts the status quo and changes the lives left behind, offering no prospect of closing the open wound, as the mourning process is stilted in limbo through impunity. Finally, finding the body and burying it provides only some of the answers, for the unresolved questions of justice and accountability make the process of mourning much more difficult. The families' helplessness not just in the face of the women's violent deaths, but also in pursuing justice is testament to their subaltern position. In spite of these haunted absences and because of them, the grieving process continues, seeking outlets through any accessible means.

One of the ways in which the Juárez murders and disappearances are publically acknowledged, remembered and mourned is through placing pink crosses in public places and on the crime scenes. One of Maya Goded's photographs (Figure 4.14) depicts two women standing in the middle of the desert, where one of them plants

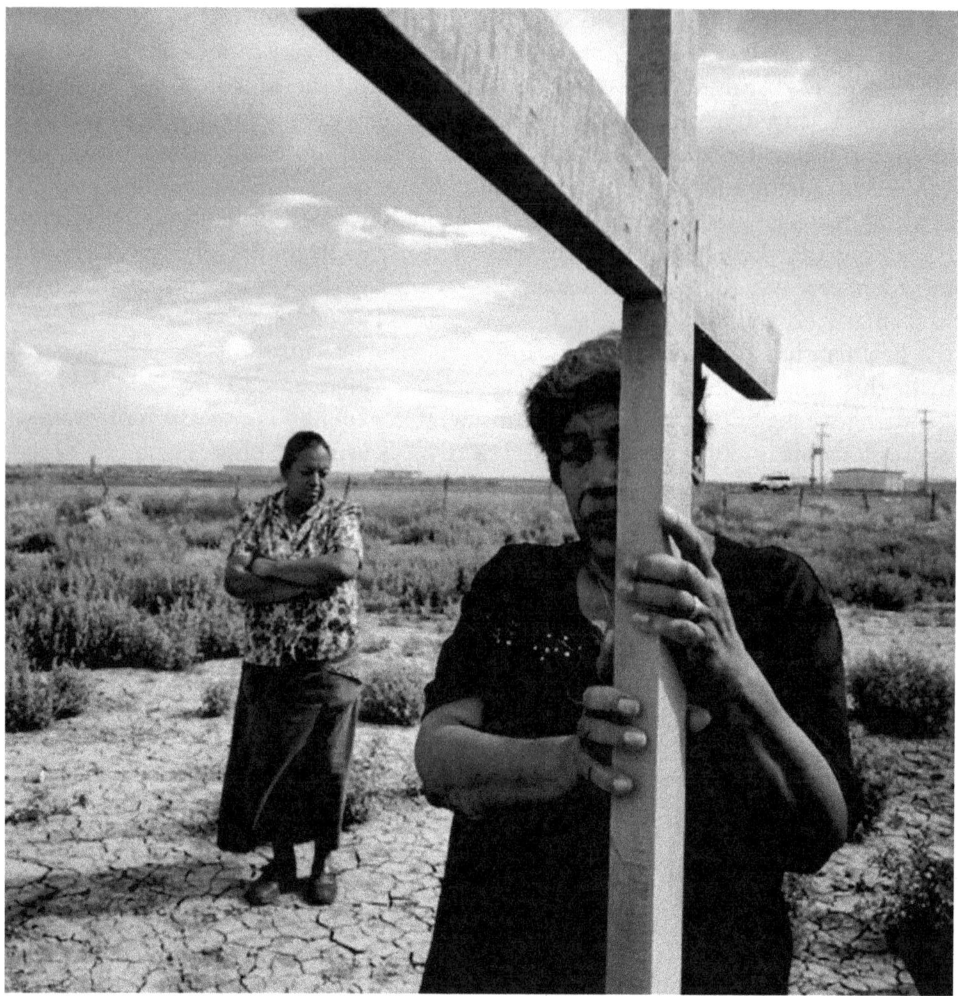

FIG. 4.14. M. Goded, Work for Justicia para nuestras hijas (2007).

a tall pink cross. The shot is very long, encompassing a sweeping, flat landscape, but the cross held by the woman in the foreground dominates the perspective. The vertical arm of the cross runs from the top edge of the frame to the bottom edge, splitting the photograph in two and obscuring part of the woman's face. The other woman pictured stands a little distance away, framed in between the background and the foreground staring at the cracked, dry ground. The windswept high clouds in the sky above the women meet the horizon in the background of the photograph, where one can discern the faint outlines of the *maquilas*. The dominant location of the cross within this composition makes it a focal symbol of the mother's sorrow caused by the death of her daughter. The woman literally bears the cross of her daughter's absence, holding it with both hands as a symbol of her daughter's and her own suffering. In this case, Catholicism provides a legitimate outlet for recognising the loss, which would otherwise go unacknowledged, and the cross provides a

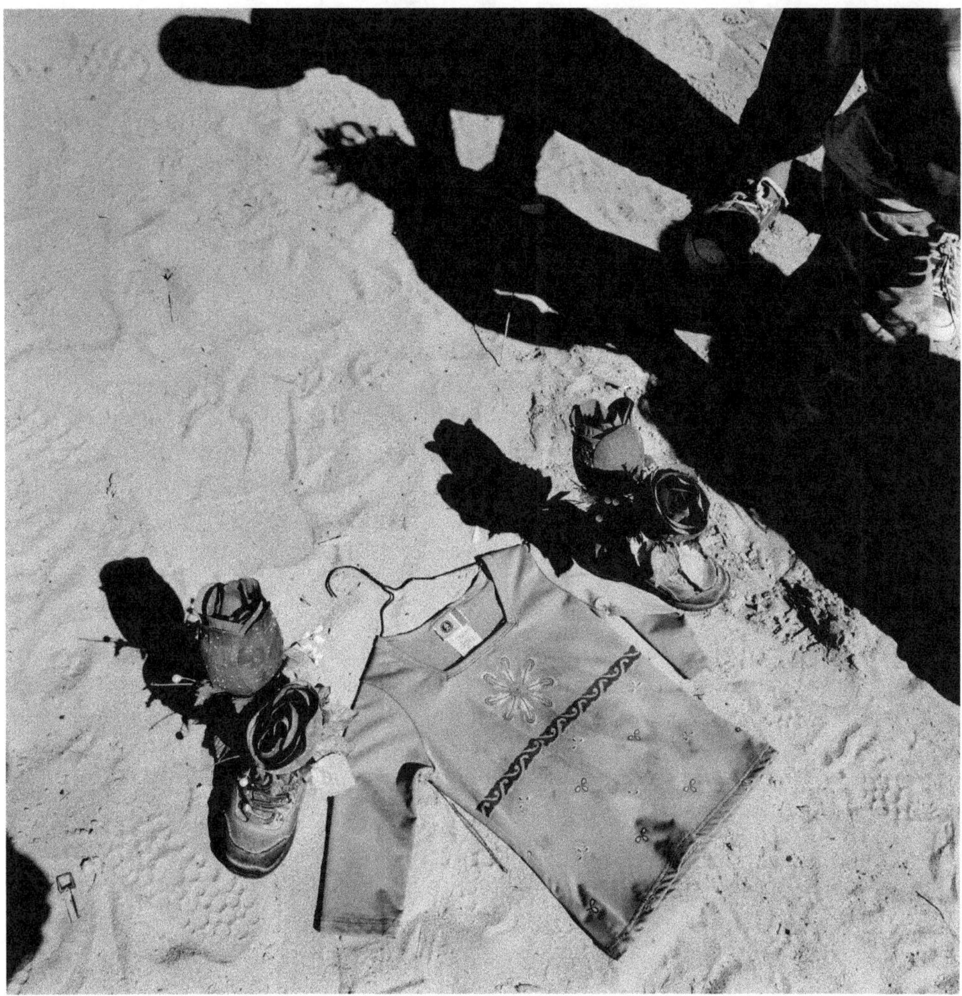

Fig. 4.15. M. Goded, Work for Justicia para nuestras hijas (2007).

tangible symbol of pain both of the grieving mother and of the dead child. After all, the Virgin Mary is present at the scene of the crucifixion, watching her son die on the cross. The woman's face also bears witness to her pain through its many lines and a tired, anxious expression. Within the haunting absence of her daughter, Goded photographs the mother paying tribute in one of the few ways available to her. Both women avoid looking into the camera's lens — their gazes criss-cross the ground under the burden of the absence that they have to live with.

If one cannot count on the authorities to bring the perpetrators of violence to justice, then how can one account for the absence left behind by the victim? Goded photographs an intimate attempt at remembering in a simply composed image of a *mise en scène* arranged from the belongings of one of the victims (Figure 4.15). It is a close up of a blue top on a wire coat-hanger lying on the sand in between two shoes filled with plastic flowers. Both the shirt and the shoes are only big enough for a child. The ground surrounding the items is filled with traces and footprints and in the top right corner of the image a person's and a child's feet are framed. Their presence is marginal within the composition, but they do cast a short shadow to the side of the items at the centre of the composition. They are left behind to remember the girl, who used to wear the small blue shirt and the shoes that have become vases. Everyday items of clothing have been turned by loss into a haunted space, made useless by the acute absence of someone who will never need them again. The family, whose shadowy presence is now marked by grief, find themselves trying to account for a voiceless void with a proliferation of objects, which have changed their use. They can no longer serve the same purpose, since dead bodies have little need for clothes, and therefore become relics, tangible symbols of absence which otherwise cannot be accounted for, but which demands to be acknowledged. The photographic representation becomes Azoulay's emergency claim, a visual message of loss and impunity. This acknowledgement of grief and longing for a missing person is necessarily an acknowledgement of their life. Goded's presence and her ability to document it validates the life of the victim as well as the grief and hurt left behind, despite the authorities' wish for them to remain silent and invisible.

Maya Goded's photographic examination of alterity exposes different ways of categorising others within hierarchies of discourse, power and cultural visibility. Her concern with race, the commoditised body and death betrays a desire to create a space for the subaltern groups which form the underbelly of the modern Mexican state, sustaining it and threatening it through their abjection. If her photography can be construed as exploitative, then it is so not just through the inequitable personal relationship between a photographer, vested with economic and socio-cultural power, and a destitute, objectified subject. Rather, it can be read as an attempt at visual reiteration of Susie's Linfield assertion that every document of barbarism is also a protest against it, sometimes even without deliberately being represented as such (Linfield 2010: 33). Framed in this way, her photographs become evidence of hierarchical, post-colonial and gendered influences producing concrete material effects on the bodies and in the lives of her subjects.

Nonetheless, it is crucial to note that despite the constant movement and exchange between the subject and abject domains, those who occupy the former enjoy more agency than the occupiers of the latter, which affects the way in which their bodies are discursively, socially, culturally and economically marked. Maya Goded as a photographer wields considerable power over her subjects in terms of how they are portrayed and sold as images. She has the choice of entering their domains, when they could not reciprocate with a similar intrusion. Visually, Goded works within a tradition of documentary photographers with a specific view of the abject, circumscribed by and creatively circumscribing the field of intelligible visual production, supported by the discursive regimes of art, economic and cultural power, and photographic publishing. Her contribution to the horizon of visibility reinforces her own status as firmly within the subject domain and the status of her photographic subjects as the constitutive outside of that domain, the border of what is seen.

The visual analysis of Goded's photographic representations of embodiment indicates a vulnerable and precarious experience of her subjects' lives. Their bodies, although to some extent mediated and re-appropriated by the photographer's lens to tell her own story, are still testament to an existence marked by their subaltern position, which is also mediated by Goded's representational intervention. Photographs of subaltern embodiment have an important role in counteracting its historical absence, particularly in the context of its liminal positionality set out in the previous chapter. By showing aspects of that liminal corporeal reality, Goded's photography subtly shifts the subject domain by fleshing out subaltern representations that were hitherto imagined as that domain's border and a void repository of negative identifications.

More broadly, the focus on the marginal body exposes the necessary flexibility within the matrices that make positive identifications possible, as the matrices cannot determine them fully in advance. The dialectical opposition between the subject and the abject is one of the conditions that make thinking possible at all and delineate the intelligibility of the body. Yet, despite its foundational significance, or perhaps precisely because of it, there is an extraordinary flexibility between the two domains and their mutual constitutive reliance on one another. Moreover, this dialectical opposition also exposes the latent potential for subversion within discourses, despite their attempts to sanction against it. This dynamic flexibility of human cognition is precisely the reason why meaning is subject to ongoing negotiation in relation to the visual and, more specifically, to photography. The epistemic field affects the way photographs are perceived and vice versa — images influence one's understanding of the world, constantly shifting the boundaries between the visible and the invisible. It is precisely this epistemic movement between the domains of visibility and invisibility in relation to photographing subaltern subjects that will be analysed in the chapter that follows.

Notes to Chapter 4

1. During the advertising campaign for British Airways in October 2009 entitled Every Day the World is Full of Opportunity, *Día de los muertos* was one of the exotic festivals used to entice travelling, alongside the Mumbai Fashion Week and Caribbean Carnivals. <http://www.youtube.com/watch?v=F75QEltLrAQ&feature=channel> [accessed 11 February 2010].
2. A *maquila* is a factory manufacturing or assembling products from imported raw materials or components, which are then exported out of the country. Its global competitiveness relies on its operation within a tax-free zone.

CHAPTER 5

On Subaltern Visibility and Invisibility

In the previous chapter, I positioned the photographic representation of the body as a site of resistance to hegemonic horizons of vision. Following on from Judith Butler's argument on the impossibility of separating meaning and materiality (Butler 1993: xi), it is important to consider the epistemological consequences of embodied vision on the notions of visibility and invisibility. This chapter focuses on the tension between the visible and the invisible in relation to photographic representation of subaltern groups and phenomena in Maya Goded's photography. In order to examine the relationship between vision and epistemology, I employ the phenomenological philosophy of Maurice Merleau-Ponty, particularly his ideas of embodied perception, which I then examine further in relation to Jacques Derrida's theories on blindness in relation to art and knowledge. I posit blindness as inherent in every act of seeing, photographic or otherwise, with tangible consequences for socio-cultural visibility. This chapter frames Maya Goded's interest in the subaltern, with an emphasis on her representation of women, as an attempt to challenge not just the regimes of visibility, but also the epistemic systems that enable their cognition. The close analysis of a selection of Goded's images from her photographic projects will demonstrate her awareness of blindness as part of seeing and representing others. Importantly, part of the difficulty in representing the subaltern is making their historical absence apparent in their photographic presence — a visual intervention across time, which aims to change the future image and definition of its subject, but which, in order to be intelligible, must acknowledge the lack that is one of the defining features of subalternity.

Visibility as a phenomenon is complex to analyse because of its immediacy and omnipresence. As J. W. T Mitchell emphasises in *What do Images Want?*, every culture is a visual culture, thus framing visibility as socio-culturally constitutive of human experience (Mitchell 2005: xiv). Within the Judaeo-Christian tradition, seeing is one of the most important attributes of God who, in the first chapter of the Book of Genesis, creates light and then uses it to guide his judgement of the newly established world. This view of God as omniscient through seeing, evidenced by Christian iconography which represents God as an all-seeing eye, has a crucial bearing on the concept of visibility in Western philosophy. This tradition is very important to consider in relation to the Mexican socio-cultural landscape, as it helps to illuminate aspects of Mexico's colonial legacy. More importantly, examining visibility from the phenomenological perspective of embodied vision helps to contextualise it within the liminal territory of thinking de-colonially (Mignolo 2012a).

Visibility and Epistemology

The concept of visibility was the focus of Maurice Merleau-Ponty's unfinished book entitled *The Visible and the Invisible* (1968), which was published posthumously accompanied by his working notes. His most significant contribution to French thought is his challenge to Descartes's theory of *a priori* knowledge, one that precedes existence. In *Phenomenology of Perception* he examines the primary importance of the human body in understanding our being-in-the-world, focusing on the impossibility of knowledge without embodiment. He argues that the Cartesian distinction between the mind and the body and its focus on perception and cognition ultimately leads an individual to consider their body as one of the objects in the world to be analysed and understood only in relation to other objects (Merleau-Ponty 2002: 70). The centrality of embodied perception in Merleau-Ponty's work has a crucial bearing on his concept of visibility, and, in that context, his engagement with Descartes's theories requires more analysis.

While showing its limitations, Merleau-Ponty also explains the value of Descartes's theory of cogito. He claims that Descartes's approach was necessary in liberating thinking and giving philosophers and scientists theoretical tools for organising their experience that avoids the pitfalls of thinking that is too empirically dominated and therefore unable to construct (Merleau-Ponty 1964: 10). Nonetheless, according to Merleau-Ponty, Descartes's mistake was in erecting his theory of cogito as a positive being, in idealising it as 'perfect of its kind, clear, manageable, and homogenous' (ibid.), which places limitations on what is possible to know. That mistake, however, is necessary to enable subsequent thinkers in their own quest for understanding (ibid.). In particular, the boundaries of Cartesian logic are a starting point for Merleau-Ponty's idea of embodied vision. Here it is important to acknowledge that the indispensability of Cartesian logic to subsequent developments in the history of thought is relevant only within the sphere of influence of Western philosophical tradition in order to avoid universalising and perpetuating the apparent transparency of Western thinkers. Bearing this in mind, the concept of embodied thinking, although clearly indebted to Western thought in its inception, has the potential of illuminating other perspectives, such as those that emerge from critical readings of Goded's photo-documentary work.

Indeed, the question of perspective as a concept is crucial to Merleau-Ponty's theory of visibility. He argues against the privileging of Renaissance perspective by claiming that there can be no one way to represent the world which comes from nature and can be relied upon to represent accurately all people and all phenomena. To the contrary, looking, seeing and representing must be made and remade in order to account for change. In that sense, Merleau-Ponty frames Renaissance perspective as a moment in time, a particular case of representing the world —

both representation and the world must continue after it (ibid.). Descartes's reliance on only one perspective in representing the world is, in Merleau-Ponty's view, an attempt to circumvent the enigma of vision through privileging thinking over seeing. Since it is not enough to think in order to see, for every act of vision is an embodied experience, Merleau-Ponty places the body at the centre of the enigma of visibility, pointing out that there can be no seeing or thinking without being. This focus on the body allows for the revolutionary possibility of being seen as a subaltern body, where *a apriori* disavowal and invisibility can be challenged from within subaltern embodiment.

Embodied Vision

Merleau-Ponty (2004: 254) focuses on determining how the sentient body can be thought in relation to vision. Because the 'total visible' is inaccessible in its entirety, the only way in which it can be accessed is through fragmentary experiences, which is why the idea of visibility is closely connected to that of blindness (Merleau-Ponty 2004: 253). As such, the bodily experience of the visible does not explain or clarify it, but physically concentrates it instead (ibid.). This partiality and incompleteness of 'the total visible' available through bodily experience is for Merleau-Ponty the paradox of being. The body that sees the world can also see itself and think of itself as, on the one hand, one of the objects of knowledge, and, on the other hand, as a sentient being. Indeed, the majority of Merleau-Ponty's philosophical output focuses precisely on the challenges of analysing the relationship between perception and knowledge within the realms of embodiment.

The concept of embodied knowledge is not just challenging to Cartesian ideas of human cognition. It also introduces several other dimensions to the relationship between the body and the world, rejecting 'the age-old assumptions that put the body in the world and the seer in the body' (Merleau-Ponty 2004: 255). Firstly, Merleau-Ponty (2004: 253) sees the partial, fragmentary access to visibility, and the ability to see oneself not as an exclusively human feature, but as a general characteristic of being in the world. In that sense, seeing partially is what the thinking body has in common with objects of its thoughts that lie outside it. Secondly, this fragmentary nature of embodied visibility highlights the difficulty in ascertaining boundaries between the self and the world, where the former is immersed in the latter (Merleau-Ponty 1964: 12). His analysis of the relationship between the body and the world as dynamic lays epistemological foundations for the emergence of theoretical frameworks where flesh and knowledge cannot be separated even if they can be conceptualised as different entities, as Judith Butler demonstrates in *Bodies that Matter.*

In analysing the relationship between a sentient body and its environment, Merleau-Ponty focuses on another aspect of embodied vision, namely its narcissistic qualities. He proposes that the embodied experience of vision and of looking at oneself is both active and passive, since it constitutes an awareness of being looked at, of functioning as an entity seen from the outside (ibid.). In that sense, 'the seer and the visible reciprocate one another and we no longer know which sees and which is seen' (ibid.). Derrida further develops Merleau-Ponty's ideas on the narcissism of vision in his *Memoirs of the Blind*. He argues that this awareness of oneself as seen from the outside is necessarily partial, since it is blind to one's ability to look. In other words, the limit of the narcissism of vision is the point where the seeing body sees itself looking (Derrida 1993: 53). Therein lies another paradox of embodied vision, where the seeing and knowing body can conceptualise itself as an image, but cannot witness itself look. In relation to photography and representation, the concept of thinking of oneself as being seen from the outside lies at the root of what makes photographic representation socially, culturally and politically relevant. It is crucial to remember that photography visualises and mobilises the very idea of the self as a phantom, an image to be looked at. Thinking critically about the repercussions of such a mode of representation illuminates different aspects of seeing as a socially constitutive activity existing within a spatially and temporally determined epistemological matrix.

The emphasis on the social aspects of visibility is, according to W. J. T. Mitchell (2005: 47), one of the most important developments in searching for an adequate concept of visual culture. In *What do Images Want?* he demonstrates the socially constitutive nature of seeing through examining the power of images and the ways in which they function as active agents altering the social, cultural and political landscapes of which they form a part (Mitchell 2005). Mitchell illustrates that the everyday reality of looking and being looked at is not merely a by-product of social relations, but an activity that is constitutive of it (Mitchell 2005: 47). Implicitly drawing on Merleau-Ponty's and Derrida's theoretical legacies, he argues the importance of vision to mediating social relationships, identifying it as irreducible to language or discourse (ibid.). While Mitchell is careful to stress the distinctions between the visual and the textual, he also argues that there are 'inescapable zones of transaction' between images and epistemology, between what is seen and what is known (Mitchell 2005: 55), building on John Berger's statement on the unsettled nature of the relationship between knowledge and vision (Berger 1972: 7).

Conceptualising looking as socially constitutive demands a return to the question of the dynamics between seeing and knowing. In order to analyse these, I first consider their temporal and spatial constraints. Merleau-Ponty's aforementioned concept of vision as fragmentary gains in this framework a new meaning, since embodied experience of vision is always bound by a specific time and place. Not only is seeing dynamic inasmuch as it relies on movement of the eye and movement of the body within a tactile and visible world (Merleau-Ponty 1964: 2–3), it also sees a moving world, where understanding follows perception. Merleau-Ponty (1964: 3) also argues that the body's immersion in the world means it cannot consider itself or be considered outside time: it has to have a past as well as a future. Still, the body perceives only in the here and now. This is yet another paradox of embodied vision — although the body has a past and a future, vision is only available as a present experience. Human experience of time as linear and always passing means that the phenomenon of vision in and of itself escapes analysis, because conceptualising vision can only ever mean 'substituting narrative for perception' (Derrida 1993: 104). This argument is relevant not only to the embodied perception of the world, but also to the perception of oneself. Seeing the world in flux and the self in flux means that embodied vision can only ever be fragmentary, whether in relation to self or to others.

In this context, photography as a form of mediated vision is unique in its ability to stop a moment in time. 'The photograph keeps open the instants which the onrush of time closes up forthwith; it destroys the overtaking, the overlapping, the "metamorphosis" (Rodin) of time' (Merleau-Ponty 1964: 17). Rodin's point of view, quoted by Merleau-Ponty in his analysis of the relationship between temporality, painting and photography, is resonant with a similar stance among photography criticism scholars rooted in the Frankfurt School traditions. To cite just one example, Siegfried Kracauer in his essay 'Photography' argues that although photography seemingly rescues subjects and phenomena from the clutches of time, and therefore death, it also atrophies them by removing them from their context and freezing them in an instant (Kracauer 1993: 433). Nonetheless, to conceptualise photography as a medium which in its attempt to circumvent the constraints of time only conjures up an image of death is to fail to account for the complex ways in which photography and representation intervene in the spatio-temporal matrix. A single frame, captured from a single perspective in a specific moment in time, can then be revisited from a variety of different spatio-temporal positions and through different subjectivities. If not a way of overcoming spatial and temporal constraints of embodied subjectivity, photography offers at least a glimpse of a different perspective, and a possibility of embodying vision and knowledge differently, which is potentially revolutionary for the possibility of subaltern representation. Since vision and knowledge relate to temporality on different terms through embodied experience, photography offers a specific mode of revisiting past sights through uncoupling spatio-temporal constraints from their image. By freezing a moment in time from a particular perspective, photography turns the subjective narcissism of vision into an image that can be shared among others across different times and places. Therefore, it also enables reflection that has an important bearing on two questions central to photography and representation, namely those of subjectivity and perception. The fragmentary nature of photography emphasises the fragmentary character of embodied vision. However partial, for the photographer every image they take is also an opportunity to witness their own gaze, momentarily circumventing the impossibility of seeing oneself look.

The temporal nature of vision and photography in relation to embodiment is particularly relevant to Goded's photographs of the missing women in Juárez, where she seeks to document loss. One of the images within the series is taken indoors in a house where one of the victims lived, framing a fragment of a wall (Figure 5.1). The wall is painted yellow and the artificial light illuminating the composition gives the image a warm glow. Within the frame of the photograph, two other frames have been captured. On the right-hand side, a small picture of a young smiling woman hangs in a brown fame with a cream *passe-partout*. Next to the photograph, a large mirror dominates the composition, reflecting the rest of the

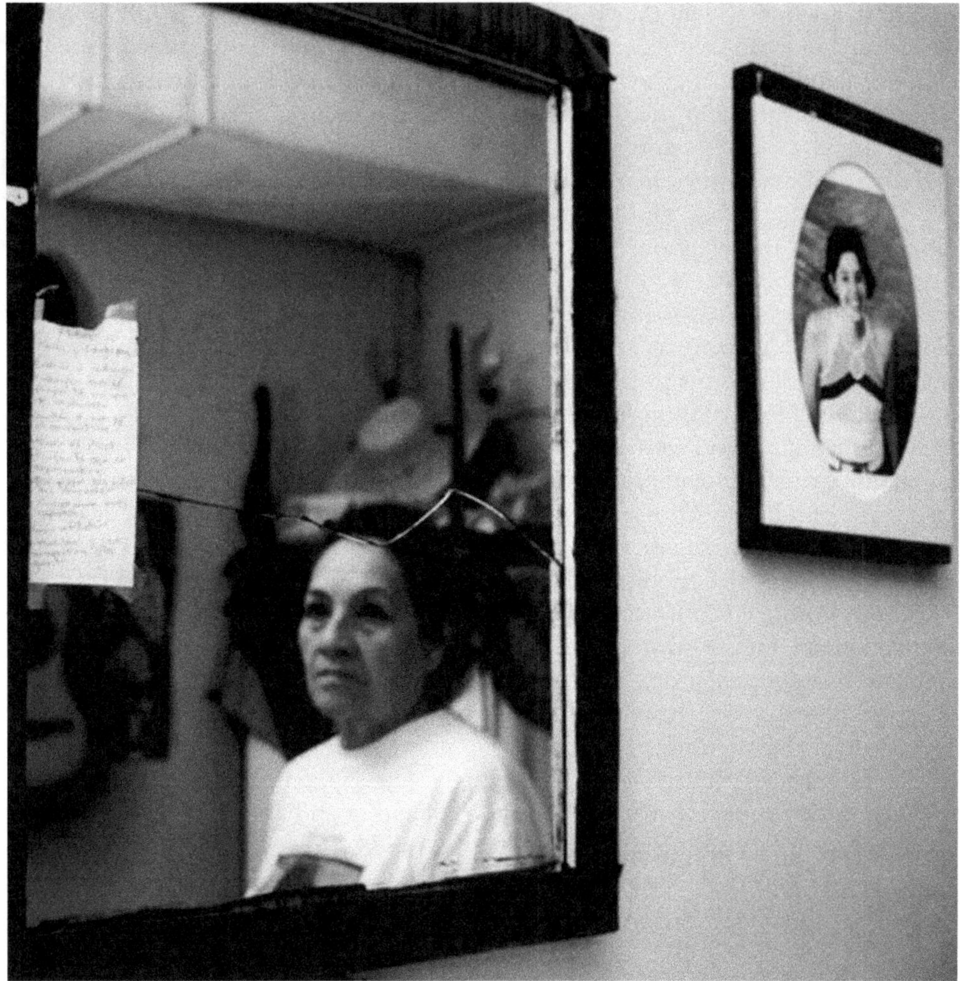

Fig. 5.1. M. Goded, Work for Justicia para nuestras hijas (2007).

room and a middle-aged woman standing in the middle of it, who is the mother of the girl whose picture hangs on the wall next to the mirror. A crack running vertically across the entire width of the glass marks her reflection. At one end of it, a small note is stuck to the edge of the mirror at which the woman is staring intently. The two women, cropped in their respective frames, come together within Goded's composition.

Using the photographs of missing women in Juárez to symbolise their loss and underline their absence is a visual method Goded uses time and again in this series. Often the photograph will act as a stand-in for a missing person in a family portrait. However, this image of the mother's reflection pictured on the same wall as a photograph of her daughter draws viewers' attention to different embodied temporalities within this one frame. The deep crack on the mirror is a metaphor of fractured time, symbolising the moment when the young woman's life was cut short, leaving her mother to contemplate her own reflection as split by grief. Three different frames isolate three distinct embodiments of temporality within the composition. First of all, the relic of memory in the shape of the missing daughter's photograph is rooted in the time before the disappearance. Secondly, the mother's reflection in Goded's photographic moment documents her palpable mourning and despair. Finally, the juxtaposition of the two temporalities creates a third one, where the image of the mother and her daughter enters a public domain through Goded's visual intervention. The lost bodily connection between the mother and her daughter is constructed here as an image of grief, emphasised by the fact that there is no one in the photograph to meet the viewer's gaze in the here and now. The mother stares sadly at a note stuck to the broken mirror; the young woman smiles into a long-absent lens. Viewers are left to contemplate a composition fragmented by loss, both in physical and in photographic terms.

Merleau-Ponty's and Derrida's theories of vision and its relationship to knowledge emphasise their fragmentary nature. Whether in relation to the world or to the self, vision is bound by spatio-temporal constraints and only ever partial, unable to perceive everything that there is (Merleau-Ponty 1964: 19). Merleau-Ponty argues that the inevitable disappointment at the human inability to represent and therefore know everything is a Cartesian legacy, which claimed 'for itself a positivity capable of making up for its own emptiness' (ibid.). He emphasises the transformative element of representation, which, without completing itself, 'changes, alters, clarifies, deepens, confirms, exalts, re-creates, or creates by anticipation' (ibid.). His argument about images that, in their passing, also 'have almost their entire lives before them' (Merleau-Ponty 1964: 19) betrays a concern with images as active socio-cultural agents capable of altering, challenging and constituting the subjects they represent. According to Merleau-Ponty, the key to understanding embodied visibility and knowledge is to accept its dynamic and incomplete nature.

The fact that every identity and every subjectivity hinges on the nexus of space and time further obscures and complicates any epistemological claims to universality. Here the concept of embodied vision enables an acknowledgement of the multiplicity of other perspectives, and makes horizons of visibility more inclusive. These horizons of visibility, and documentary photography's contribution to such horizons, are therefore not just a matter of accumulating more images within an already saturated landscape. Changing the boundaries between the visible and the invisible has a profound influence on expanding one's understanding of the multiplicity of embodied subjectivities, which photography can approximate through its apparent immediacy. Goded's photographs are in such contexts active agents of change as images that constitute new epistemologies of vision. In order to analyse further their role in expanding the horizons of vision, the next part of this chapter examines the relationship between visibility and blindness.

Visibility, Blindness and Subalternity

Derrida builds on Merleau-Ponty's concept of visibility and invisibility, but his definition of blindness is different from Merleau-Ponty's. Within Merleau-Ponty's conceptual framework, visibility relates to what is seen and invisibility to what is known (Baldwin in Merleau-Ponty 2004: 247). For Derrida, on the other hand, blindness is an inherent part of vision. In *Memoirs of the Blind* Derrida argues that even though drawing as an art form is inextricably connected to the artist's ability to see, the act of drawing itself relies on blindness, as it is through the process of turning the eyes away from the subject of the drawing that the artist is able to produce its representation (Derrida 1993). Building on Merleau-Ponty's phenomenological legacy in relation to embodied vision, Derrida emphasises not just the blindness of drawing, but also, more broadly, the blindness of representation and witnessing (Derrida 1993: 104). If vision is only possible in the here and now, fixed not only in terms of its spatio-temporal location, but also in relation to its multiple subjective embodiments, then any analysis of vision has to begin from a place of blindness (Derrida 1993). This argument has an important bearing on the relationship between vision and epistemology, since blindness has to be considered as a constitutive element that enables understanding, as opposed to an obstacle to seeing and knowing which can be overcome. That is why in the 'Translators Preface' to the English edition of the *Memoirs of the Blind* Pascale-Anne Brault and Michael Naas argue that Derrida's philosophical discussion of blindness, vision and drawing 'leaves us another way to understand the legacy of [...] vision, the legacy of representation, [and] the legacy of legacy itself' (Derrida 1993: x).

In searching for the most theoretically fruitful usage of Derrida's concepts of vision and blindness in relation to the problem of representing subalternity, it is fitting to draw a particular parallel between blindness and subalternity. Derrida's blindness is to vision what subalternity is to hegemony. The concepts of vision and hegemony are both positive notions rooted in Cartesian logic, while, on the other hand, the models of blindness and subalternity challenge that very logic. No longer locked into a theoretically paralysing position of a mere binary opposite, the concepts of blindness and subalternity have the potential to productively challenge Western epistemology from within, opening new pathways for what Walter Mignolo terms 'decolonial thinking' (Mignolo 2012a). Cartesian claims to universally applicable epistemology are a hegemonic tool that sustains a taken-for-granted ontology and holds up a specific image of the world, and a specific view of history, as its true representation (Mignolo 2005: xii). Within this positive ontology of the world, the subaltern is unacknowledged and unrepresented, sidelined by history and deprived of means of representation which could function independently of the hegemonic system. Arguably, the notions of blindness and subalternity have their roots in Western history of thought and, as such, offer limited representational options constrained by Western hegemony. Nonetheless, they also provide opportunities to question this hegemony not as a positive ontological certainty, but as a particular framework, which can be challenged, remade and deconstructed from within.

One of the main paralysing features of subaltern positions within society is their invisibility, which forecloses any potential for social, cultural, political or historical representations. In such contexts, invisibility is not a necessary by-product of vision, but a deliberate ostracising of identifications and subjectivities that do not fit within hegemonic frameworks. Documentary photography plays a very important role in such situations, a role which is specific to its character as a medium. As a particular mode of vision, photography intervenes in the dynamics between vision and epistemology, shifting boundaries of what is shown and known. Merleau-Ponty underlines the importance of thinking about vision as a specific mode of human access to being and not merely as a variant of intellectual thinking, as Descartes would have it (Merleau-Ponty 1964: 8). Vision, and photography as a specific mode of vision, is a way of learning about the self and the world, and not merely a visual confirmation of what is already known. The camera makes it possible to overcome at least some of the spatio-temporal constraints of vision, lifting particular perspectives out of their specific limits and into different contexts.

At this point, it is important to note that, just as blindness is inherent in vision, it is also one of the constitutive elements of photography. Firstly, using a camera to photograph a particular moment results in a paradoxical situation whereby the photographer has to obscure their view of what they are about to capture in order to shoot and preserve it. Secondly, the very mechanism of the shutter means that traditionally photographers could never simultaneously witness and capture the exact same moment, as the shutter would have to close in order to record the image, effectively blinding them to it for an instant. Although technological advances mean that some digital cameras no longer have mechanical shutters, the vast majority of photographic equipment does not allow the photographer to see and capture simultaneously. Furthermore, photographs are only ever partial images taken from a particular perspective and, as such, always involve a number of omissions and blind spots. For every perspective, person or phenomenon photographs show, there are countless others to which they remain blind.

How does this concept of blindness as part of seeing influence the intervention of documentary photography within socially and culturally constitutive horizons of vision? Ariella Azoulay in *Civil Imagination: A Political Ontology of Photography* (2012) examines how photography can transform seeing with significant consequences for the social and political environments in which it intervenes. The book builds on Azoulay's theory of photography published in *The Civil Contract of Photography*, which was outlined in Chapter 2. This specific view of the medium as one which requires civil imagination in order to fulfil its function of witnessing and intervening in the lives of people bound by its contract (i.e. subjects, photographers, viewers) is relevant to considering the blindness inherent in every act of seeing and the relationship between vision and epistemology. The concept of civil imagination is for Azoulay a key aspect of the nature of social relations and communication, not only in relation to photography. She argues that, although imagination is 'part of our structure of consciousness', and is indispensable to every communicative act 'we do not consciously experience it for what it is' (Azoulay 2012: 4). Although she does not explicitly challenge the Cartesian notion of cogito, the very idea that an imaginative process, which cannot be understood or experienced in its entirety, underpins human understanding demarcates the limited application of Cartesian reason. Moreover, Azoulay underlines the social and collective nature of human imagination. While acknowledging the importance of individual imagination for effective communication with others, she also argues that 'we are not the sole source of our imaginative capacities. The imagination is always shot through with splinters of images which have their source in the outside world and in other people' (ibid.). This is where Azoulay's analysis of civil imagination is particularly useful to examining blindness within the socially constitutive visibility. If individual imagination is dependent on collective imagination for its social viability and usefulness, then the individual field of vision is also similarly contingent on the wider horizon of vision. That is not to say that people or phenomena under the radar of shared socially constitutive visibility cannot be perceived by individuals, but rather to stress the collective nature of blindness. Photographers such as Goded disrupt this collective blindness by their intervention within the horizons of vision.

Maya Goded, through her choice of subjects, is already consciously working against what is seen and what is hidden within Mexico's socio-cultural landscapes, therefore using her art partly as an exercise of civic duty to witness the marginalised lives of her subaltern subjects. Through her photography, Goded weaves images of hitherto invisible communities and individuals into the socio-visual fabric, exposing not just their differences as evidence of their subaltern otherness, but focusing on the similarities between their lives and the lives of those who chose to view them, including them in a field of visual reciprocity. Her contribution to the field of vision challenges what is present in and absent from the socio-cultural landscape and provides a representation of the subaltern, which had been hitherto missing.

In order to examine the relationship between visibility and invisibility in Goded's photographs, it is crucial to focus on the issue of perspective. Her photography, despite its visually, culturally and socially transformative potential, composes a visual narrative which is told from only one perspective, namely that of the photographer. Although, as Azoulay argues in *The Civil Contract of Photography*, the photographer does not have complete power over what appears in the photograph or how it appears (Azoulay 2008: 11), the visual content of the photograph is always shown from a particular perspective because of the physical limits of the medium itself. While experimental images may layer two or more perspectives onto one photograph, they do not overcome this physical necessity to photograph from a particular perspective. Goded's explicit commitment to Mexico's marginalised communities and her evident interest in the documentary genre and its social and cultural significance are accompanied by her awareness of her individual standpoint and viewpoint. In an interview for *Revista 7.7*, a digital Spanish-language magazine dedicated to documentary photography, she explains the creative process of photography as a slow educational journey, where reading and gathering information have eventually to give way to developing a personal perspective. Far from making any claims to objectivity, she declares that she is interested in telling stories from her own perspective, however deeply they are rooted in Mexico's cultural and socio-economic circumstances.

> No creo en el documentalismo directo, en el que se supone que el fotógrafo no está y dice la verdad, la única verdad. ¡Ahí no te ves! Y, de alguna forma, siempre te ves en las fotografías. (Goded 2008: 8)
>
> [I don't believe in straightforward documentary, where the photographer is assumed to be transparent and showing the truth, the only truth. You don't see yourself this way! And you always see yourself in the photographs in different ways.]

The above statement about always seeing oneself in one's photographs acknowledges Merleau-Ponty's concept of the fundamental narcissism inherent in embodied vision (Merleau-Ponty 2004: 255). Even mediated through a photographic camera, a personal perspective is always linked to a particular body from which it originates. Perspective is therefore both a physical matter of seeing or representing others from a particular viewpoint, and of being able to conceptualise that vision from within one's own epistemological standpoint, which once again demonstrates the impossibility of separating materiality from meaning.

It is crucial to emphasise that Goded's perspective is not a subaltern one. She is a privileged, upper class and comparatively wealthy white woman of European and US descent who has the cultural and socio-economic advantages most of her subjects never enjoy. Nonetheless, the direction of her photographic gaze and her impetus to notice and represent subaltern people and phenomena in Mexico produces subaltern representations. It is important not to see this intervention as a paternalistic attempt to create another cohesive socio-visual landscape with subaltern representations providing images that, instead of disrupting visual hierarchies, merely reinforce them by providing photographic templates for shoring up the borders of socially acceptable identifications. Instead, Goded's photography creates a personal narrative that exposes the shortcomings of any visual landscape, which presumes to show it all. By embracing fractures, difficulties and invisibilities inherent in the medium and in the lives of her subjects that she witnesses, Goded finds new ways of simultaneously adding to and questioning the socio-visual landscape of which she forms a part. She includes new agents previously excluded from the field of social reciprocity and through photography demonstrates the way they participate in the Mexican socio-cultural landscape and how they reinterpret it, implicitly questioning the issue of representation in relation to issues of gender, national identity and belonging.

Representing Women

Goded has a very keen photographic interest in her own gender and its socio-cultural manifestations in Mexico. Most of her photographic work focuses on women and their lives; men are only included inasmuch as they relate to the women who remain in the centre of the image. This is a conscious reversal of the male-dominated discourse that marginalises women, who were historically only seen as important in relation to men and not as people in their own right. Judith Butler's theories on gender, previously examined in relation to the body, are relevant here because they explain that embodied meaning and knowledge are in the Western history of thought a profoundly masculine concept, which excludes femininity (Butler 1993: 33). Shifting the focus radically from men to women allows for a different theory to emerge as looking intervenes in cognitive processes and alters civil imagination. Representation plays a crucial role in this process. Goded's photography is a starting point for examining the questions of visibility and invisibility and their relationship to the idea of the feminine in the context of Mexico. Moreover, even though her primary focus is on gender, she also exposes a variety of other cultural and socio-economic factors that contribute to her subjects' subalternity, thus demonstrating a complicated interplay of different factors that affect the people she photographs, showing different facets of their marginalisation. Whether in relation to her projects with sex workers, witches or crime victims, viewers have a chance to see a myriad of abjections in a single snapshot.

Goded's largest photographic project focused on prostitution, part of which was published in the album *Plaza de la soledad*, resulted in a large amount of photographic material. As I discussed previously, Goded foregrounded her own first pregnancy as a main motivation for being interested in the bodies of other women, particularly those who are marginalised due to their sexed bodies and their sexual functions. After giving birth to her daughter and while still working on her project concerning prostitution, Goded took a self-portrait, which has weaved itself in and out of her internet-based publicity, appearing in an interview with Goded for *Revista 7.7* (Figure 5.2) and featuring on her website (2018). Shot in the same style as the photographs within *Plaza de la soledad*, the black-and-white image taken in 1995 portrays the photographer with her baby daughter María.

The young mother and her baby daughter are captured together in a bath full of water. The self-portrait's subject matter is thematically consistent with the rest of Goded's work on prostitution, where she clearly expresses an interest in the prostitutes' relationships with others, particularly their children. Both the mother and the child are naked as they are pictured floating in the bathtub, the baby lying on the mother's torso. They meet the camera with relaxed expressions on their faces, although the baby's look appears a little more quizzical than the mother's. Their mouths are slightly open and the corners of the lips are gently turned up. The edge of the water in the bathtub draws an irregular semi-circle just above the woman's head. The water surrounding the mother and her daughter is clear with gentle ripples reflecting the light. The woman appears to be holding onto the baby's legs, although they are outside the frame. The girl has both her arms raised, allowing them to float up freely. The composition of the photograph bears an uncanny resemblance to two popular devotional images painted by traditionalist painter William Bouguereau in the second part of the nineteenth century. The painting entitled *Our Lady of the Angels* (Figure 5.3) depicts the Virgin Mary holding the baby Jesus as she is standing on a throne in heaven and they are both surrounded by angels; the other one, entitled *Virgin of the Lilies* (Figure 5.4), depicts Mary and Jesus in a very similar pose against a flowery background, their heads surrounded

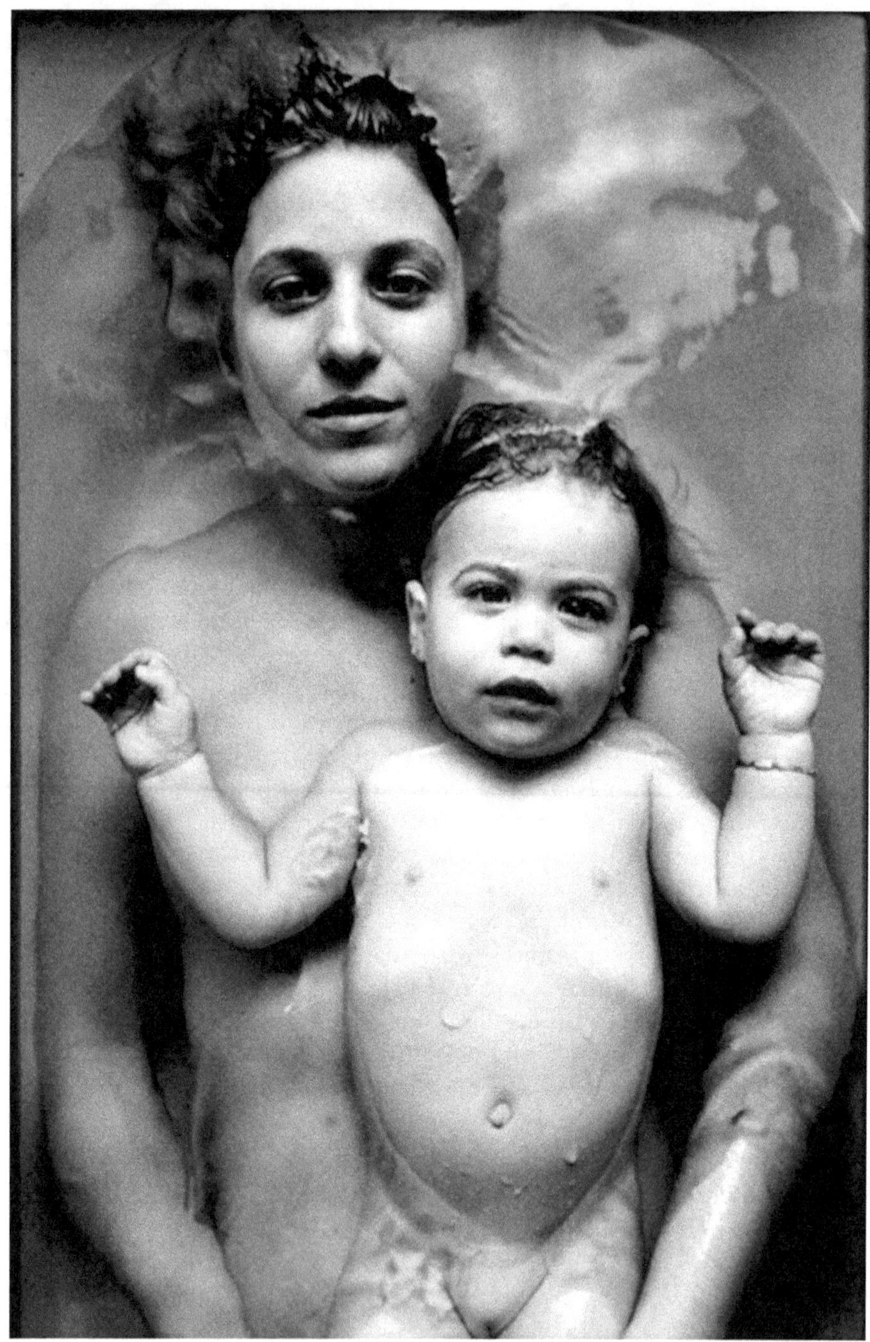

Fig. 5.2. M. Goded, *Autoretrato* [Self-portrait] (2006).

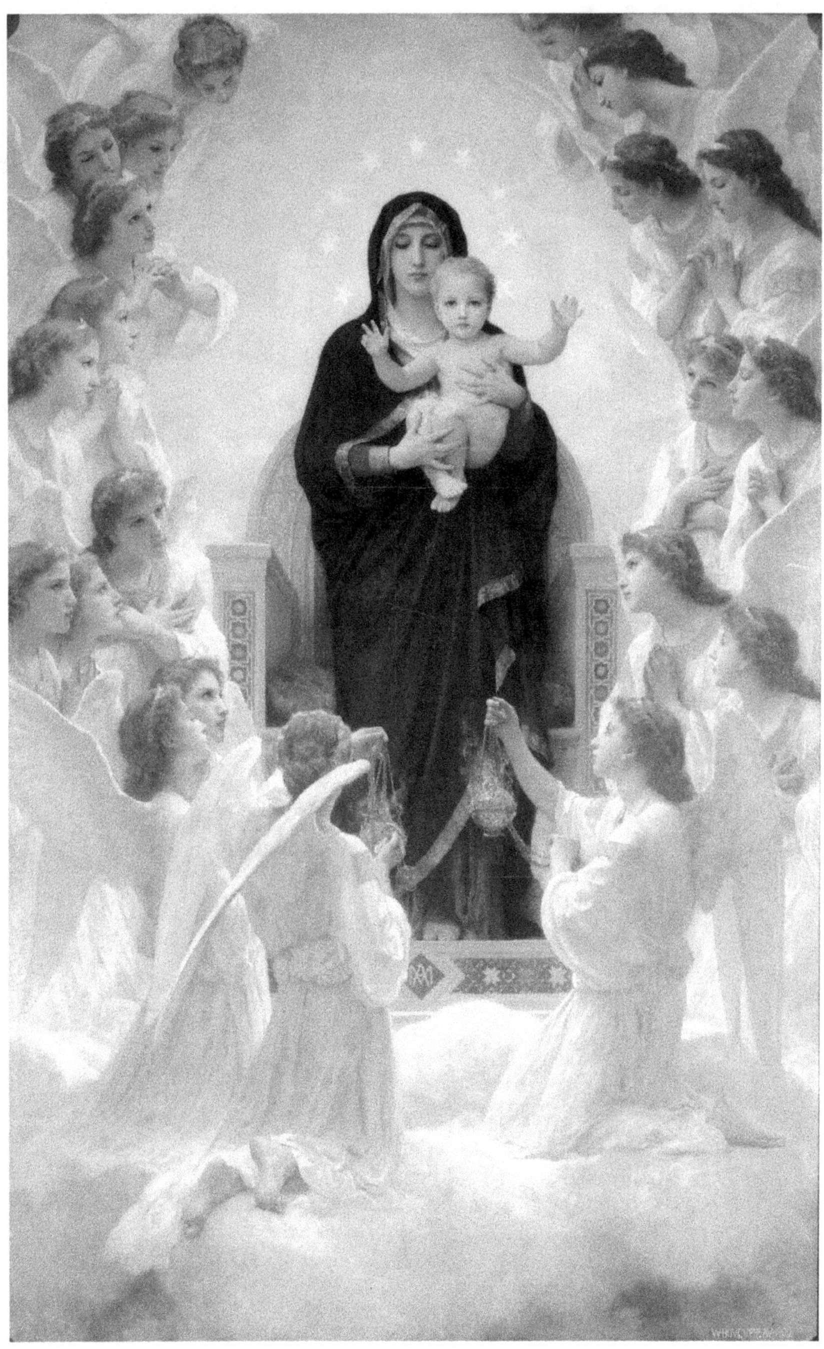

Fig. 5.3. W. Bouguereau, *Our Lady of the Angels.*

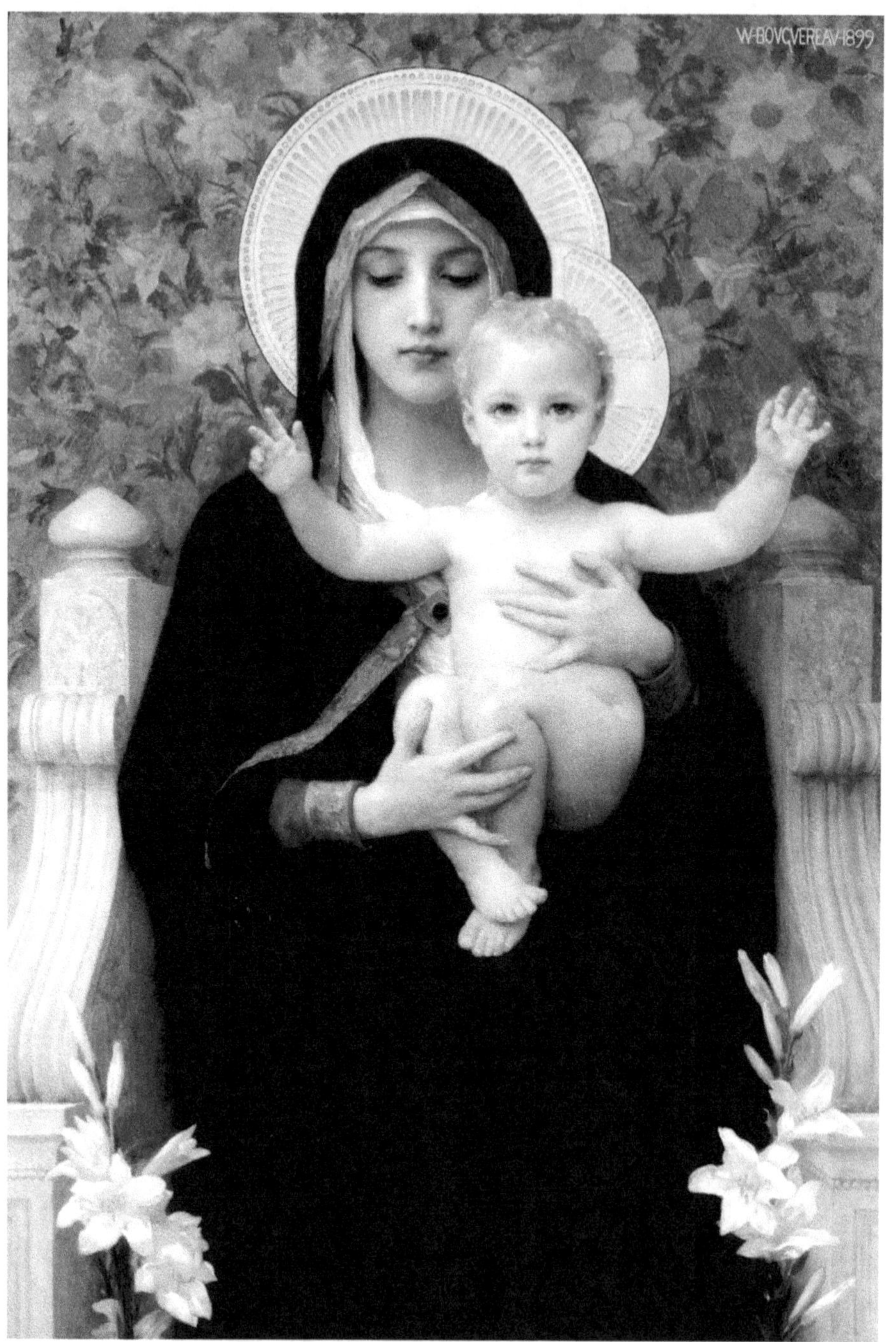

FIG. 5.4. W. Bouguereau, *Virgin of the Lilies.*

by halos. The child's pose, his proximity to the mother, and the compositional regularity of the semicircle of angels surrounding the pair in one the paintings are mirrored in Goded's photograph. How does this visual reference affect the balance between visibility and invisibility in relation to representations of subaltern women?

Because of the hegemonic status of Bouguereau's paintings, Goded's reference to the artworks' existence makes apparent the interconnected web of images and meanings that form part of the cognitive mechanisms that make visibility intelligible. By composing an everyday image of a small child and its parent taking a bath together in this way, Goded emphasises the importance of outside influences on identity formation and on one's own sense of self. She relies on the reciprocity of gazes produced by the social field of visibility for the dramatic effect of the photograph in its accurate resemblance to the well-known painting. The similarity between the images is not only relevant with regard to the meanings they produce, but also in relation to the medium of photography itself since Goded's photograph produces a visual metanarrative clearly pointing to the medium's origins in painting. The images also share a quality of serenity as their composition is classical and the face expressions of their subjects are calm and gentle. It is the similarity between the photograph and the paintings that provokes the most pressing questions with regards to gender and visibility.

The most obviously provocative effect of such a resemblance is Goded's substitution of the Virgin Mary for herself and of baby Jesus for her naked daughter named María. By showing herself and the girl unclothed this photograph lays bare the embodied intertwining of materiality and meaning, which is the epistemological foundation of the construction of gender as a social category, in Mexico so closely linked with motherhood. The corporal connection between the two subjects is visceral, the baby's belly button a bodily memory of having been formed on the inside of her mother's uterus not long before the photograph was taken. The exposed flesh of the mother and her child as well as their engagement in an intimate, regular ritual, which normally is only featured in family albums, hints at the everyday intimacy and co-dependency of raising children, where the well-being of children and carers is interlinked. This process is still mainly a female domain, and especially so in countries where patriarchal influences remain strong, such as Mexico. The paintings, however much they influence the compositional features of this photograph, offer an entirely different narrative of motherhood. First of all, the Virgin Mary is depicted fully clothed, since female flesh is inherently sinful in Catholic theology and iconography. The Baby Jesus, on the other hand, is depicted naked, but because of his gender and his status as the Son of God, the bareness of his flesh is not a sign of sin, but a sign of innocence and divinity instead. Moreover, his flesh serves as proof of his father's love of humanity, as God offers his only Son in order to redeem the faithful. The painting emphasises the epistemological connection between the baby and his father, sidelining the mother as a mere human vessel made pure, and therefore able to give birth to God, only by divine intervention. Since Mary's virginity is a crucial part of Catholic dogma, the paintings' depiction of the connection between flesh, sex and meaning is channelled through a restrictive prism of patriarchal values. The meaning here does not hinge on bodily connections and therefore is not embodied — it is dependent instead on divine ability to bestow meaning, on abstract ideas about flesh and belonging, which protect the father's lineage.

One of the most striking differences between Bouguereau's paintings and Goded's photograph is the gaze of the photographer. In the painter's depictions, Virgin Mary is looking down, as if she is purposefully avoiding the gaze of the viewer in a gesture that is meant as a sign of modesty and humility. The direction of her gaze is crucial to the idea of femininity as self-effacing, a wilful surrender of one's ability to see, and therefore one's ability to know. In *Our Lady of the Angels* and *Virgin of the Lilies* blindness that results from averting one's eyes is portrayed as a virtue of femininity, a part of female surrender to a higher, masculine force. With her eyes closed to the gaze of the viewer, the figure of Virgin Mary does not invite reciprocity of gazes. Moreover, this wilful avoidance of looking suggests a surrender of one's embodied cognition in favour of faith or knowledge passed on from a higher being, which clearly indicates women's inferior position within epistemic hierarchies. Not only does this blindness result in necessary reliance on *a priori* ideas, it also prevents the narcissism of vision from developing into introspection. To paraphrase Derrida (1993: 53), a body that cannot see cannot witness itself look. Additionally, the inability to exchange gazes with the Mother of God in Bouguereau's paintings renders her on a different symbolic and epistemic plane from God and from her own son, whose gaze is fixed firmly on the viewer despite the fact that he is depicted as an infant. The cognitive power that is associated with seeing is in these two Bouguereau's paintings clearly split along gender lines.

The Virgin Mary's averted gaze produces another symbolic effect, which was described by Derrida in *Memoirs of the Blind.* He argues that there is a significant difference between the fascination by the sight of the other and by the eye of the other. Although these two phenomena are not mutually exclusive, but haunted by one another, Derrida argues that the fascination with the other's ability to see as well as the ability to exchange looks with the other dissimulates 'up to a certain point' the 'body of [their] eye' (Derrida 1993: 106). This suppression of the fascination with the flesh by the fascination with its embodied ability to see is at the root of appreciating the subjectivity of the other as different from one's own. Eye-contact between two people implies reciprocity precisely because an exchange of looks implies two subjectivities, two ways of seeing and two perspectives. In that sense, Bouguereau's depiction of Mary renders her as a two-dimensional vessel, inscribed with the significance bestowed upon her by a higher power, defined by what she is in relation to others and how her flesh is figured not from within but from without. This is why Goded's decision to substitute the blind Virgin with her own image gazing directly into the camera, while keeping other compositional similarities intact, has important implications for the interpretative possibilities of this photograph.

According to Derrida (1992: 106), the gaze, or a possibility of meeting the gaze of the other, can be framed as a meeting of two embodied subjectivities, mutually appreciative of their singular perspectives and seeking a connection. His theory is pertinent to examining how witnessing embodied subjectivity affects one's own view of the seeing other: '[W]e are all the more blind to the eye of the other the more the other shows themselves capable of sight, the more we can exchange a look or gaze with them' (ibid.). In other words, perception of the body of the other as an agentic as opposed to a symbolic being is underlined by an implicit appreciation of their subjectivity, although these two perceptions are difficult to disassociate from one another. In Goded's photograph, her own direct gaze as a mother is powerful in its quiet insistence on considering her as a thinking, agentic subject, especially since she is also the author of the image. There is a curious visual tension between the composition of the photograph being based on classical religious paintings, where men depict women, and the intensity of the woman's gaze, in an image where she depicts herself and her daughter. Her gaze resists the classical composition and the religious references.

The image's visual similarities to Goded's depictions of sex workers are significant because they explicitly insert the naked photographer into her own work on womanhood. The cropping, focus and saturation levels as well as the intimate setting of the image are stylistically coherent with those often used in *Plaza de la soledad.* It is a visual declaration of vulnerability and solidarity with her marginalised subjects, whose flesh she exposes in her intimate photography. It is also a meta-photographic visual reiteration of Goded's belief that sharing the private and vulnerable moments of her subjects exposes her own privacy and vulnerability (Goded 2013). While projecting vulnerability, this exposure also mediates Goded's embodied, cultural power. Her ability explicitly to make her own image part of the narrative evidences her awareness of her role as a witness and a mediator, who is self-consciously and critically in charge of her own artistic output. This image, however, is also an important departure from conventional depictions of photographers, usually with a camera in hand or in front of their faces. Goded's replacement of her professional prop for her baby daughter foregrounds a different, embodied power within her own flesh. The carnal connection between the photographer and her child, with the infant foregrounded atop her mother's torso, represents motherhood as a source of empowerment.

This intertextual pictorial reference to Bouguereau's religious paintings also demands a questioning of Catholic discourses surrounding motherhood in Mexico. By framing herself in a way which mirrors the framing of Virgin Mary, Goded makes visible the interplay of gender restraints against individuality captured in her own ability to return the camera's and the viewers' gaze. It is a challenge to the self-effacement customarily expected of mothers, on Bouguereau's paintings clearly marked by the averted gaze of the Virgin Mary. Goded's replacement of the mother of God with her own seeing flesh requires an imaginative leap on the part of the photographer and the viewers to allow for an image to intervene in a cultural landscape where identities are narrowly demarcated, becoming a space where civil imagination (Azoulay 2012) can redefine visual tropes and symbols from a new perspective. Within that intersection of gazes, a subjective figurative space emerges where a representation of the photographer compared to the Virgin Mary need not mean straightforward condemnation hinged on a binary view of female identifications. It is the figure of Mary, understood here as a model of self-effacing motherhood and submissive femininity, which is explicitly questioned by its compositional and implicit juxtaposition with the naked mother and her baby, and found lacking in its ability to account for the embodied vision, knowledge and power of women. Read as an attempt to redefine gender characteristics, Goded's photograph invites an imaginative rereading of socio-cultural gendered expectations within the field of visual reciprocity, to which this book aims to contribute.

As part of the analysis of this photograph's visual questioning of gender models, it is also important to acknowledge its reliance on those models for its intelligibility. Although composing the image to resemble that of the Virgin allows for exposing the pervasive restrictive influence of praising self-effacing womanhood, ultimately it still positions the woman photographed within the patriarchal virgin–whore dichotomy. Moreover, capturing the subject with her daughter places emphasis on the idea of motherhood, still visually defining the woman according to her role as a parent. Goded's photograph is not a radical break with the concept of gender stereotyping, rather a creative reworking of existing, shared patterns which still require imagination to be reinterpreted. As Azoulay (2012: 4) claims, most of the time civil or political imagination does not work particularly hard to break or reinforce boundaries. Although inevitable, this photograph's reliance on shared gender patterns for its intelligibility and relevance is not politically, socially or culturally neutral, for it relies on the socially constitutive power of reiteration (Butler 1993: 95), which reinforces hegemonic patterns.

This shared inability to define oneself on one's own terms and the shared reliance on social patterns to recognise others and self is most striking in this photograph in the representation of the baby girl lying on her mother's torso. Her biological sex is obvious enough from the photograph since her genitals are pictured. What is also apparent from the image is the fact that despite her young age and the lack of personal agency stemming from it, her body is already being culturally demarcated as female. The baby girl has her ears pierced and is wearing little stud earrings as well as a small bracelet on her wrist. Adorning baby girls with jewellery from an early age and not doing the same for small boys is a sign of gender differentiation imposed from without. As the pictured girl's consciousness develops, it will not only involve the awareness of her body, but also the way her body is perceived by others, since reciprocity in looking and understanding is crucial for identity formation. What is the implicit message in desiring baby girls to look pretty to the extent of modifying their young bodies in the name of attractiveness and ability to display wealth? The very fact that ear piercings for girls, often done at an age when children cannot consent to them, are commonplace in many cultures around the world is a measure of how much gender as a socially constitutive category determines the way bodies are thought. Internalising societal expectations about one's own embodiment is an unavoidable part of developing awareness of one's

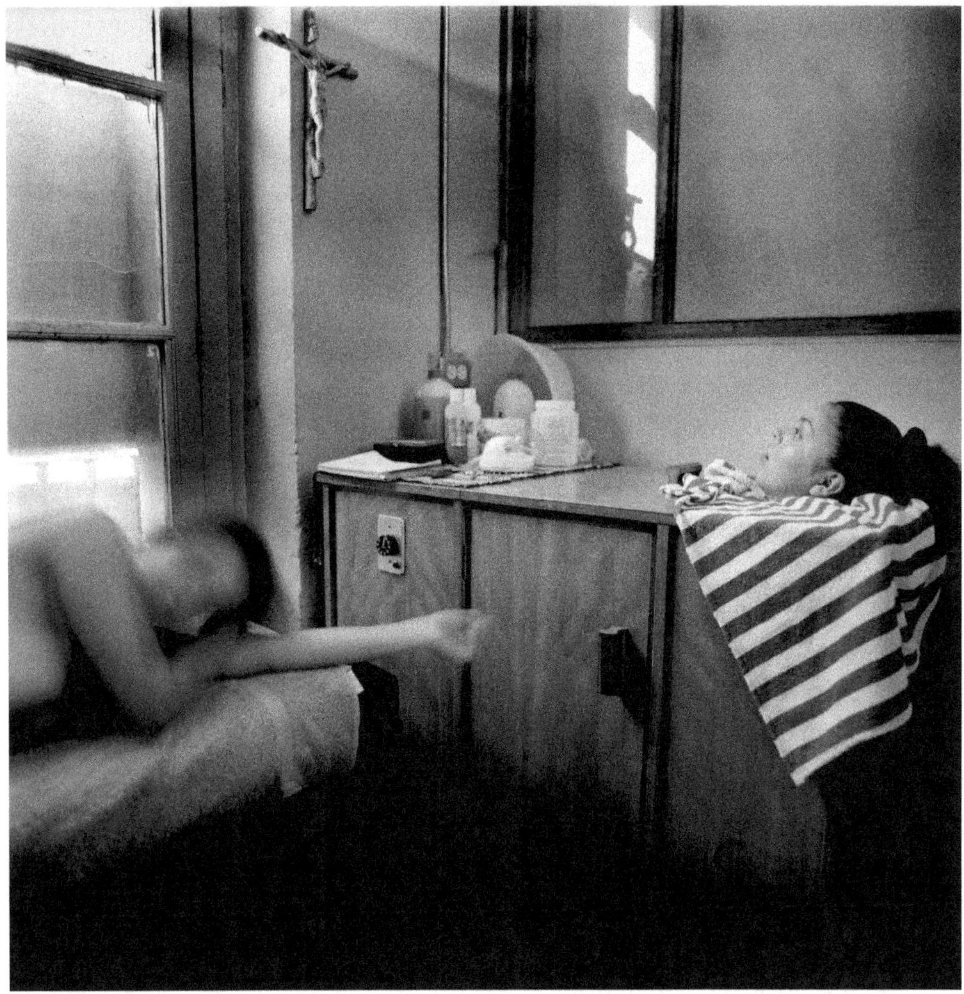

Fig. 5.5. M. Goded, Image from La Merced (2006).

gender. That is why the striking emphasis on the carnal in Goded's photograph forces viewers to reconsider the conventional ways of thinking about femininity in Mexico and ways in which idealising femininity falls short of accounting for the variety of different female subjectivities and experiences and considering women as people in their own right. Within the visual field of reciprocity, Goded questions the classical image of the Virgin from the point of view of its omissions, directing her gaze and her camera towards the lived experience of women.

Another photograph taken during Goded's work in La Merced, but not published in *Plaza de la soledad*, which figuratively questions the ideas of femininity, is an image taken in a beauty salon (Figure 5.5). It shows a corner of a bright room with a large window facing onto the street, which is partly obscured to preserve the privacy of the clients. Below the window, there is a massage bed, where a naked woman is lying on top of her towel. Her body is captured mid-motion and therefore appears blurred. The frame of the photograph cuts her off just below her breasts. In the corner of the room, there is a wooden chest, which is a small personal sauna with a round temperature gauge and a switch on the side. There is a young woman sitting or lying inside it, but the only part of her body that is visible outside the wooden box is her head, perched on the right hand-side of the sauna top, a little further along from a few bottles and jars with cosmetics. Above her there is an empty glass panel or an obscured window and she is facing a cross that is hanging next to the window. A stripy towel covers the top of the sauna surrounding the woman's head and makes it appear even more disembodied from the rest of the room and from the woman's own hidden body. The high contrast of the photograph makes the floor of the room indiscernible, and the base of the sauna box and the legs of the massage bed disappear in a dark shadow at the bottom of the frame.

Small personal saunas, such as the one pictured on this photograph by Goded, are common in many Latin American countries, although they may appear unusual to Western viewers. The angle from which this image was taken and its framing de-familiarises this everyday situation by emphasising the visual separation of the woman's head from her body. The wooden box is reminiscent here of devices used during magic tricks, where a male magician appears to cut through a container in which his female assistant is trapped. The role of the man is to saw through the device without harming the woman, while the woman's role is to appear pretty and vulnerable, confirming patriarchal expectations. The woman in the photograph is also trapped, for this particular beauty ritual requires her to stay still inside a hot container with her head immobilised by a specially designed wooden bracket. Higher personal grooming standards expected of women in comparison to men within most patriarchal settings are a sign of gendered differences between what is visible and what is hidden in relation to embodied ideas of beauty. Although a personal choice with regard to one's own grooming regime is not impossible, it is always permeated by social expectations and circumscribed by a variety of factors, not least the socio-visual landscape, which determines desirable appearances by visually perpetuating them. So powerful is this regime of representation that the appearance of female body hair, to name just one example, is virtually absent from mainstream visual culture, unless as a deliberate statement of difference, where no such widespread prejudice exists against men's body hair. Even though popular culture often portrays beauty rituals as pampering and relaxing activities, particularly for women, in fact they demand a significant time commitment and often involve subjecting the body to painful and potentially dangerous therapies. There is, therefore, another tension between the visible and the invisible at play in terms of the processes of body modification resulting from cosmetic intervention, where the effects of such intervention are naturalised and quickly become expected as the cultural norm, but the processes themselves are seen as intimate and therefore often hidden from view. It is Goded's presence and her ability to record such everyday personal processes that contribute to the intimacy for which her photographs are often praised.

Ann Cahill (2003) sets out to problematise the issue of beautifying rituals from a feminist perspective. She examines two main approaches to such processes. The first one is exemplified by references to work of Mary Wollstonecraft (1983 [1792]) and Susan Bordo (1993) who argue that beautification is an oppressive demand made on women within patriarchal structures (Cahill 2003: 42). The second one aims to analyse the re-examination of the processes of beautification by scholars such as Nancy Friday (1996) as an empowering subjective experience of embodiment (Cahill 2003: 42). Cahill underlines that as

> [a] source of both intense anxiety and deep pleasure for women, feminine beautification raises issues concerning coercion, internalization of misogynist values and beliefs, and aesthetic creativity. Underlying and connecting these disparate issues are enduring questions of women's subjectivity: does participation in socially demanded forms of beautification necessarily hinder women's ability to function as equal, autonomous beings? (ibid.)

She then continues to answer these questions from within her own subjectivity by examining a beautifying family ritual before her brother's wedding. Despite her analysis being rooted in a hegemonic context in terms of class, race, as well as economic and cultural capital, the basic theoretical questions pertaining to the value of beautifying rituals are useful for analysing representations of subaltern subjects. In moving away from either condemning or endorsing beautifying practices, Cahill's main interest is in activities that 'can create a communal experience that furthers feminist aims' (Cahill 2003: 43). The fact that Goded's subjects are often isolated when she photographs them points to a deliberate strategy aimed to diminish a sense of beautifying rituals as collective experiences.

The idea of conforming to a widely accepted definition of beauty through a series of cosmetic processes has another important consequence for reinforcing the differences between genders. Through the emphasis on the appearance of the female body, hegemonic cultural forces create a socio-visual paradigm where the female body is not respected as the source of vision, knowledge and lived experience, but instead reduced to its appearance and its function for others, an extreme example of which is prostitution. Caring for one's body in accordance with patriarchal expectations of female beauty in the context of prostitution is difficult to consider as a process of self-care. Instead, it is a preparatory ritual for the enjoyment of the prostitute's clients, reducing the body to a marketable commodity. That is why the implicit comparison between the woman in the sauna box and a magician's assistant waiting to appear to be sliced open is particularly salient. It hints at the physical danger of performing either role, and it helps viewers to appreciate the sense of vulnerability and oppressiveness in being perceived as an attractive commodity, and ways in which such perception reduces one's value as a human being to one's entertainment value. Goded's imagery proves subtly subversive, precisely because it refuses to hide the laborious, time-consuming and tedious processes that are necessary in order to conform to societal expectations of femininity, showing the prostitute in a box not as a fetishised young beauty, but as a person trapped, both literally and figuratively, in a socio-cultural matrix of acceptable female identifications.

Within the frame of the photograph, the cross hanging by the side of the window is fixed in a position which makes it impossible for the person using the sauna to avoid looking at it. The sex worker forced to contemplate a figure of Christ on the cross as she prepares for her clients is a visual allegory of the wider situations of prostitutes in Catholic Mexico. The significance of the symbol's presence is at least twofold. On the one hand, it can be seen as a source of spiritual comfort for women who find themselves in need of solace. Regardless of the prostitutes' evident lack of adherence to the Catholic moral code in relation to sex, the central part of the Christian doctrine focuses on the idea of Jesus dying on the cross in order to redeem people's sins, which, for believers, is proof of God's love. On the other hand, one cannot fail to consider the socio-cultural impact of Christianity's prohibitive attitude to sex, which produces unattainable ideals of female sexuality and motherhood that inform gendered expectations. In that sense, Christian redemption is only necessary because of Christian condemnation. Ingrained in the social fabric of Mexico through the process of imperialistically motivated conquest Catholicism is a powerful political and socio-cultural force. Hence the woman's extremely fixed position in front of the cross in the photograph is an apt visual commentary on the impossibility of escaping the restrictive codes that ostracise women such as her. The fact that her body is hidden in front of the cross is a visual reference to the Catholic perception of the female form as intrinsically sinful, which underpins the importance of the virgin birth to the doctrine. Whether the woman photographed draws comfort from the presence of the cross or feels condemned by it is impossible to know, but the situation she finds herself in, figuratively as well as literally, leaves her no other choice but to position herself in relation to the Catholic matrix.

It is important to return to the uncomfortable photographic effect produced by the visual separation between the woman's head and the rest of her body, concealed within a box. As argued above, it is a destabilising tactic making viewers reconsider the woman's position in relation to society's expectations with regard to beauty, religion and morality. The discomfort of seeing the head visually severed on top of the chest is relevant for at least two reasons. By splitting the body at the neck, Goded plays on viewers' expectations with regard to the bodily integrity of the people she photographs. In relation to the woman's job, it also becomes a visual representation of the separation of the mind and the body required of prostitutes, who have to put aside their preferences with regard to their own bodies for the sake of fulfilling someone else's. The boxed body therefore becomes a commodity, as the head ghoulishly perched on top of the box does not have dominium over it, rendering it doll-like and inhuman in its constricted invisibility. Moreover, hiding the body where one expects to see it forces viewers to think about the hidden flesh, which underlines the crucial role of civil and political imagination in the visual field. Contemplating the peculiarity of seeing a head without a body also makes visually apparent the fallacy of Descartes's concept of human cognition, which ignores the bodily aspect of both vision and knowledge in favour of abstract ideas. Far from introducing clarity, separating the thinking head from the rest of the body produces an epistemological conundrum that Merleau-Ponty aimed to question when he asked for the age 'age-old assumptions that put [...] the world and the body in the seer as in a box' to be rejected (Merleau-Ponty 2004: 255). In Merleau-Ponty's work and in Goded's photography, the metaphor of a body in a box helps to explain the concept of embodied vision and knowledge as an approach which aims to produce a different way of understanding ourselves and the world, one that is not dependent on *a priori* principles, but stems from embodied experience of vision and knowledge. By bringing out subaltern people and phenomena in her photographs, Goded makes apparent the socio-cultural invisibility which plagues her subjects, thus exposing the current visual as well as epistemological regimes as incomplete and in need of constant visual and theoretical intervention in order to become more inclusive and more able to account for the intersubjective variety of embodied experiences.

Goded's project on witchcraft in northern Mexico entitled *Tierra de brujas* is another example of her artistic intervention as a photographer who seeks to visualise invisible phenomena. The title of this photo-essay is significant because it links the idea of land to the women who occupy it, when historically women were excluded from holding any stakes in real-estate and, to this day, only 1 per cent of wealth belongs to women (Reddy 2011). Therefore, before looking at photographs, viewers are forced to consider the concept of ownership differently, not from the viewpoint of the state or of the land-owning classes, but from the subjective point of view of embodied reality, which necessarily involves occupying a physical space on this earth, regardless of one's legal status with regard to that space. The witches, despite their liminal status as outcasts who are feared and needed in equal measures by the communities who rely on them for healthcare, are in the title framed at the centre of their space. Moreover, *Tierra de brujas* is another of Goded's attempts to picture women considered socially undesirable or dangerous in a different light, already seen in her work on prostitution. According to Kaja Finkler (1994: 80), the notion of witchcraft in the popular imagination in Mexico often becomes the symbolic repository for unexplained or incurable ailments and various misfortunes, thereby shifting responsibility for the bodily or social ills onto a particular group of ostracised women.

In using the word *bruja* in the title of her photo-documentary Goded makes a political statement, because, as Irene Lara argues, calling a woman *bruja* marks a desire 'for her social death, an attempt to silence her bodymindspirit' (Lara 2005: 2011). Including that word in the title makes apparent the subaltern positions of women labelled as *brujas* and exposes the difficulties in forging their representation in terms unrelated to pejorative, sexist terms aimed at circumscribing desirable female identifications within patriarchal paradigms. Lara also argues that in Latin America the association with sorcery carries an additional racialised neo-colonial stigma, where women practising 'transgressive knowledge about nature, spirit, and the erotic' are also labelled as 'superstitious' and 'primitive', ostensibly standing in the way of progress by upholding 'indigenous *conocimientos*' (Lara 2005: 12). Thus the title itself reveals a multiplicity of female subaltern positionalities of Goded's subjects, who are actively excluded not just from their immediate environments but also from the social field of visual reciprocity.

The exclusion of women from the field of social reciprocity has a long tradition in Mexico that reaches back to colonial times. Jean Franco in *Plotting Women: Gender and Representation in Mexico* (1989) claims that colonial society made every effort to contain women, who were neither in convents nor under the care of their male relatives, in *recogimientos*, although it was not always successful (Franco 1989: 55). Even before the arrival of the Inquisition in New Spain, there was no legitimate social space for a woman with no family and no estate, unless she could rely on the charity of the clergy (Franco 1989: 68). Franco argues that because the Inquisition was founded to maintain 'the purity of the system' (Franco 1989: 56), examining its proceedings reveals how subalternity is produced in the quest for discursive and symbolic hegemony. In her study of Inquisition trials from New Spain, Franco examines how the Holy Office began persecuting women at the time when the power of the confessional as a source of control began to decline, and describes the fear instilled by the prosecutions as a powerful effect of power (Franco 1989: 58–59). The Holy Office's lack of tolerance towards any female transgression or form of independence was especially apparent in its persecution of *ilusas* — women, who could not be labelled witches, but who were not under the control of their husbands or fathers or in a convent. By underlining the importance of embodiment for transgressive women in New Spain, Franco argues that the body can be a powerful site of resistance 'when the official institutions have closed off or monopolized all other discursive space' (Franco 1989: 76). Seeing Goded's work within this historical legacy illuminates the intersectional subalternity of her subjects in *Tierra de brujas* and explains the origins of the social ostracism they suffer.

One of the photographs from the series depicts an old woman getting dressed in her room (Figure 5.6). The frame is tight and constrained to the extent that the woman's bent back is cut off. The photograph is shot from below, emphasising the compositional dominance of the woman pictured. She is sitting down in a grey plastic chair, bending down to pull her shoe on. The contrast of the photograph is high, where a wide beam of light illuminates the central figure, but the rest of the room remains rather dark. There is a small chest of drawers with a mirror on top against the wall, next to a small pile of boxes with swathes of fabric on top that are mostly obscured by the figure of the woman. The woman's face, only partially visible at the top of the frame, is concealed by her own hair and by dark shadows making her facial features indistinguishable apart from a prominent nose and a sunken cheek. The woman's skin is a deep olive colour. Her hand stretches down towards her heel in order to pull on a light-coloured, worn loafer. The skin on her forearm appears aged and wrinkled. She is wearing light-coloured tights as well as a skirt and a blouse made out of shiny material in pale pink. How does this photograph of an old woman getting dressed help in an analysis of gendered visibilities and invisibilities in Goded's work?

The photograph's colourful chiaroscuro makes the woman's dress the most prominent part of the photograph, as the shiny material reflects light, drawing attention to its baby pink hue. The woman's top is pleated and her skirt is smooth.

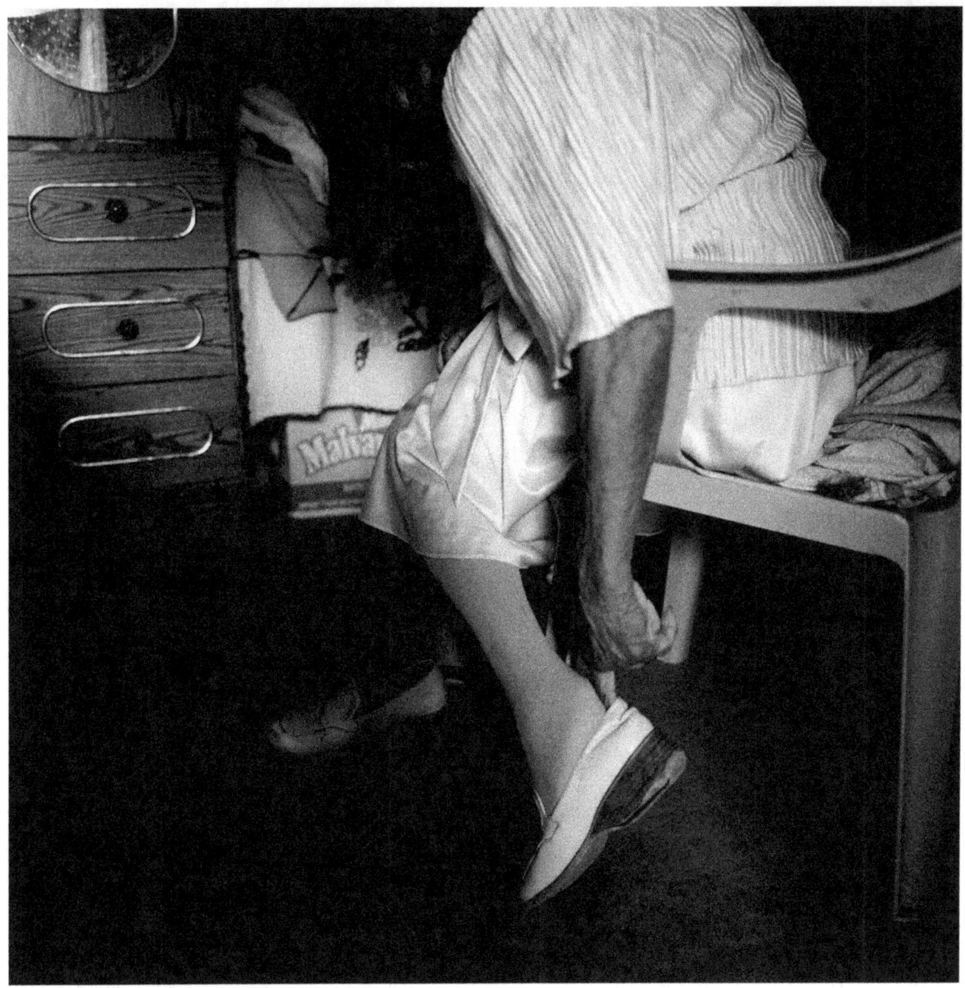

Fig. 5.6. M. Goded, *Tierra de brujas* (2008).

The contrast between the woman's aged skin and the infantile colour of her clothes strikes at the centre of viewers' assumptions about age-appropriate dress. Once more Goded probes the socially constrained ideas of feminine beauty, where clothes play a significant part in dressing women as objects to be admired, and are highly conventionalised through the fashion industry. The dominance of pink as a girl's colour, only prevalent in Western societies in recent decades, is now part of gender-specific expectations globally, influenced by the West's hegemonic position and its effects on worldwide fashions and markets. It is a striking example of how quickly trends can become naturalised and materialise as an expected part of gendered expectations influencing ideas of childhood and parenthood, when, to state the obvious, there is no intrinsic need for girls to wear pink any more than for boys to wear blue. Yet, this socially driven need to differentiate between genders from an early age produces strong visual associations between certain colours and situations, which Goded is implicitly questioning in this photograph. Framing the old woman in a dress which seems out of kilter with her age and her socially ostracised function as a witch points to the invisibility of older women within the field of visual reciprocity. The surprising effect of the unexpected attire in this photograph suggests that there is freedom in social ostracism resulting from occupying a liminal social position. If following gendered social conventions is a manifested desire for conformity and inclusion, then defying it is 'tantamount to civil disobedience' (Koo and Reischer 2004: 302), which can be read as both a cause and a result of social ostracism.

The socio-cultural importance of the woman's dress is emphasised in this photograph by the fact that she is captured while putting her shoes on. By taking the picture in such circumstances, Goded visually references countless photographs of women and girls preparing themselves or being prepared for rituals such as weddings, first communions, *quinceañeras*, etc. Since the woman's appearance is indicative of her family's social position and wealth, their presence on days of special symbolic significance is highly fetishised, to an extent that often photographs will be taken of girls and women as they are readying themselves for the event, even though normally such preparations are hidden from view, as argued above. Therefore, female social visibility is intertwined with the way women's physical appearance is linked to rituals, which usually only occur in their youth. That is why seeing an old woman dress herself is breaking the visual mould and challenging the socio-cultural implications of the highly conventionalised field of visibility. Goded turns her camera precisely towards the subaltern, neither a nurturing mother nor a young beauty, a blind spot across the socio-visually constituted choices of acceptable gendered identifications. The theme of the family album is employed here again, where Goded subverts viewers' expectations once more by copying conventions of domestic photography with unconventional subjects, normally excluded from such photography. Goded's witnessing enables the woman to become visible and, through her mediated presence, exposes the conventions of portraying femininity as well as the invisibilities they create through the expected emphasis on youth and beauty.

Another aspect that makes Goded's series on sorcery in northern Mexico significant in terms of visualising gender constraints concerns motherhood. Her other photo-documentaries, particularly her work on prostitution and the Juárez murders, are often focused specifically on the bonds between mothers and children and in that sense *Tierra de brujas* constitutes a stylistic and thematic departure. In my interviews with Goded, she emphasised the way the witches differ from other women in their area in their independence and childlessness (Goded 2013). The restrictive gender roles, which provide socio-cultural templates for women mainly in terms of their physical appearance or servitude to others, leave old and childless women on the margins of socially acceptable feminine identifications. Once more, Goded's visual intervention is ethically complex. On the one hand, *Tierra de brujas* shows independent women practising their healing power despite the disapproval of the wider society, which can be framed as an act of defiance against patriarchy and against the imposition of neo-colonial values (Lara 2005: 12). On the other hand, her portrayal of the women is conventional inasmuch as they are photographed as childless outcasts engaged in exotic healing rituals. This is a common difficulty in visually exposing subaltern positionalities, recurrent through Goded's work, which stems from the impossibility of creating a representational regime on one's own terms. There is an ethical contradiction in images of subalternity that, often at the same time, provide hitherto missing representation but also mark out their subjects as others within hegemonic representational regimes, which they rely on for their intelligibility. It is precisely this ethical contradiction that requires analysis in order to illuminate the collective blindness inherent in socio-cultural fields of visual reciprocity.

The Blind Spot of Gendered Perspectives

The ethical problem of whether an image of subalternity is a tool that either undermines that subaltern position or helps to constitute it is a question of perspective, both visually and critically. Once again, Ariella Azoulay's concept of a civil contract of photography is indispensable in analysing socially engaged documentaries. In relation to Goded, it is pertinent to analyse Goded's choices in terms of her subjects, since they broadly determine the content of her images, and contrast them with her own view of her work. Goded is acknowledged through many humanistic photography awards as a photographer with a particular interest in shunned communities, which is evident in her artistic output and the responses it elicits. Although she describes her work as documentary, in interviews she also acknowledges her subjectivity in framing the themes that interest her (Goded 2008: 8). In acknowledging the partiality of her vision and perspective, she emphasises the socially constitutive intersubjective nature of looking, which then allows her to mediate embodied perspectives of her subaltern subjects, normally shunned and denied the opportunity for representation.

Moreover, Goded is also aware of the limitations of the medium itself in terms of its ability to provide a coherent narrative, for photography is perceptibly partial in spatio-temporal terms. The photographer's propensity for capturing the same sights and the same subjects from different perspectives and during different events, but within the same documentary narratives, is a meta-photographic device aimed at de-familiarising images. Through showing various frames of the same people, places or events from different perspectives, Goded emphasises that her photographs are partial accounts of her witnessing. The tight framing and cropping of so many of her images also contribute to the impression that the visible image is fractional. Such tactics resist building a coherent, totalising visual narrative and point at the absences which are a constitutive part of representation, thereby building visual awareness of partiality in seeing and representing. This awareness is crucial since it indicates not only the blindness of Goded's documentaries, but also the invisibilities within the visual landscapes of which she forms a part. Furthermore, Goded's particular focus on the subaltern shows the material consequences of invisibility enforced by a hegemonic representational system with claims to universality. She builds a complex visual narrative where she creatively reworks representational regimes without making totalising claims, thus producing a more egalitarian socio-visual landscape, introducing new agents into the field of photographic reciprocity.

All of Goded's major photo-essays attempt to explore the spatio-temporal constraints of the medium of photography. Whether in capturing a baby's funeral in *Tierra Negra*, documenting a relationship between a mother and her daughter in the run-up to the child's first communion in *Plaza de la soledad*, photographing prison walls in *La vida oculta* or fragmenting landscapes in *Tierra de brujas*, Goded's photography is dynamic in showing people and communities in flux. Her propensity to frame the same people and the same sights from different perspectives introduces an element of polemical multiplicity into her photographic practice. It also practically shows perspective as a shifting tool in representing others, not a static technique that offers objective access to the captured photographic referents. By visually revisiting the same people and situations, Goded prevents viewers from quickly moving onto other images, since this purposeful repetition builds familiarity and invites questioning of the unseen.

One of the most dramatic effects produced by this technique of photographing similar situations from different perspectives or at different times are two images captured by Goded in the red light district of La Merced (Figures 5.7 and 5.8). They both show a young woman sitting on the edge of a bed. Both are framed to show her head, torso and hips as she is sitting down on the bed cover, leaning back slightly on her left arm. They are both taken in a room in one of the hotels in La Merced, and the furniture as well as the room's sparse décor is the same. On both photographs the girl is wearing a black bra and a pair of black, high-waisted trousers. She is wearing a watch on her left wrist and subtle make-up on her face. Both images are shot at eye-level and have very similar chiaroscuro, lit from the right-hand side of the photographs by natural light, most probably coming through a window. The girl's face and her body are well lit from the right, but a lot more shaded on the left, and she has a very similar, neutral face expression on both images. One of the images is taken from a slightly shorter distance than the other, but the most striking difference between them is the fact that the girl appears to be wearing a wig on at least one of the photographs. The image that is more close-up shows the girl with long, flowing and relatively fair wavy locks, cascading down to her waist from a hairnet fixed at her hairline. The photograph taken a little further away shows the same woman with her black, thick hair chopped into a short bob with a fringe, the hairstyle reaching just above her earlobes.

The difference in hairstyles between the two photographs highlights the importance of physical appearance and conventionally defined attractiveness for young women, particularly those who rely on their sexual appeal for their livelihood, as the prostitutes in La Merced do. There is also an element of transformative surprise to the images, where, despite all the similarities, the different haircuts transform the girl's face and parts of her body, drawing viewers' attention to her agency over her physical appearance. The fact that on at least one of the photographs the young

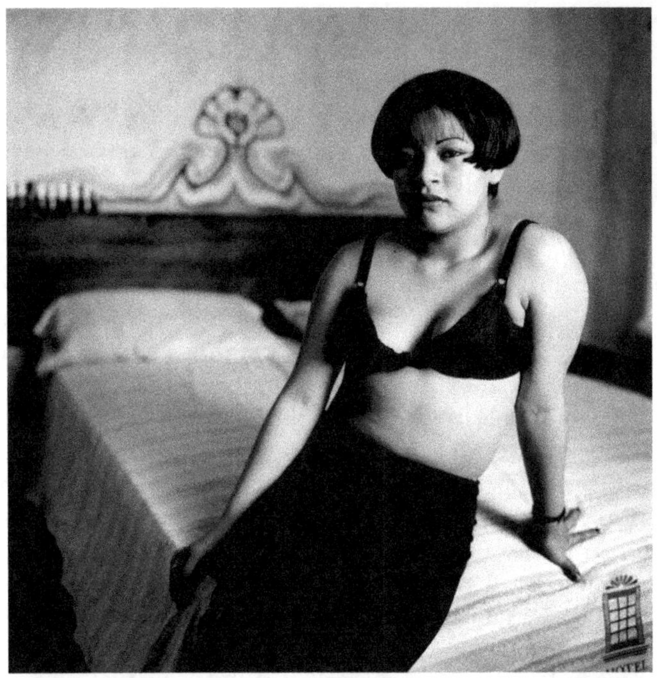

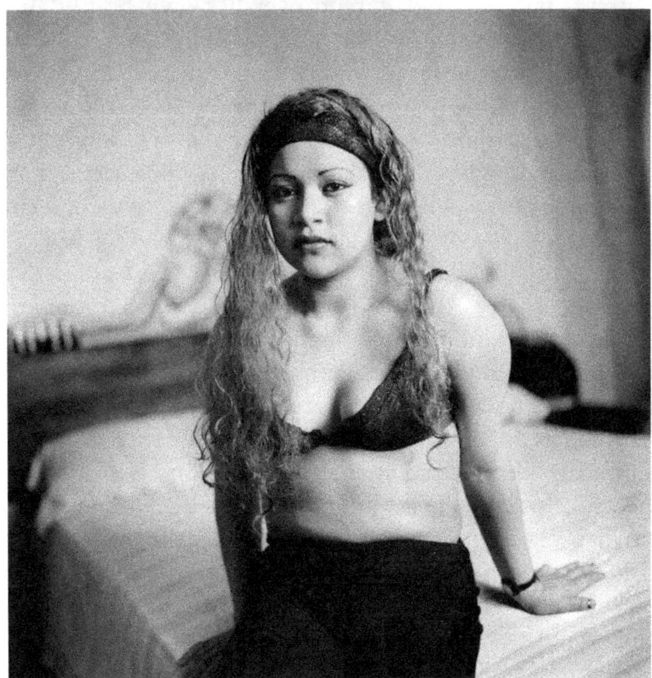

Figs. 5.7 and 5.8. M. Goded, Images from La Merced (2006).

woman appears to be wearing a wig shows how ways of achieving an expected level of attractiveness are a performative spectacle requiring props to showcase supposedly natural sexual appeal (Wolf 2002, Butler 2008).

What the photographs also achieve in their similarity is an impression of entrapment. While the woman's hair may change, the rest of her surroundings remain eerily similar, symbolising her fixed position as an ostracised sex worker in a predominantly Catholic, traditional society. Her agency over her appearance is a poor substitute for the lack of agency she suffers over her environment. The focus on hairstyles also helps to underline the superficiality of society's concern with women's beauty, as here the change in appearance between the two photographs reduces their subject to a doll-like figure waiting passively on the same bed with the same dispassionate facial expression. In framing the two photographs in almost the same way and by publishing them both, Goded (2008: 8) again hints at the repetitive nature of the work of her subjects, who have a high quota of clients per day that must be met on pain of beating from their procurers. The young woman meets the camera's and the viewers' gaze in the same way she would meet the gaze of yet another client. Figuratively speaking, that embodied gaze draws every viewer into the same exchange of flesh for money. Although Goded explicitly tries to avoid victimising her subjects, the story she tells with these two images is one of entrapment and limitations, where the field of personal expression is confined to the girl's haircut, but does not extend over her own bodily autonomy or her ability to change her circumstances. The images expose the contrast between the body as a symbol and the body as an agent, where reducing the photographed subject to the former inhibits its potential as the latter (Wolf 2002). Nonetheless, through the repeated exposure of Goded's photography, the woman's young face and body become an embodied statement of her subalternity and a stance against invisibility, haunted by the collective social blindness which forms part of the stigma of prostitution.

Goded's resistance to building a coherent image of the lives of her subjects and her insistence on stylistic devices that de-familiarise the conventions of documentary photography have important epistemological consequences for ways of understanding her output. Since she is a photographer interested in women and their lives, her techniques also challenge accepted norms in gendered terms. By representing women normally excluded from the social gaze, Goded implicitly questions the notions of femininity that guide such a gaze, posing a challenge to gendered roles and expectations through a variety of embodied subjective positionalities she presents in her photography. Although the statement Goded's photography makes on sexism is not explicitly combative, it does question the notion of human worth as tied to gender. That Goded's ambition to represent disenfranchised and marginalised communities should produce several collections of photographs where women dominate visually is, in and of itself, a visual acknowledgement of radical inequalities. The women's embodied, mediated testimony is politically charged because of their clear inability to fulfil socially expected norms, which is a judgement on the suitability of those norms rather than the value of subaltern subjects unable or unwilling to comply with them.

Nonetheless, although Goded clearly engages with politically charged social issues such as racism, sexism or impunity, she is also framing them from individual embodied perspectives of people over whom she holds a socio-cultural form of hierarchical power in her role as an educated, privileged, white photographer. This is where chosen perspectives are crucial to analysing Goded's ethical engagement with her subjects. In her awareness of her own photographic practice as partial witnessing, Goded confesses to carefully choosing situations and frames.

> [W]hen you get to a place where you want to work, I think you first have to be very *respetuoso*, respect the people, and it's a relationship of equals. You can never feel that you are superior because you are taking the photos. It's like you need to really live with the people that you are photographing, and to learn, and to really get inside that something that you want to work with. (Goded 2013)

This is particularly apparent in her treatment of the victims of Ciudad Juárez murders and their families. The series is filled with empty rooms, grieving families and mothers holding onto photographs of their young daughters, but the mutilated bodies of the murdered women are never shown. That choice to avoid showing a crime for fear of further objectifying its victims as a spectacle of violence, as well as Goded's admission to not taking photographs in situations she deems too ethically challenging (Goded 2008: 8) demonstrates a heightened awareness of photography's agency within the field of visual reciprocity and its effects on individual subjects. Taking photographs as partial documentary accounts is not a simple choice between visibility and invisibility, for it also has to take into account the complex relationship that vision and blindness have with epistemology and the socially constitutive nature of looking. In ethically challenging circumstances, Goded's approach is to be open and honest about her intentions as a photographer and cooperate with her subjects (ibid.), pointing, on the one hand, to the idea of photography as a social practice, and, on the other hand, to challenging paternalistic assumptions that would deem subaltern subjects incapable of informed consent.

In order to examine further Goded's photography and its relationship to socially constitutive vision as a partial and time-constrained phenomenon, an analysis of one of her photographs from *Tierra de brujas* will conclude this chapter on visibility and invisibility. It is a colour photograph of an old couch abandoned in a desert (Figure 5.9). Both the saturation and the contrast of this image are relatively low and its colour palette consists mainly of different shades of rosy beige. The old couch dominates the image, placed to the right of the composition on the side of a desert track. It is barely recognisable as a comfortable piece of furniture, since all that is left of it is a wonky wooden frame and rudimentary springs that would have once supported the seat and the backrest from within. On the left-hand side of the couch there are broken planks of wood or medium-density fibreboard (MDF), sticking through the gaps between the springs. Two long-abandoned plastic bottles, which are almost exactly the same colour as the sand, lie by the bottom of the couch, their white caps clearly visible against the ground. The atmosphere of the photograph is calm but also very desolate, partly through the sparseness of the landscape and

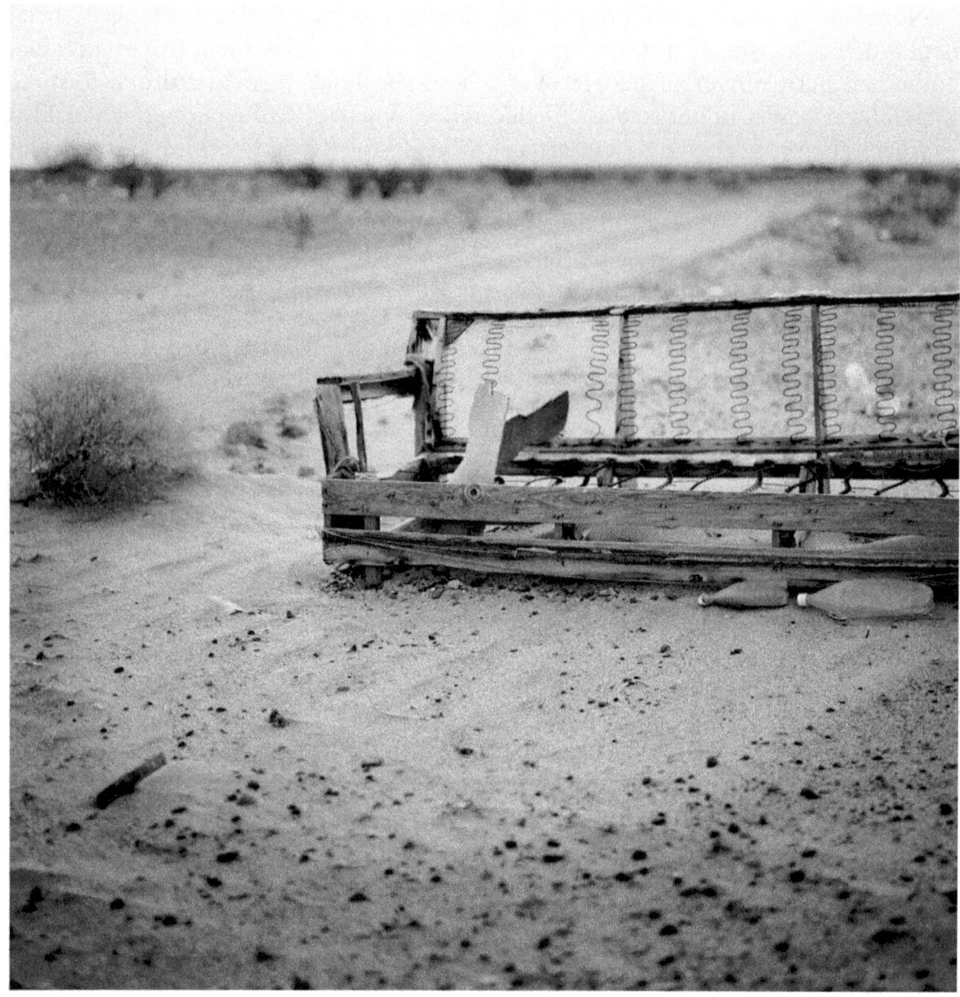

Fig. 5.9. M. Goded, *Tierra de brujas* (2008).

partly through the lack of evidence of any animal or human life, apart from the dusty road and the old couch.

Photographing a piece of familiar, everyday furniture normally associated with comfort and relaxation in the middle of a desert and in a state of disrepair is visually arresting and surprising. It draws viewers' attention to the everyday partiality of vision by de-familiarising an everyday object, showing precisely what is normally hidden. In that sense, the old, dilapidated coach may be seen as a metaphor for the socio-cultural position of Goded's subaltern subjects. Despite forming part of the social fabric, their lack of representation renders them invisible, much like the inside of the couch normally hidden by a cover. Human invisibility, in contrast to that of the inside of the sofa, has crucial effects on horizons of vision and their socially constitutive nature, which determine hierarchies and structures of power with significant socio-cultural influence. Nonetheless, the two invisibilities, one in relation to an old piece of furniture, the other concerning subaltern positionalities, are both an intrinsic part of human vision, which is a partial and temporal phenomenon. The couch's location in the middle of a dusty desert, as well as its poor condition, references the biblical promise of everything turning to dust, reminding Western viewers of their reliance on Christianity for their understanding of time. It visualises not just the limited lifespan of household items, but also photography's relationship to death and its ability to fragment the passage of time into single frames. Moreover, this lyrical photograph of the dishevelled couch is a stylistic reminder that photography is a construct of visibility, a particular visual narrative controlled, at least to some extent, by the photographer. The imagery can only encompass a few moments in time that are then, in Goded's case, collated to form a narrative. The photographer herself thus relays some of her subjects' take on her perspective in their representation: 'Lo que me dijeron las prostitutas es que mi visión era muy bonita, cuando la realidad era mucho más dura' [The prostitutes told me that my vision was very beautiful, while the reality was much harder] (Goded 2008: 8). It is precisely this tension between 'visión' and 'realidad' that lies at the heart of the relationship between seeing and knowing.

AFTERWORD

Working on photography made by contemporary artists, who are alive while research is being conducted, is both delightful and daunting. Nearly a decade after I first saw Goded's images, I found myself sitting at her kitchen table in her house in Coyoacán, a beautiful part of Mexico City, talking through the practicalities of reproducing her images in this book. In the course of researching this volume, we met each other on several occasions during my two trips to Mexico City in 2013 and 2018. We immediately found an easy understanding. Goded welcomed my interest in her documentary work with openness, sharing her time and her work with me. One of the most gratifying aspects of our relationship was her ease with my interpretation of her work and the comfort with which she accepted her images taking on new meanings once they were out in the public domain and open to interpretation. It is partly her openness that made weaving the dialogue between photography and critical theory in this book possible.

I wrote the book with the sense of responsibility not only towards Goded as a photographer, but also towards her marginalised subjects. In my role as a cog in the Western academic machine, writing in the current lingua franca with all its colonial and neo-imperialistic implications, I searched for ways in which academic discourse could account for its own omissions. By mobilising the concept of subalternity in relation to photography criticism, I investigated ways to connect the blind spots of epistemology with gaps in our shared horizons of vision. Making links between what is seen and what is known allowed me to find new ways of thinking through the power of photography and representation, examining how Goded's work resonates with Mexican realities and wider epistemic trends and their exclusions.

Instead of providing a definitive reading of Goded's art, I sought interpretative tools that embraced ambiguities, dissonances and ethical dilemmas. Relying on the concept of subalternity, I examined how Goded's work, despite its ability to represent only a small fragment of its subjects' lives, managed to transform their invisibility into photographic permanence. Her intense focus on the corporeal reality of her subjects' experiences works against the civil imagination that designates the subaltern as a cultural repository of social danger, thereby forging for them a new liminal space within the constraints of photographic encounters. That symbolic space, which transports subaltern representations across different times and contexts, and makes them part of documentary tradition, is in sharp contrast to the liminal structures and landscapes represented by the photographer as the physical spaces in which her subjects dwell. The relationship between the realities of Goded's subjects and their representations is by no means unproblematic. However, the photographs' emergence into the cultural field of vision is at least an opportunity to analyse the role of hegemony and subalternity in the intertwining of materiality and meaning.

Ways of thinking that embrace ambiguity and account for their omissions fit well with writing about a living artist, whose story is open-ended. Although this book focuses on Goded's photographic output, she was already making her first feature-length documentary, *Plaza de la soledad* (2016), during our initial interviews in 2013. This film, a final chapter in her decades-long engagement with the subject of sex-work (Goded 2018), secured a nationwide theatrical release in Mexico and garnered attention on the international film festival circuit. Its success raised the profile of Goded's photographic work as well, leading to new exhibitions and a renewed public interest in some of her older projects. As of 2018, Goded is working on a transnational project photographing traditional women healers throughout Latin America. After years of working with women for whom abuse is a daily experience, seeking out healers is a personal curative strategy and a way of bringing women's resilience and resistance into the spotlight (Goded 2018).

In recent years, Goded's persistent interest in marginal women found new resonance because of the cultural shifts resulting from the media exposure of sexual abuse and harassment scandals. The experiences captured by her camera, often presenting her subjects as vulnerable, can no longer be seen as isolated stories from the fringes, because grass-roots campaigns such as #metoo and #niunamenos have exposed and resisted the scale and commonplace nature of abuse, harassment and violence committed against women. These stories underline the saliency of gender in environments such as the Hollywood film industry and expose abuses behind hegemonic modes of visual production. Precisely because of its lack, Goded's photographs make apparent the persistent dominance of the male gaze in representing women. In shining a spotlight on Goded's documentary production, which is focused on women's marginalised lives, this book theorises photography's power as a form of resistance against the sedulous silencing of women's voices and stories.

REFERENCES

Achugar, H. 1998. 'Leones, cazadores e historiadores: A propósito de las políticas de la memoria y del conocimiento', in *Teorías sin disciplina (latinoamericanismo, poscolonialidad y globalización en debate)*, ed. by S. Castro-Gómez and E. Mendieta (Miguel Ángel Porrúa: México), pp. 169–205

Amnesty International. 2005. 'Mexico: Justice fails in Ciudad Juárez and the city of Chihuahua', <http://www.amnestyusa.org/node/55339?id=5AB197BCEE37D92D80256 FB600689A74> [accessed 7 February 2012]

Arce, C. 2018. *México's Nobodies: The Cultural Legacy of the Soldadera and Afro-Mexican Women* (CUNY Press: New York) Kindle Edition

Azaola, E. and Bergman, M. 2007. 'Cárceles en México: Cuadros de una crisis', in *URVIO: Revista Latinoamericana de Seguridad Ciudadana*, 1, Quito, mayo 2007, pp. 74–87 <http://www.flacsoandes.org/urvio/img/INV_MX_Urv1.pdf> [accessed 20 March 2013]

Azoulay, A. 2008. *The Civil Contract of Photography* (New York: Zone Books)

——2012. *Civil Imagination: A Political Ontology of Photography*, trans. by L. Bethlehem (London: Verso)

Bakhtin, M. 1984a. *Problems of Dostoyevsky's Poetics*, trans. by C. Emerson (Minneapolis, MN: University of Minnesota Press)

——1984b. *Rabelais and His World*, trans. by H. Iswolsky (Bloomington, IN: Indiana University Press)

Barthes, R. 2000. *Camera Lucida* (London: Vintage)

Baudrillard, J. 1994. *Simulacra and Simulation* (Ann Arbor: University of Michigan Press

Benjamin, W. 1968. 'Theses on the Philosophy of History', in *Illuminations*, ed. by H. Arendt (New York: Schocken Books), pp. 253–64

——1999. *The Arcades Project*, trans. by H. Eiland and K. McLaughlin (Cambridge, MA: Belknap Press)

Berger, J. 1972. *Ways of Seeing* (London: BBC and Penguin Books)

——2001. *Selected Essays* (London: Bloomsbury Publishing)

——2003. 'Photographs of Agony', in *The Photography Reader* ed. by L. Wells (London: Routledge), pp. 288–90

Berman, D. 2012. 'Prison Population Statistics', House of Commons Library <www.parliament.uk/briefing-papers/sn04334.pdf> [accessed on 15 March 2013]

Beverley, J. 1999. *Subalternity and Representation: Arguments in Cultural Theory* (Durham, NC and London: Duke University Press)

Bhabha, H. 1994. *The Location of Culture* (New York and London: Routledge)

Blackburn, S. 2001. *A Very Short Introduction to Ethics* (Oxford: Oxford University Press)

Bordo, Susan. 1993. *Unbearable Weight: Feminism, Western Culture, and the Body*. Berkeley: University of California Press.

Butler, J. 1993. *Bodies that Matter: on the Discursive Limits of 'Sex'* (London: Routledge)

——2004. 'Endangered/Endangering: Schematic Racism and White Paranoia (1993)', in *The Judith Butler Reader*, ed. by S. Salih and J. Butler (Oxford: Blackwell Publishers), pp. 204–12

——2008. *Gender Trouble: Feminism and the Subversion of Identity* (London: Routledge)

CADAVA, E. 1997. *Words of Light: Theses on the Photography of History* (Princeton: Princeton University Press)

CAHILL, A. 2003. 'Feminist Pleasure and Feminine Beautification', *Hypatia*, 18.4: 42–64

CALDERÓN, F. 2013. 'Todos Somos Juarez: An Innovative Strategy to Tackle Violence and Crime', Commentary in *Latin American Policy Journal* <http://isites.harvard.edu/icb/icb.do?keyword=k85105&pageid=icb.page507915> [accessed 5 November 2013]

CANO, G. 2006. 'Unconcealable Realities of Desire: Amelio Robles's (Transgender) Masculinity in the Mexican Revolution', in *Sex in Revolution: Gender, Politics and Power in Modern Mexico*, ed. by J. Olcott, M. K. Vaughan and G. Cano (Durham, NC and London: Duke University Press), pp. 35–56

CANON PROFESSIONAL NETWORK. 2008. News, 'Magnum Photos elects three new Members' (authorless text) <http://cpn.canon-europe.com/content/news/magnum_members.do> [accessed 20 April 13]

CARRERAS, C. 2004. *Conversaciones con fotógrafos mexicanos* (Barcelona: Fotoggrafía)

CASANOVA, R. and KONZEVIK, A. 2006. *Luces sobre México: Catálogo selectivo de la Fototeca Nacional de INAH* (Mexico: Editorial RM)

CASTILLO, D. 1998. *Easy Women: Sex and Gender in Modern Mexican Fiction* (Minneapolis, MN: University of Minnesota Press)

Centro Nacional de Servicios de la Pastoral Penitenciaria Católica Pontifica Comisión para América Latina. 2012. <http://www.americalatina.va/content/americalatina/es/experiencias/centro-nacional-de-servicios-de-la-pastoral-penitenciaria-catoli.html> [accessed on 16 March 2013]

CHALLENGER, T. 2010. *400 Women* Exhibition <http://www.tamsynchallenger.co.uk/work/400-women/> [accessed 14 March 2012]

Corbis Corporate. 2012. <http://corporate.corbis.com/uk/company-fact-sheet/> [accessed 27 August 2012]

DEBROISE, O. 2001. *Mexican Suite: A History of Photography in Mexico* (Austin, TX: University of Texas Press)

DERRIDA, J. 1993. *Memoirs of the Blind: The Self-Portrait and Other Ruins*, trans. by Pascale-Anne Brault and Michael Naas (Chicago: University of Chicago Press)

ESCORZA RODRÍGUEZ, D. 2010. *Casasola: El fotógrafo y su colección* (Madrid: La Fabrica Editorial)

FANON, F. 1986. *Black Skin, White Masks* (London: Pluto Press)

——2001. *The Wretched of the Earth* (London: Penguin Classics)

FERRER, E. 2006. *Lola Álvarez Bravo* (Aperture: London)

FINKLER, K. 1994, *Women in Pain: Gender and Morbidity in Mexico* (Philadelphia: University of Pennsylvania Press)

FORGACS, D. (ed.). 2000. *The Gramsci Reader* (New York: New York University Press)

FOUCAULT, M. 1995. *Discipline and Punish: The Birth of the Prison* (London: Vintage)

FRANCO, J. 1989. *Plotting Women: Gender and Representation in Mexico* (New York: Columbia University Press)

FRIDAY, N. 1996. *The Power of Beauty* (New York: HarperCollins)

GABARA, E. 2008. *Errant Modernism: The Ethos of Photography in Mexico and Brazil* (Durham, NC and London: Duke University Press)

GENNEP, A. VAN. 1960. *Rites of Passage*, trans. by M. Vizedom and G. Caffee (Chicago: The University of Chicago Press) Kindle Edition

GODED, M. 1994. *Tierra Negra: Fotografías de la Costa Chica en Guerrero y Oaxaca, Mexico* (Mexico City: Consejo Nacional para la Cultura y las Artes)

——2006A. *Good Girls* (New York: Umbrage Editions)

——2006B. *Plaza de la soledad* (Barcelona: Lunwerg Editores)

——2008. Interview with Maya Goded in *Revista 7.7* <http://www.7punto7.net/?nu=03> [accessed 5 June 2013]

——2011a. Interview with Maya Goded, Animal Político, 'La fotografía acompaña mi soledad' (2011), <http://www.animalpolitico.com/2011/08/la-fotografia-acompana-mi-soledadsegunda-parte/#axzz2W2H48PSG> Part 2 [accessed 5 May 2013]

——2011B, 'Land of Witches', *International Review of Photographs: Private*, 55: 34–35 <http://www.privatephotoreview.com/private-photographers/maya-goded-land-of-witches/> [accessed 27 March 2013]

——2013. Personal Interviews with Maya Goded, Mexico City, June–July 2013

——(dir.). 2016. *Plaza de la soledad*

——2018. Personal Interviews with Maya Goded, Mexico City, May 2018

GOLDBERG, D. and SOLOMOS, J. 2002 'General Introduction', in *A Companion to Racial and Ethnic Studies*, ed. by D. Goldberg and J. Solomos (Oxford: Blackwell Publishers), pp. 1–12

GONZÁLEZ RODRÍGUEZ, S. 2010. *Huesos en el desierto* (Barcelona: Editorial Anagrama)

GRAMSCI, A. 2000. *The Gramsci Reader*, ed. by D. Forgacs (New York: New York University Press)

GUHA, R. 1998. *Dominance without Hegemony: History and Power in Colonial India* (Cambridge, MA: Harvard University Press)

HADDU, M. 2008. 'Henri Cartier-Bresson and a photographic Mexico', *Journal of Romance Studies*, 8.1 (2008), 7–17

HIRSCH, M. 1997. *Family Frames: Photography, Narrative and Postmemory* (Cambridge, MA: Harvard University Press)

INTER-AMERICAN COMMISSION ON HUMAN RIGHTS. 2012. The Situation of the Rights of Women in Ciudad Juárez, Mexico: The Right to Be Free from Violence and Discrimination <http://www.cidh.org/annualrep/2002eng/chap.vi.juarez.htm> [accessed 2 February 2012]

INTERNATIONAL CENTRE FOR PRISON STUDIES. 2013. World Prison Population, BBC News <http://news.bbc.co.uk/1/shared/spl/hi/uk/06/prisons/html/nn2page1.stm> [accessed 15 March 2013]

ITURBIDE, G. 2010 [1989]. *Juchitán de las mujeres: 1979–1989* (Mexico City: RM/Editorial Calamus)

IVES, P. 2004. *Language and Hegemony in Gramsci* (London: Pluto Press)

KAEL, P. 1969. 'Trash, Art and The Movies' <http://www.paulrossen.com/paulinekael/trashartandthemovies.html> [accessed 12 September 2013]

KELLY, P. 2008. *Lydia's Open Door: Inside Mexico's Most Modern Brothel* (Berkeley, CA: University of California Press)

KOO, K. and REISCHER, E. 2004. 'The Body Beautiful: Symbolism and Agency in the Social World', *Annual Review of Anthropology*, 33: 297–317, <http://www.jstor.org/stable/25064855> [accessed 12 June 2013]

KRACAUER, S. 1993. 'Photography', *Critical Inquiry*, 193:421–36 <http://www.jstor.org/stable/1343959> [accessed 25 March 2013]

KRISTEVA, J. 1982. *Powers of Horror: An Essay on Abjection*, trans. by L. S. Roudiez (New York: Columbia University Press)

LAMAS, M. 2017. *El fulgor de la noche: El comercio sexual en las calles de la Ciudad de México* (Mexico City: Océano) Kindle Edition

LARA, I. 2005, 'Bruja Positionalities: Toward a Chicana/Latina Spiritual Activism', *Chicana/Latina Studies*, 42: 10–45 <http://www.jstor.org/stable/23014464> [accessed 11 June 2013]

LATIN AMERICAN SUBALTERN STUDIES GROUP. 1993. 'Founding Statement', *The Postmodernism Debate in Latin America*, 110–21

Legrás, H. 2004. 'The Latin American Subaltern Studies Reader (Review)', *The Americas*, 61.1 (2004), 125–27

Levi Strauss, D. 2005. *Between the Eyes: Essays on Photography and Politics* (New York: Aperture)

Lewis, L. 2000. 'Blacks, Black Indians, Afromexicans: The Dynamics of Race, Nation, and Identity in a Mexican "moreno" Community (Guerrero)', *American Ethnologist*, 274: 898–926

——2004. 'Modesty and Modernity: Photography, Race, and Representation on Mexico's Costa Chica (Guerrero)', *Identities: Global Studies in Culture and Power*, .4: 471–99

<2-em rule>Lieberman, I. 2009. *Niño Perdido*, Exhibition <http://www.drawingcenter.org/viewingprogram/share_portfolio.cfm?pf=742> [accessed 14 March 2012]

Light, K. 2010. *Witness in Our Time: Working Lives of Documentary Photographers* (Washington, D.C.: Smithsonian Books)

Linfield, S. 2010. *The Cruel Radiance: Photography and Political Violence* (London: University of Chicago Press)

Lomnitz, C. 2001. *Deep Mexico, Silent Mexico: An Anthropology of Nationalism* (Minneapolis: University of Minnesota Press)

MacKinnon, C. 2006. *'Are Women Human?' and Other International Dialogues* (London: The Belknap Press of Harvard University Press)

Magnum Photos. 2012. <http://www.magnumphotos.com/Archive/C.aspx?VP=XSpecific_MAG.PhotographerDetail_VPage&pid=2K7O3R148ZF1&nm=Maya%20 Goded> [accessed 12 February 2008]

Marx, K. 1964. *Economic and Philosophic Manuscripts of 1844* (New York: International Publishers)

——1982. 'The Economic and Philosophic Manuscripts', in *Classes, Power, and Conflict: Classical and Contemporary Debates*, ed. by A. Giddens and D. Held (Berkeley: University of California Press), pp. 12–19

McAfee, N. 2004. *Routledge Critical Thinkers: Julia Kristeva* (London: Routledge)

Merleau-Ponty, M. 1964. 'Eye and Mind', in *The Primacy of Perception*, ed. by J. M. Edie, trans. by C. Dallery (Evanston, IL: Northwestern University Press), <http://www.biolinguagem.com/biolinguagem_antropologia/merleauponty_1964_eyeandmind.pdf> [accessed 15 May 2013]

——2002. *Phenomenology of Perception* (London: Routledge)

——2004. 'The Visible and the Invisible: The Intertwining — The Chiasm', in *Basic Writings* ed. by T. Baldwin (London: Routledge), pp. 247–71

Mignolo, W. 2005. *The Idea of Latin America* (Oxford: Blackwell Publishing) Kindle Edition

——2012a. *The Darker Side of Western Modernity: Global Futures, Decolonial Options (Latin America Otherwise)* (Durham, NC: Duke University Press)

——2012b. *Local Histories/Global Designs: Coloniality, Subaltern Knowledges, and Border Thinking* (Oxford: Princetown University Press) Kindle Edition

Mitchell, W. J. T. 2005. *What do Pictures Want? The Lives and Loves of Images* (Chicago and London: The University of Chicago Press)

Monsiváis, C. 2006. 'Foreword', in *Sex in Revolution: Gender, Politics and Power in Modern Mexico*, ed. by J. Olcott, M. K. Vaughan, and G. Cano (Durham, NC and London: Duke University Press), pp. 1–20

Mora, S. 2006. *Cinemachismo: Masculinities and Sexuality in Mexican Film* (Austin, TX: University of Texas Press) Kindle Edition

Moreno Figueroa, M. 2010. 'Distributed Intensities: Whiteness, Mestizaje and the Logics of Mexican Racism', *Ethnicities*, 10.387, online version <http://etn.sagepub.com/content/10/3/387> [accessed 10 February 2013]

Mraz, J. 2001. 'Photographing Mexico', *Mexican Studies/Estudios Mexicanos*, 17.1: 193–211
——2009. *Looking for Mexico: Modern Visual Culture and National Identity* (Durham, NC and London: Duke University Press)
——2012. *Photographing the Mexican Revolution: Commitments, Testimonies, Icons* (Austin, TX: University of Texas Press)
Naggar, C. and Ritchin, F. (eds). 1993. *Mexico through Foreign Eyes* (New York and London: W.W. Norton & Company)
Nair, P. 2011. *A Different Light: The Photography of Sebastião Salgado* (Durham, NC and London: Duke University Press)
Navarrete, J. A. 2003. 'Del tipo al arquetipo. Fotografía y tipos nacionales en América Latina. Segunda mitad del siglo XIX y comienzos del XX', *Extra Cámara*, 21: 34–43
Noble, A. 2000. *Tina Modotti: Image, Texture, Photography* (Albuquerque: University of New Mexico Press)
——2010. *Photography and Memory in Mexico: Icons of Revolution* (Manchester: Manchester University Press)
Oliver, A. 2011. 'Mestizaje, Mexicanidad, and Assimilation: Zea on Race, Ethnicity, and Nationality', in *Forging People: Race, Ethnicity, and Nationality in Hispanic American and Latino/a Thought*, ed. by J. Gracia (Notre Dame, IN: University of Notre Dame Press), pp. 249–71
O'Neill, M. 2001. *Prostitution and Feminism: Towards a Politics of Feeling* (Cambridge: Polity Press) Kindle Edition
Ortega, M. 2013. 'Photographic Representation of Racialized Bodies: Afro-Mexicans, the Visible, and the Invisible', *Critical Philosophy of Race*, 1.2: 163–89
Pateman, C. 1988. *The Sexual Contract* (Stanford, CA: Stanford University Press)
Paz, O. 2008. *El laberinto de la soledad* (Manchester: Manchester University Press)
Pelàez Ferrusca, M. 2011. 'Derechos humanos y prisiòn. Notas para el acercamiento', *Revista Jurídica Boletín Mexicano de Derecho Comparado* (Instituto de Investigaciones Jurídicas de la UNAM, Biblioteca Jurídica Virtual), <http://www.juridicas.unam.mx/publica/rev/boletin/cont/95/art/art8.htm> [accessed 21 March 2013]
Peteet, J. 1996. 'The Writing on the Walls: The Graffiti of the Intifada', *Cultural Anthropology*, 11.2: 139–59 <http://www.jstor.org/stable/656446> [accessed 19 April 2013]
Phillips, W. E. 2009. 'Representations of the Black Body in Mexican Visual Art: Evidence of an African Historical Presence or a Cultural Myth?', *Journal of Black Studies*, 39.5: 761–85 <http://www.jstor.org/stable/40282595> [accessed 15 October 2013]
Prince Claus Fund. 2010. 'Network — Maya Goded' <http://www.princeclausfund.org/en/network/maya.html> [accessed 21 January 2014]
Prosser, J. 2005. *Light in the Dark Room: Photography and Loss* (Minneapolis: University of Minnesota Press)
——2010. 'Introduction', in *Picturing Atrocity: Photography in Crisis*, ed. by G. Batchen, M. Gidley, N. K. Miller and J. Prosser (London: Reaktion Books), pp. 7–14
Quintana, V. 2013. 'Juárez: lo que Calderón no enseña en Harvard', *La Jornada*, Opinión (1 March 2013) <http://www.jornada.unam.mx/2013/03/01/opinion/026a1pol> [accessed 6 November 2013]
Rabasa, J. 2010. *Without History: Subaltern Studies, the Zapatista Insurgency, and the Specter of History* (Pittsburgh: University of Pittsburgh Press)
Rancière, J. 2009. *The Emancipated Spectator* (London: Verso Books)
Reanda, L. 1991. 'Prostitution as a Human Rights Question: Problems and Prospects of United Nations Action', *Human Rights Quarterly*, 13.2: 202–28
Redclift, N. 2003. 'Re-reading gender: Comparative Questions, Situated Meanings, Latin American Paradoxes', *Bulletin of the School of Oriental and African Studies*, 66: 486–500

Reddy, S. 2011. 'New Facts on the Gender Gap', *Wall Street Journal Blogs*, <http://blogs.wsj.com/economics/2011/09/18/new-facts-on-the-gender-gap-from-the-world-bank/> [accessed 16 June 2013]

Rodríguez, I. 2001. 'Reading Subalterns across Texts, Disciplines, and Theories: From Representation to Recognition', in *The Latin American Subaltern Studies Reader*, ed. by I. Rodríguez (Durham, NC and London: Duke University Press), pp. 1–34

Rodríguez, J. 1994. *Our Lady of Guadalupe: Faith and Empowerment among Mexican-American Women* (Austin, TX: University of Texas Press) Kindle Edition

Rodríguez Ortiz, E. 2010. *Crímenes de odio por homofobia: Los otros asesinatos de Ciudad Juárez* (Mexico City: Universidad Autónoma Metropolitana) Kindle Edition

Rommens, A. 2006. 'In Other Words: Subaltern Epistemologies or How to Eat Humble Pie', *Image and Narrative*, Online Magazine of the Visual Narrative, 14 <http://www.imageandnarrative.be/inarchive/painting/Aarnoud_Rommens.htm> [accessed 3 June 2012]

Rosenblum, N. 1993. 'Strand/Mexico', in *Mexico through Foreign Eyes*, ed. by C. Naggar and F. Ritchin (New York and London: Norton & Company), pp. 27–30

Rosler, M. 2003. 'In, Around and Afterthoughts (on Documentary Photography)', in *The Photography Reader*, ed. by L. Wells (London: Routledge), pp. 261–74

Rulfo, J. 1992 [1953]. *El llano en llamas* (Mexico City: Fondo de Cultura Económica)

Ryan, P., Moore, C., van Franeker, J., and Moloney, C. 2009. 'Monitoring the Abundance of Plastic Debris in the Marine Environment', *Philosophical Transactions of the Royal Society B: Biological Sciences*, 364, doi: 10.1098/rstb.2008.0207 <http://rstb.royalsocietypublishing.org/content/364/1526/1999.full.pdf+html> [accessed 20 March 2013]

Said, E. 1988. 'Foreword', in *Selected Subaltern Studies*, ed. by R. Guha and G. Spivak (Delhi: Oxford University Press), pp. v–xii

Sanders, T., O'Neill, M., and Pitcher, J. 2009. *Prostitution: Sex Work, Policy and Politics* (London: Sage Publications)

Saldívar, J. D. 2012. *Trans-Americanity: Subaltern Modernities, Global Coloniality, and the Cultures of Greater Mexico* (Durham, NC and London: Duke University Press)

Saynes-Vázquez, E. 1996. 'Galán Pa dxandí'."That would be great if it were true": Zapotec women's comment on their role in society in Identities: Global Studies in Culture and Power', *Identities: Global Studies in Culture and Power/Special Issue: Indigenous Peoples/Global Terrains*, 3.1–2: 183–204

Snow, R. 2001. 'Goodbye to All That', in *American Heritage*, 52.3 <http://www.americanheritage.com/content/goodbye-all> [accessed 26 August 2012]

Sontag, S. 2005 [1973] *On Photography* (New York: RosettaBooks)

Sosa, M. 2010. 'En aumento, nivel de violencia en México: AI', *El Universal*, <http://www.eluniversal.com.mx/notas/682802.html> [accessed 21 March 2013]

Spivak, G. 1995. *Can the Subaltern Speak?* <http://www.mcgill.ca/files/crclaw-discourse/Can_the_subaltern_speak.pdf> [accessed 14 May 2010]

—— 1999. *A Critique of Postcolonial Reason: Toward a History of the Vanishing Present* (London: Harvard University Press)

Stutzman, R. 1981. 'El Mestizaje: An All-Inclusive Ideology of Exclusion', in *Cultural Transformations and Ethnicity in Modern Ecuador*, ed. by N. Whitten (Chicago: University of Illinois Press), pp. 45–94

Szakolczai, A. 2009. 'Liminality and Experience: Structuring transitory situations and transformative events', *International Political Anthropology*, 2.1: 141–72

Tagg, J. 1988. *The Burden of Representation: Essays on Photographies and Histories* (Basingstoke: Palgrave Macmillan)

Tejada, R. 2009. *National Camera: Photography and Mexico's Image Environment* (London: University of Minnesota Press) Kindle Edition

Thomassen, B. 2009. 'The Uses and Meanings of Liminality', *International Political Anthropology*, 2.1: 5–28

Tierney, D. (2007). *Emilio Fernández* (Manchester: Manchester University Press)

Trejo, E. 2013. 'La crisis penitenciaria in México', *Cámara: revista de los centros de estudios de la cámara de diputados* (Centro de Estudios Sociales y de Opinión Pública: Ciudad de México) <http://comunicacionsocial.diputados.gob.mx/camara/mayo/revista/index.php?option=com_content&view=article&id=93:la-crisis-penitenciaria-en-mexico&catid=43&Itemid=230> [accessed 24 March 2013]

Turati, M. 2012. '...Y Todos Somos Juárez, gran negocio', *Proceso* (8 November 2012) <http://www.proceso.com.mx/?p=324641> [accessed 5 November 2013]

Turner, V. 1974. 'Liminal to Liminoid, in Play, Flow and Ritual: An Essay in Comparative Symbology', *Rice University Studies* <http://scholarship.rice.edu/bitstream/handle/1911/63159/article_RIP603_part4.pdf?sequence=1> [accessed 10 March 2013]

——2008. *The Ritual Process: Structure and Anti-Structure* (New Brunswick and London: Aldine Transaction)

Uribe-Zúñiga, P. Hernández-Tepichín, G. Del Río-Chiriboga, C. Ortiz, V. 1995. 'Prostitución y SIDA en la Ciudad de México', *Salud Pública Mexicana*, 37: 592–601

Wade, P. 1993. *Blackness and Race Mixture: The Dynamics of Racial Identity in Colombia* (Baltimore, MD: Johns Hopkins University Press)

Warren, J. and Twine, F. 2002. 'Critical Race Studies in Latin America: Recent Advances, Recurrent Weaknesses', in *A Companion to Racial and Ethnic Studies*, ed. by D. Goldberg and J. Solomos (Oxford: Blackwell Publishers), pp. 538–60

Wells, L. 2011. *Land Matters: Landscape Photography, Culture and Identity* (London: I. B. Tauris) Kindle Edition

Wolf, N. 2002. *The Beauty Myth* (London: Harper Perennial)

Wollstonecraft, Mary. 1983 [1792]. *Vindication of the Rights of Woman* (New York: Penguin Classics)

Žižek, S. 2000. 'Looking Awry', in *Film and Theory: An Anthology*, ed. by R. Stam, T. Miller (London: Blackwell Publishers), pp. 524–38

INDEX

www.ingramcontent.com/pod-product-compliance
Lightning Source LLC
LaVergne TN
LVHW081300100826
845148LV00005B/926
9781781887967